THE NEW SECTARIANISM

THE NEW SECTARIANISM

THE ARAB UPRISINGS AND THE REBIRTH OF THE SHI'A–SUNNI DIVIDE

GENEIVE ABDO

OXFORD
UNIVERSITY PRESS

OXFORD
UNIVERSITY PRESS

Oxford University Press is a department of the University of Oxford. It furthers
the University's objective of excellence in research, scholarship, and education
by publishing worldwide. Oxford is a registered trade mark of Oxford University
Press in the UK and certain other countries.

Published in the United States of America by Oxford University Press
198 Madison Avenue, New York, NY 10016, United States of America.

Library of Congress Cataloging-in-Publication Data
Names: Abdo, Geneive, 1960-, author.
Title: The new sectarianism : the Arab uprisings and the rebirth
of the Shi'a-Sunni divide / Geneive Abdo.
Description: New York : Oxford University Press, 2016. |
Includes bibliographical references and index.
Identifiers: LCCN 2016023454 | ISBN 9780190233143 (hardback) |
ISBN 9780190233167 (epub)
Subjects: LCSH: Sunnites—Relations—Shī'ah. | Shī'ah—Relations—Sunnites. |
Arab Spring, 2010- | BISAC: RELIGION / Islam / General. | RELIGION / Islam / Sunni.
Classification: LCC BP194.16 .A24 2016 | DDC 297.8/042—dc23
LC record available at https://lccn.loc.gov/2016023454

1 3 5 7 9 8 6 4 2
Printed by Sheridan Books, Inc., United States of America

For my mother, Rosemary Rizk Abdo

CONTENTS

ACKNOWLEDGMENTS

Many people in the United States and the Middle East contributed to this book. Throughout the research and writing, my life-long friend Jonathan Lyons, author and scholar, generously offered his feedback and knowledge. In my 25 years of writing books and other publications, his talent still goes unmatched.

Researchers stretching from Bahrain to Lebanon, and Iraq offered their enormous insights and skills, and are examples of the young generation in the Arab world that is the best (and maybe only) hope for the region in the near future. In the Middle East, Zeina Najjar, Lulwa Rizkallah, Nadine Ali, and Suzan Haidamous provided very useful contacts and knowledge. Lamia Estatie in Lebanon and now in the United Kingdom spent months researching related papers and doing social media research for this book. In Washington, DC, Yasir Zaidan was extremely kind and generous with his time and often worked on a moment's notice. His knowledge and very positive work ethic helped me through many deadlines.

Also in Washington, DC, Ellen Laipson, former president of the Stimson Center and now distinguished fellow, offered support for my work and ideas during the early years when most scholars and regional experts did not agree that sectarianism would play a significant role in Arab societies. Ellen gave me confidence and courage in a town that rarely thinks outside the box. Stephen Grand at the Atlantic Council has also been a great support. At the Brookings Institution, where some of the material contained in these pages was the subject of two monographs, I am grateful for the support of Tamara Cofman Wittes, director of the Center for Middle East Policy, and Daniel Byman, director of research at the Center.

I am also grateful to the institutions in the Middle East that offered me a home to conduct fieldwork. The Lebanese American University, and particularly Imad Salamey, provided resources in Lebanon in 2016. In Iraqi Kurdistan, I am grateful to Zeina Najjar and Christine Vandentoorn who gave me a home at the American University in Sulaimaniya in 2015.

The Earhart Foundation awarded a series of grants to make my frequent travel to the Middle East possible for 4 years. The Foundation supported my work for more than a decade and I am especially thankful to the board of directors.

Last, but certainly not least, I am forever grateful to Cynthia Read, my editor at Oxford University Press. This is our third book together and she has trusted in my work for 16 years.

THE NEW SECTARIANISM

INTRODUCTION: OF
HISTORY AND MEMORY

The Arab uprisings began with seemingly secular cries of *al sha'b yurid isqat al nizam*: The people want to overthrow the system. In most countries, religious motivations were, at first, conspicuously absent; but, 5 years on, the initial unity has eroded into societal conflict in some countries and all-out war in others. Instead of agreed-on goals of social justice and a different form of governance, religious differences and how Muslims define themselves have emerged as newly salient characteristics throughout Arab society.

Throughout history, competing groups, sects, and schools of Islamic law (the *madhabs*) all struggled to define the faith for a diverse and often-contentious community of believers, but the Arab uprisings brought identity and religion once again to the fore. A core issue in the post-Arab uprising era is the question: Who is a true believer and who is a nonbeliever? This exclusionist mind-set is most evident in the sectarian conflict between Shi'a and Sunni Muslims, which poses a serious threat to the stability of regional states and to stakeholders in the wider world, including the United States and its allies.

One of the many reasons sectarianism is so intractable and will, unfortunately, plague the Middle East for years to come, is that all players in the violent conflict claim to have a monopoly on religious truth. *Whose Islam is it?* Is it that of the Salafist, who wants to return to how he says Islam was practiced during the time of the Prophet Mohammad 1,400 years ago? Or that of the banned Muslim Brotherhood leader in Egypt? Or the leader of a Shi'a militia in Iraq? Or the Islamic State of Iraq and Syria (ISIS), the Islamic State? Each party believes its religious knowledge is sacred and true.

From its beginnings in the 1970s until today, a key to the power and appeal of modern Islamism—encompassing an array of groups from the nonviolent Muslim Brotherhood of Egypt to the violent al Qaeda and ISIS—has been the process of defining "the Other." Members of traditional religious institutions have been left behind in what has become an interpretive free-for-all. As one cleric put it, during an interview in April 2015 in Erbil, Iraq: "People pick and choose from the Koran in a way that is convenient for them. But they have no education, as opposed to us, who have studied and have PhDs and understand the true principles of Islam."

This exclusionist claim to religious truth is not new, nor is it exceptional to Islam. This historical phenomenon shares some characteristics with other revealed faiths. As sociologists of world religions have long noted, the death of a charismatic leader, prophet, or seer deprives the nascent community of immediate access to revelation and its meaning sets the stage for the rise of a caste of priests, lawyers, and bureaucrats who claim the authority to interpret the holy teachings. The sacred texts remain the same whereas how they are interpreted—and by whom—become questions of utmost importance.

These same circumstances also introduce the very real likelihood of dissent, fragmentation of the community, and the emergence of distinct sects or groupings, each asserting a monopoly on religious truth. In the world of Islam, this problem has proved particularly acute. With the arguable exception of the era of the Rightly Guided Caliphs, the *khulafa al rashidun*, during the earliest days of Islam, there has never been anything resembling a consensus figure or institution of religious authority among the Muslims.[1] As a result, Muslims worldwide have been left vulnerable to a succession of claimants, many backed by the use of force, in what have proved ultimately to be doomed efforts to secure such a mandate. Much of the social and political unrest that characterizes Islamic history, from the murders of its earliest leaders, to medieval rebellions, to the rise of Osama bin Laden and the birth of the self-proclaimed Islamic State in our own century, reflects this same internal logic.

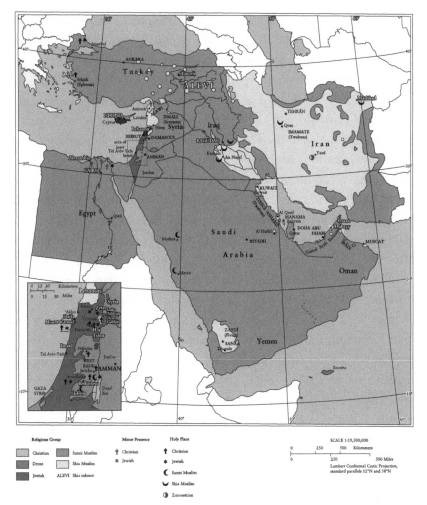

Figure I.1 Distribution of religions in the Middle East. Courtesy of the University of Texas Libraries.

In other words, the longing for Muslim religious identity reflects an internal debate that has been, quite literally, centuries in the making. Since the death of the Prophet Mohammad in 632 CE, the question of legitimate religious authority has plagued the worldwide community of believers. *Who, then, is a good Muslim? And who gets to decide?* These questions are no less relevant today than they were in the seventh century, and differing responses during the intervening centuries

3

have brought forth aspiring prophets, visionaries, and revolutionaries demanding the right to dictate the proper contours of the faith to their fellow Muslims, often with the threat of death or damnation.

During the postcolonial period, a new generation of essentially secular leaders—such as Egypt's Gamal Abdel Nasser and Libya's Muammar Gaddafi—backed their nationalist policies with claims of religious sanction and used local religious institutions to solidify their hold on power. It is no accident that Egypt and Libya later emerged among the most prominent battlegrounds between dictatorial state power and popular demands for self-determination. Even before the Arab uprisings began, the Middle East had been headed in a direction polarized between society's demands for self-determination and the autocrats' desire for regime survival at any cost.

Today's charismatic religious ideologues first began to make their presence felt during the 1970s, laying the foundation among Arab societies for a religious revival that continues to the present. Shi'a and Sunni communities—the former in reaction to the Iranian Revolution in 1979 and the latter in response to the developing power of the Muslim Brotherhood in Egypt—began to associate their long-established religious beliefs and practices with personal identity, supplanting a largely manufactured and fragile loyalty to the relatively new phenomenon of the nation state. Moreover, Iran's Islamic Revolution proposed a theocratic state as an alternative to the Western-style nationalism then offered across the region.

As these religious revivals gathered momentum—often as the only real outlet for dissent under authoritarian leaders claiming the nationalist or pan-Arab mantle—the efforts by states to invent traditions to secure the idea of nationhood began to collide with societies' growing Islamism. Over time, this battle between nationalism and Islamism steadily eroded the power of many of the region's rulers, but also challenged established religious institutions, which were widely, and correctly, seen as having placed the interests of the state over those of the *ummah*, the larger community of Muslim believers.

By the time the Arab uprisings erupted into their full fury in early 2011, there was already fertile ground for instability, insecurity, and violence. The struggle over the degree to which religion would determine how countries are governed gained new intensity. Although it is imprecise to say the Arab uprisings alone produced violence in the name of religion, it should be understood that the overarching ideologies of Islamism and nationalism, which had been developing for decades, locked horns.

In addition to this state–societal competition, a struggle has developed within Islam, primarily between Shi'a and Sunni Muslims, but also within each of these communities, penetrating many aspects of Arab society. In 2015, Naser Ghobadzdeh and Shahram Akbarzadeh wrote:

> Once othering becomes part of politico-religious discourse, it moves to all levels of society, transforming itself into as much a bottom-up as a top-down process. Over the course of time othering rhetoric has expanded beyond theology to become a decisive part of political, social, religious and economic reality.[2]

In each Arab country, this "othering" competition has a different history and is now being played out in different ways. There is no consistent frame and thus the Shi'a–Sunni conflict must be analyzed separately in each country.

So, is the Shi'a–Sunni conflict fundamental? Can the gulf be bridged? These questions divide academics and other experts in the East and West. The fundamental question is whether religious identity now trumps other identities, including ethnicity, tribe, and national affiliation. If so, because the religious difference is, by its nature, unresolvable, this would mean the violence now sweeping the Middle East is intractable. If, however, other struggles over other identities are just as important to stability, then there is hope the conflict will subside or be subsumed into other less combustible and more manageable arenas.

The argument I put forth in these pages, through narratives, rhetorical analyses of nonstate actors, and interviews with a variety of religious figures, is that even if there ever should be agreement over what constitutes being an Iraqi, a Syrian, an Egyptian, a Bahraini, or a Lebanese, the recent uprisings have brought religious identity to a place of new importance in Arab societies—a development with at least 30 years of history behind it.

Granted, the intensification of religious identity, a lack of security resulting from state failure or even outright collapse, and an erosion of the notion of citizenship as shared membership in a nation state have all led the Arab world to where it is today. Those who argue that religious difference is not the fundamental cause for violence posit another theory: it is the geopolitical rivalry between Shi'a Iran and Sunni Saudi Arabia, and their proxies and clients doing their bidding on the ground, that are shaping and directing the conflict. Although this is certainly a significant driver of the conflict, the violence would not be as profound if religion were not also being contested. Essentially, longstanding notions of religious identity and sectarian affiliation have supplanted the postcolonial project of Arab nationalism, thereby creating the opportunity for violent extremist groups, such as ISIS and al Qaeda, to fill the resulting vacuum.

Contrary to conventional wisdom, extremist groups such as the Islamic State did not appear out of nowhere. Rather, these extremists are benefiting from all the conditions described earlier. They have also found support from those who have been marginalized economically and politically—not necessarily from the Arab uprisings alone, but from everything that helped spark the revolts in the first place.

This significant development took Western governments by surprise. It was not until the civil and sectarian wars in Iraq and Syria became so bloody that Western scholars and governments acknowledged the Sunni–Shi'a conflict was real and that it probably had something to do with religion. What is most alarming is that Western thought, having experienced 30 years of modern Islamism, did not understand that religion and ideology were destined to become the main currencies among societies in the Arab world.

As the Arab uprisings toppled dictators, Western media outlets, political leaders, and others viewed the turmoil as being led exclusively by secular actors and groups engaged in civil disobedience in the name of Western-style democratic reform. Herein lies the origin of the seductive but highly misleading notion of an "Arab Spring," a dangerous misnomer that has led many a politician and commentator astray. Now, it is clear that those who led the revolutions in some countries will not finish them.

Sectarianism in the Arab world remains an inescapable presence that ignites whenever there are social or political upheavals, such as the Islamic Revolution, the US invasion of Iraq, or the more recent Arab uprisings and the resulting Syrian and Iraqi civil wars. Yet, many analysts, government experts, political leaders, and academics refuse to see extremist religious sentiment and practices as anything but an epiphenomenon of more familiar and more comfortable factors, such as institutional failings, economic backwardness, traditional geopolitics, ethnic difference, entrenched antimodern attitudes, and so on. Although these conditions certainly are playing a role in some Arab states, without religious identification the conflicts would not have flared to the degree they have done today.

At the same time, it is vital that scholars, analysts, and others in the field not shy away from acknowledging the role that some prominent contemporary readings of Islam have in the propagation of violence and extremism. It must be possible to distinguish between the faith as a whole—that is, the faith as Scriptural command—and its various and conflicting interpretations throughout the many centuries following the Revelation.

So what does religion have to do with it? It should be understood that the role that changing interpretations of religion play in violent conflict varies significantly between the leaders in groups, who might use religion as an instrument, and their foot soldiers, who may be sincere in their belief in an idealized notion of Islam that is a perversion of accepted doctrinal interpretations issued by qualified religious scholars. They believe their actions are protecting the faith.

Today's Shi'a–Sunni animosity displays some characteristics that differ from historical sectarianism in the Middle East. Traditionally, sectarianism can be understood as a set of institutional arrangements determining familial, local, regional, and even broader kinds of loyalty and affiliation.[3] Today, however, the increase in sectarian conflict is primarily the result of the collapse of authoritarian rule and a struggle for political and economic power, and over which interpretation of Islam will influence societies and new leaderships.

In states such as Bahrain and Lebanon, where the Shi'a make up approximately 70% and 40% of the population, respectively, the prospects of democratic governance alarm the Sunni. As a result, democracy is viewed largely as part of a subversive Shi'a agenda, "rather than as a universal principle which would advance modernity and development in those countries."[4] Although the underlying goal of the Arab uprisings was to move toward a more just style of governance, the Shi'a "threat" may provide those Sunni-dominated governments still standing with powerful justification to retain authoritarian rule.

The Shi'a have long been a poignant reminder to Sunni Muslims of the unresolved differences within Islam since the death of the Prophet Mohammad. For centuries, the differences between these two major sects have crystallized around the question of the rightful succession to the Prophet as head of the early religious and political community: should the new leader be chosen from among Mohammad's closest Companions or from his direct bloodline only? The Shi'a telling of the death of Hussein, grandson of the Prophet and champion of the future Shi'a, at the hands of the Umayyads in a battle near Karbala in 680 CE, has created the narrative many Shi'a have lived by ever since.

During the past three decades, as Sunni Islamist movements gained widespread popular support, the Shi'a also began to mobilize, despite restraints imposed by their governments. According to Max Weiss, as the Shi'a of Lebanon became better capable of articulating their political demands, they transformed themselves from a "sect-in-itself" to a "sect-for-itself."[5] Broadly speaking, the Shi'a, once a seemingly weak and alienated community within Arab Islam, are now demanding their rights and reaching for greater political influence—from Saudi Arabia to Bahrain and Kuwait.

Just how profound are the challenges still facing the Shi'a was documented recently in an opinion survey conducted by the Pew Forum on Religion and Public Life, a Washington, DC–based research institute.

The study showed a widespread belief in most Arab countries that Shi'a are not real Muslims.[6] This was true particularly in countries where Shi'a represent only a small minority. According to the survey, at least 40% of Sunni do not accept the Shi'a as fellow Muslims. In many cases, even greater percentages do not believe that some practices common among some Shi'a, such as visiting holy shrines and praying to dead religious figures, are legitimate Islamic traditions.[7]

Western analysis of the Arab world generally suffers from two intellectual developments that grew out of the European Enlightenment: (1) the flagrant tendency to dismiss the abiding importance of religion and (2) the more obscure inclination to see the Western nation state as the proper vehicle, even the only vehicle, for orderly "modern" governance. When applied to Muslim societies, these two established discourses interact with one another in subtle but powerful ways that distort our understanding, undermine policy proscriptions, and, effectively, prevent any fruitful interaction between East and West.

European notions of history and progress, and of the decline of religiosity that inevitably accompany them, are all too often applied reflexively to the experience of Islam. Sociologists who first articulated and helped establish the intellectual primacy among Western scholars—and among Western-educated Arab elites—of so-called secularization theory have largely abandoned the idea altogether in the face of overwhelming evidence that religion matters as much today as it ever has. It is time for other fields, including terrorism studies and its associated disciplines, to follow suit.

To appreciate fully the complexity of the Sunni–Shi'a relationship today, we must look back not so much to the times of the so-called First Muslims of the mid-seventh century as to the sacred histories these two rival communities have told themselves ever since. Such historical fast-forwarding beyond the immediate days of the Prophet Mohammad and the earliest generations of believers is not only useful but largely unavoidable; there are simply no extant accounts from the period available to the student of Islamic history. The early histories—including the popular lives of the Prophet (the *sira*), the chronicles of the early struggles, military campaigns, and ultimate victory of the

young community of believers, and other such works—are later recon-
structions viewed through the lens of thriving and vital religious traditions. Walter Benjamin's classic observation that "history is written by
the victors" is no less true of the theological realm.

So, too, the accounts of the splits, civil wars, deviations, and heresies
that bedeviled the early Muslims. It was only after the death of the
Prophet Mohammad that the Revelations themselves were compiled,
edited, or preserved in any organized, comprehensive, and canonized
version, traditionally said to be the work of a committee of experts
assembled at the behest of Caliph Uthman (644–656). And it was only
centuries later that the great legal commentaries, hadith collections, and
works of exegesis, among the glories of Islamic intellectual and cultural
life, spelled out how most believers practice their faith to this day.

As a result, tracing the origins, circumstances, and consequences
of the Sunni–Shi'a rift is an exercise not so much in history as in
historiography—that is, in a critical reading of those traditions that
have come throughout succeeding generations to define the separate
experience of the two largest Muslim communities. Down through the
centuries, the formation of historical tradition and religious, political,
and social developments have continued to exist in a symbiotic relationship, each reinforcing the other.[8] The history of the Sunni–Shi'a rift
is, essentially, a history of the present, with communal memory and tradition shaped by facts on the ground today. This can be seen clearly, for
example, among the Shi'a communities in Bahrain and eastern Saudi
Arabia and their minority Sunni rulers: "In both countries, Shi'a and
ruling elites offered different interpretations regarding the emergence
of modern Bahrain and Saudi Arabia, each trying to lay claim to the
homeland," reports Yitzhak Nakash after conducting fieldwork interviews among the Arab Shi'a.[9]

The second conceptual challenge to addressing this sectarian conflict
is a logical extension of the first—that is, the Western failure to take
religion seriously, especially when it comes to the teachings, experience, and practice of Islam. Among the most prominent casualties is
recognition of the complete integration within Islam's worldview of
the religious and political realms. Despite frequent calls from Western

critics, echoed by some Muslim intellectuals, for "reform" that would somehow replicate the early modern European experience and formally separate the two spheres, Islam has remained consistently true to its holistic approach.

This has led much of the Muslim world today into a dead-end, reflecting what Wael B. Hallaq calls the very "impossibility" of an Islamic State, in the modern meaning of the term:

> There can be no Islam without a moral–legal system that is anchored in a metaphysic; there can be no such moral system without or outside divine sovereignty; and, at the same time, there can be no modern state without its own sovereignty and sovereign will.... The modern state can no more be Islamic than Islam can come to possess a modern state.[10]

Imposed from without by European colonial power during the 19th century and with no regard for Muslims' beliefs, practices, or modes of communal governance throughout the preceding 1,100 years, the apparatus of the modern state failed to take root in the region. Instead, postcolonial rulers floundered to cobble together systems that mimic elements of the modern sovereign state, grounded in nationalist and pan-Arab claims of legitimacy, while simultaneously pledging fealty to the Sharia, in which the ultimate sovereign is God.[11]

The relative ease with which the recent Arab rebellions toppled many of these regimes and badly shook others merely underscores their fragility, instability, and illegitimacy. Yet, among many Westerners, the nation state remains the preferred frame through which to view the conflicts raging across the Arab Middle East. This book challenges this predominant discourse. The increasing power of nonstate actors—who are even more influential after the Arab uprisings—makes any notion of the nation state essentially irrelevant.

The outside observer, then, must resist the reflexive impulse to parse the many expressions of Sunni–Shi'a contestation—whether political, social, or economic—into discrete, independent units in such a way as to ignore or downplay the dispute's fundamentally *religious* nature. In other words, this sectarian conflict may be, and often is, expressed in forms that appear recognizable to the outsider as simple rivalry between communities over, say, land use, water rights, political power, economic opportunity, or access to education. However, its very persistence and seeming intractability must be understood as flowing directly from religious differences and their associated religious identities that this difference has conferred on both Shi'a and Sunni. This same fundamental tension infuses meaning, form, and purpose into all natures of disputes. Thus, the Iran–Iraq War of the 1980s and today's geopolitical struggle between Iran and Saudi Arabia are both cast by all parties as recapitulations of the Shi'a–Sunni rivalry, the origins of which lie in idealized notions of the seventh century.

For decades, the Shi'a–Sunni difference was contained by sheer numbers that placed the former at a great disadvantage. Recent estimates put the world's Muslim population at around 1.6 billion, with the Shi'a representing between 10% and 13% of that figure.[12] The overwhelming majority of Shi'a, perhaps as many as 80%, are concentrated in just four countries: Iran, Pakistan, India, and Iraq. Iran and, to a less certain degree, Iraq are the only modern states in which Shi'a political power predominates. Like many other minority groups, the Shi'a have safeguarded their traditions, practices, and identity zealously from dangerous encroachment by the large Sunni majority while at the same time staking out their rightful place within the totality of the Muslim *ummah*.

This perceived need for self-assertion, generally in the face of prejudice, persecution, or even outright repression throughout the centuries at the hands of the Sunnis, has served to sharpen Shi'a attitudes and to reinforce their communal sense of self. This, in turn, provokes a hardening of religious identity and exclusion on the part of the Sunni. "The responsibility for the salience of Shi'ite identity in society and politics lies not with the Shi'a alone, but at least as much with the Sunnis who dominate social and political attitudes," write Graham Fuller and Rend Rahim Francke in their study of the Arab Shi'a.[13]

As a result, the Shi'a have produced a rich and powerful tradition that spells out not only their claim, against the radical Sunni position— that they are in fact Muslims—but also asserts that their long history of innocent suffering and unwarranted deprivation as an underclass, and an associated sense of existential sorrow and martyrdom, are grounded in the religious upheavals that attended the first, formative years of Islam. The Shi'a historical memory—what one scholar has termed a "historiographical monument"[14]—not only defines the past, but also interprets and explains the present, and shapes the community's hopes and fears for the future.

Although this book focuses on the societal dynamics of sectarianism, it is important to note how outsiders—namely, states—encourage and drive this conflict. The US invasion of Iraq in 2003 and its subsequent role in creating a Shi'a-led government ignited a sectarian conflict that eventually spread to other Arab states. Although Iran, Saudi Arabia, Bahrain, and other Gulf States advance a sectarian agenda for their own political purposes, domestically and regionally, they also blame one another. In Bahrain, for example, a Shi'a-led uprising that began with some local Sunni support was transformed quickly into a government narrative of loyal Sunnis pitted against an Iranian-backed Shi'a opposition. This influential propaganda discouraged any further Sunni support for the uprising, which at the beginning in 2011 was focused on political and economic reform to end the regime's authoritarian monopoly on power.

For the Sunnis, the shift in the political dynamics in the Arab world, placing the Shi'a as rulers over them in some countries, produced feelings of anxiety and even fears of extinction. The Sunni response came from many different quarters—from the Salafists, who for decades had resisted politics but now felt a need to enter the fray to combat the perceived Shi'a threat, to Muslim Brothers in Egypt, who overplayed their hand in seeking religious and political supremacy in the region, to the explosions of wars in Syria and Iraq.

My goal here is to illustrate how Shi'a and Sunni perceive one another after the Arab uprisings, and how these perceptions have affected Arab life. Chapter 1 focuses on the Shi'a in Iraq and how the formation of Shi'a militias, backed by Iran and unleashed in 2014 by Grand Ayatollah Sistani, the leading Iraqi Shi'a authority, added a new dimension to the Shi'a–Sunni relationship. Here are Arab Shi'a taking orders from a Persian Shi'a militia, Iran's Islamic Revolutionary Guard Corps, to combat the Sunni Islamic State that has at least some support from Iraqi Sunnis. This chapter shows how, despite Iran's heavy hand in Iraq, the Shi'a in the holy Iraqi city of Najaf are fighting to preserve the historical difference between their religious traditions and how Shi'ism is practiced and interpreted in Iran. The Shi'a of Najaf are facing a threat on the one hand from the Sunni extremists in the Islamic State, and on the other from the onslaught of Iranian Shi'a domination in the rest of the country.

Chapter 2 explains how Salafism has changed during the post-Arab uprising era. It explores the entrance into politics of a brand of Islamists who had, for the most part, shunned such activity in the past but changed course as a result of the war in Syria and the revolutions. This chapter also offers a discussion of the categories of Salafists and how and why they have shifted since the Arab uprisings. Historically, their tradition required, for example, that they support a ruler regardless of the conditions, but this changed after the uprisings, as Salafists became more politicized and joined in the rebellions within their own countries.

Chapter 3 is a study of sectarian discourse among a select group of influential Salafists. I have chosen leading, nonviolent Salafists as an indicator of Sunni attitudes toward the Shi'a for a number of reasons. This is not to say they are representative of mainstream Sunni thought; however, they are at the forefront of new thinking, particularly after the Muslim Brotherhood in Egypt was banned and forced underground. As one Salafist told me in Cairo in 2012: "Our aim is to redefine how Islam is practiced." Although their numbers are too few and their influence is too little for such a grand ambition, they have nonetheless made a dramatic impact on how Sunnis perceive their Shi'a brethren. Chapter 3 profiles these most influential Salafists, many of whom are completely unknown to the Western audience and operate in what might as well be a parallel universe to our own. Because their Twitter feeds are in Arabic, as are their satellite shows and YouTube videos, they are often unknown quantities in the West, although some have millions of Arabic-speaking Twitter followers. The analysis of the

Twitter-sphere in this chapter also shows the transnational nature of sectarian attitudes, which have no borders or boundaries. In the appendix of the book, I have included a selection of the actual tweets, which I provide in English with the Arabic links, to show the literal sectarian discourse.

Chapters 4 and 5 are case studies of the sectarian conflicts in Lebanon and Bahrain, respectively. In both countries, the tension between Shi'a and Sunni has a long history. But the Arab uprisings altered social and political conditions, causing both communities to perceive one another in a new and different light. In Bahrain, a Shi'a-led uprising that began with some Sunni support degenerated quickly into a degree of polarization between the two such as few Bahrainis can remember in modern times. Self-segregation now runs deep in Bahrain society from the universities to cafés to internal family relations. Meanwhile, the ruling Sunni government fuels the religious difference by convincing the minority Sunni population that the uprising had no merit, but was simply an Iranian–Shi'a plot to topple the regime.

In Lebanon, Hezbollah's direct intervention in Syria to help keep President Bashar al Assad in power transformed the movement from a militia and a party fighting the Israeli resistance for the benefit of all Lebanese to a Shi'a fighting force that lost support among Sunnis at home, but managed to remain a strong political force inside Lebanon. Today, Hezbollah is seen largely as advancing Shi'a interests.

The tensions being played out in the region cannot be analyzed effectively without acknowledging the geopolitical conflicts among Iran, Saudi Arabia, and other states with sectarian agendas. Chapter 6, the conclusion, is a discussion of state rivalry. The conflict on the ground is highly influenced by geopolitics at the state level. Much media attention is focused on Iran and Saudi Arabia as two countries with a longstanding rivalry that tried to ramp up sectarian tension after the Arab uprisings for their own political purposes. But in fact, other states—Bahrain among them—also played the sectarian card to their own benefit. Although from the beginning, in 2011, Iran's political elites conveniently referred to the Arab uprisings as a pan-Islamic awakening that would ultimately unite Shi'a and Sunni, the country's military apparatus drew sectarian battle lines in Iraq and Syria almost immediately after conflicts got underway in those countries.

In the final chapter I conclude that the state rivalry feeds societal sectarian sentiment and vice versa. This combustible top-down and bottom-up bigotry along sectarian fault lines will, ultimately, alter the map of the Middle East from what it has been since the fall of the Ottoman Empire. This is the reason to draw world attention to the sectarian conflict. Although the idea of a reconfigured Middle East has now become a media cliché, the long-term, significant effects of the shifting boundaries should not be lost in punditry. Shifting borders along sectarian lines could end in a partitioned Iraq and Syria with Shi'a and Sunni living separately; a more divided Syria than exists today; an increasingly polarized Lebanon; and the further marginalization of the Shi'a in Bahrain and Saudi Arabia, and confinement to their own communities in both countries.

Last, on a personal and intellectual level, I must note that I wrote this book as further evidence that religion in Arab society matters—not only in how it is exploited and instrumentalized by extremists, moderate Islamists, and dictators alike for political purposes—but also how it evolves perpetually and is perceived and practiced among the vast majority of Muslims. Arab women do not wear headscarves because of pressure from their husbands or because they cannot afford to buy shampoo, as one prominent Egyptian leader tried to convince me during the 1990s. Similarly, Shi'a and Sunni today are not battling it out over territory alone; they are fighting for history and memory.

Beirut, Lebanon
February 2016

CHAPTER ONE

MULLAHS AND THE MILITIAS

At first glance, the unsuspecting visitor could be excused, perhaps, for mistaking the twisting alleyways of the remote Iraqi desert city of Najaf for those of the equally dusty Iranian religious center of Qom, 365 miles to the northeast. Shi'a clerics in long robes, their backs ramrod straight, glide elegantly in starched clothing through muddy streets, seemingly immune to the surrounding hubbub of nonstop religious tourism. Both Najaf and Qom play host each year to small armies of pilgrims who flock to the cities' respective holy shrines, seeking intercession with God and remission of their sins. And both house thousands of young seminary students and the large cohort of mid-level and senior scholarly clerics who guide their charges through the long and arduous curriculum of traditional Shi'a religious and secular learning.

And yet, Najaf can, in many ways, lay claim to both greater symbolic significance and greater theological purity than Qom, its Iranian counterpart and on-again, off-again rival as the fount of Shi'a scholarly thought and religious influence. After all, Najaf is one of the four Shi'a "sublime thresholds," holy sites that, for the faithful, exist as intermediary spaces between the divine and earthbound worlds. Here, in a practice that is bitterly denounced by many Sunni theologians as polytheism—and, thus, as heretical—Shi'a believers gather to pray at the tombs of their earliest leaders, the semidivine and infallible Imams.

At the center of Najaf's religious life sits the burial site of Imam Ali ibn Abi Talib, revered by Shi'a Muslims as the commander of the faithful. Ali was the son-in-law and companion of the Prophet Mohammad and the first to be regarded by the Shi'a as his legitimate successor. In Shi'a eyes, he is second only to the Prophet in religious and political importance; in contrast, Sunni Muslims view Ali as the last—and in the minds of some, the least worthy—of the four "rightly guided" successors, or Caliphs, who were chosen to lead the Muslim community in the immediate years following the death of the Prophet Mohammad.

On any given day, the past meets the present in Najaf, 90 miles due south of the Iraqi administrative capital Baghdad. Shi'a pilgrims wail at Ali's tomb, set in a shrine made of gold and crystal so bright it almost blinds the eye. Chandeliers hang garishly from the ceilings, and ornate tiles in the ancient Persian colors of cobalt blue and green encase the walls. The tomb itself is covered in gold and green, the traditional color of the Prophet and his family, the *ahl al bayt*. Such is popular devotion to Ali that Najaf is the third most visited site in Islam, after Mecca and Medina, despite the fact that Shi'a make up only a little more than one tenth of the world's Muslims. Here, the pilgrims kiss the sacred walls and mourn Ali's passing almost 1,400 years ago.

Just as the tomb of Ali outshines Qom's shrine to Fatemeh Masoumeh, the sister of the Eighth Imam who fell ill in eastern Iran during the early ninth century and asked to be buried among the local Shi'a, so, too, can Najaf's supreme religious authorities, represented in the person of Grand Ayatollah Ali Sistani, be seen in something of a superior light. Throughout the centuries they have largely avoided the reliance on state support and the patronage of the social elite that has long characterized clerical life in the Iranian religious centers of Qom and Mashhad. This is an important distinction, one that lies at the intersection of Shi'a religious thought and historical experience—and one that is playing out today in the ongoing rivalry for power and influence throughout the Shi'a world between the senior clergy of Iran and Iraq.

Traditional Shi'a thinking, shaped by the community's long experience as a distinct and often-persecuted minority under Sunni domination, dismisses the exercise of political or executive authority by ordinary mortals as inherently corrupting and religiously illegitimate. As such, the clerics should have nothing to do with worldly affairs, unless the Shi'a community were to face an existential threat or significant hindrance to the proper practice of the faith. In such cases, the clergy must step forward and address the danger, before retreating to their seminaries and returning to their books. Since its establishment as a prominent center of Shi'a learning during the 19th century, Najaf has largely adhered to this reading of the faith, and its leading thinkers have passed along these notions to legions of colleagues and students.

The history and social makeup of Najaf as a center of Shi'a teaching and scholarship have served to reinforce this quietist tendency. Unlike their Iranian or Ottoman counterparts, the religious centers of the "sublime thresholds," such as Najaf and nearby Karbala, were funded traditionally by private donations rather than by direct state sponsorship or the awarding of landed endowments, the *awqaf*, by the central authorities. As a result, the clergy of Najaf were not faced with demands to provide religious legitimacy to government policies. Nor were they called on to staff the state judiciary or provide pathways to social advancement among Qajar or Ottoman elites.[1]

Absent top-down oversight by the state or undue pressures from its ruling circles, the clerics of Iraq have pursued their own religious and scholarly work in line with both traditional Shi'a thinking and the day-to-day concerns of ordinary believers. This has kept the religious community there relatively free of corruption and nepotism, and allowed it to serve as a powerful source of upward mobility in which scholarship, personal integrity, and charisma generally trump wealth or political and social connections.[2]

At the same time, the Shi'a community in Iraq has distinguished itself through its Arab identity rather than through its ties or interactions with the Persian *ulama* in Iran. The Iraqi Shi'a flourished centuries after Shi'ism became grounded in Iran during the 16th and 17th centuries. In Iraq, the Shi'a population began to establish itself only beginning in the mid-18th century. The result was an Iraqi Shi'a community in modern times that built an identity that is neither Iranian–Persian nor Sunni Arab.

Taken together, the social fabric of Najaf's religious center, with its bottom-up orientation, and the establishment of a strong Arab Shi'a identity, separate and apart from that of its Iranian brethren, have provided the Iraqi clergy with a degree of insulation and protection in even the most turbulent of times. The Iraqi Shi'a authorities, for the most part, survived the brutal rule of Sunni strongman Saddam Hussein, just as they earlier dismissed attempts by Ayatollah Khomeini to extend his so-called Islamic revolution and his own religious authority into neighboring Iraq.

In many ways, Ayatollah Khomeini's religious radicalism posed a greater fundamental threat to the integrity of the Najaf religious establishment than even the aggressive secularizing policies, not to mention the murderous tendencies, of Hussein and his Sunni-dominated Baath Party. During his exile from Iran in the 1960s and 1970s, much of it in Najaf, Khomeini developed a new and expansive reading of traditional Shi'a clerical responsibility to oversee not only those too weak to care for themselves, such as widows, orphans, or the infirm, but society as a whole.

In Khomeini's vision, the senior-most religious jurist, or *faqih* (in this case, Khomeini himself), was duty-bound to assume political and executive authority, the *velayat*, in place of Iran's corrupt and Westernized secular rulers. Such direct clerical power violated the very notion of authority in Shi'ism, which ultimately rests on a scholarly consensus that no one, absent Ali and the other perfect Imams, is sufficiently free of sin to exercise such power legitimately. This doctrine of *velayat-e faqih*, which holds official sway in post-Khomeini Iran, continues to horrify traditionalist Shi'a clerics—in Iraq as well as in Iran.[3]

Today, however, it is unclear whether this Shi'a clerical ideal of noninterference in worldly affairs, championed in the past by Iraq's religious establishment under the supreme religious authority, Grand Ayatollah Sistani, can survive when confronted with raging regional instability and mounting sectarian violence now consuming the region in the wake of the 2003 US invasion of Iraq and its tumultuous—and, sadly, all-too-predictable—aftereffects. Already, Sistani has found himself crossing that line more than once, driven, say his aides and supporters, by necessity because of the war, the persistent weakness of the Iraqi central state, and the accompanying violence that plagues the country. The question remains: Is there any turning back? Or has the sheer scale of the challenges facing Iraq—corruption, sectarian hatred, rampant instability, and the expanding threat from ISIS—pushed the

Shi'a clergy into a permanent role in the political life of the nation? In other words, has the *jinn* of direct clerical rule in Iraq been loosed from its bottle?

Given the complex nature of Iraqi life, it is perhaps fitting that the problem of the clergy's place in politics can best be illustrated by a meeting that never happened. One afternoon in November 2015, Prime Minister Haider al Abadi arrived in Najaf to consult the grand ayatollah, hoping to seal the latter's support for key government policies; but, Sistani refused to see him—a snub with huge symbolic and political significance. Najaf clerics said publicly no such meeting had been planned, but privately they acknowledged the affair was a major setback for the embattled prime minister in his struggle with parliament over proposed political, economic, and social reform. An entourage of cars and men outside the house of Ayatollah Fayad was all abuzz with the news, and there was a certain sense of pride that Iraq's grand ayatollah stood up to the prime minister.

The incident points to the murky position of Iraq's clerics: although they are outside politics officially, they hold great political weight. Sistani, for example, has been instrumental in guiding Iraq's future since the US invasion. He influenced US government decision making and he continues to be a leader in trying to build a better life for Iraq's Shi'a, who represent about 60% of the country's population. His views on domestic affairs, often relayed in the Friday prayer sermons delivered by trusted surrogates or through published statements, are helping to shape post-Saddam Iraq, while his son is said to a maintain a direct telephone line to Abadi's office.

Complicating Sistani's relationship to the Iraqi body politic is a seemingly intractable problem that intermingles relatively obscure questions of Shi'a theology and more familiar notions of nation-state geopolitics: How should the Iraqi Shi'a deal with Iran, a rich, powerful neighbor and home to the political mullahs who have pushed Khomeini's notion of religious rule to the extreme? With the fall of Saddam Hussein and the end of minority Sunni domination, the Shi'a of Iraq are no longer just an opposition force led by clerics; they are politicians running a government. But, Iraqi government decisions are often dictated by Iran's demands. The al Quds Force, which is under the Islamic Revolutionary Guards Corps, Iran's primary military, has deep roots in Iraq. Even when Iraq's clerical establishment makes decisions, there is no guarantee Iran will cooperate or resist co-opting and manipulating the conflicts that engulf Iraq.

The most recent and significant example of this dilemma emerged when Sistani issued a *fatwa*, or religious decree, June 13, 2014, calling on all Iraqis to fight against ISIS, the heavily armed Sunni movement that has seized considerable territory in Iraq and neighboring Syria. On that day, during the Friday sermon at the Imam Hussein Shrine in Karbala, Sheikh Mahdi al Karbalai announced that Sistani had issued a call to arms for all Iraqis—Shi'a and Sunni alike—to roll back ISIS advances into Iraqi territory.[4] At the time, ISIS had just seized the major provincial city of Mosul, in its first big victory, and announced the creation of what they call their caliphate, or Islamic State.

The Sistani *fatwa* was followed by another statement a week later on June 20, during a Friday prayer sermon given by another representative of the grand ayatollah, Sayyed Ahmad al Safi:

> The call to arms is directed towards all Iraqi citizens regardless of religious sect, since the goal is to confront this *takfiri* [heretical] group called ISIS which has secured an upper hand in many provinces and has declared frankly and clearly its plan to target others, such as Najaf and Karbala, and all Shi'a sacred sites and shrines.... The call to arms has no sectarian basis, and it cannot be so because the Supreme Religious Authority [Sistani] has demonstrated over the past years and in the most difficult circumstances that it is far from any sectarian practice, proved by the famous line about the Sunnis: "Sunnis are not our brothers, they are us."[5]

Responding to Sistani's call for *al hashd al shaabi*, or "popular mobilization," against ISIS, Iraqis rushed to volunteer centers in many provinces. In Basra, volunteer centers received more than 30,000 volunteers, according to Ali al Edani, Director of Citizens Affairs in Basra

Province.[6] Immediately, an estimated 60,000 to 90,000 citizens had enlisted. But, despite Sistani's assertions that his order was not sectarian, nearly all volunteers were Shi'a, determined to defend the country from the Sunni militants of ISIS. They considered the call from Sistani a religious duty and responsibility because they no longer believed the Shi'a-led Iraqi government or army—both weak after many years of incompetent governance—could save them.[7]

And it was not fear of ISIS alone, but of what had become a widespread fear that Sunnis across Iraq, and throughout the wider region, were intent on conquering the Shi'a communities that dot the Middle East. The Shi'a believed, not without justification, that ISIS would not have succeeded in taking control of Mosul if the militants had not had the support of the local Sunni population. And, in interviews in Jordan and other parts of Iraq months later, Sunni tribal leaders admitted to me they had turned their support to ISIS and instructed their tribes to do the same to avenge what they believed was years of marginalization and repression by the Shi'a-dominated Iraqi government, the Iraqi military and Iranian-backed Revolutionary Guards.[8] Another reason Iraqi tribal leaders give for the ISIS takeover in parts of Iraq is the collapse of state security. "Initially, the citizens of Anbar were peacefully protesting before ISIS was a phenomenon," explained Sheikh Majid in an interview in Erbil, Iraq, in 2015. "Daesh took advantage of the situation by taking advantage of people's grievances," said Majid, who is from Anbar Province, now an ISIS stronghold. "The Sunnis have no recourse. They are stuck between ISIS and the Shi'a militias."[9]

Such characterizations became clear in 2014, prompting one scholar of contemporary Iraqi politics to describe the Shi'a–Sunni dynamic aptly as "Shi'a-centric state building and Sunni rejection." Scholar Fanar Haddad wrote:

> Sectarianization will continue to define Iraqi politics. The spread of the self-proclaimed Islamic State across much of Iraq in 2014 represents the most extreme form of Sunni rejection. The state-sanctioned *hashd al shabi* ... embodies the most serious defense of Shi'a-centric state building as of late 2015.[10]

For scholars such as Haddad, the drivers of sectarianism are more about a battle for political control and trading in notions of citizenship for a communal rather than a religious identity. They do not see conflict as a permanent reflection of religious identity, but rather of communal sentiment. Haddad refers to a road map written by a prominent Iraqi Shi'a politician, Ali Allawi, which stated, "Iraq is the Shi'a . . . and the Shi'a are Iraq."[11]

Although the political class has no reservations about their objective to retain Shi'a-centric state building, the clerics try to deemphasize communal differences. Although the *hashd al shabi* ended up as a predominantly, although not fully, Shi'a military force, this was never Sistani's intention. Since the *fatwa*, an array of armed militias have emerged, not all of which acknowledge the authority of the grand ayatollah to the point of following his decrees—another unanticipated problem.

Two such groups follow the veteran Iranian commander Qasem Soleimani, who first gained notoriety in the Iran–Iraq War (1980–1988) and has since become the point man for Iran's military operations in Iraq and Syria. Soleimani boasts of his victories by sending out through social media photos of himself standing on tanks. He is a persistent thorn in Sistani's side, and rumors circulated in Najaf in 2015 that Sistani had written a letter to Iranian Supreme Leader Ali Khamenei complaining that Soleimani was an unwanted guest.

Another faction of the militia movement is loyal to former Prime Minister Nouri al Maliki, who once enjoyed Iranian patronage and support. In 2015, Haddad wrote:

> Indeed, given the *hashd's* popularity, it seems all but inevitable that an increasing number of Shi'i political figures will try to position themselves as patrons of the *Hashd*. Already Vice President and former Prime Minister Nuri al Maliki has badly attempted to absorb the *hashd's* organic popular appeal.[12]

Clearly, the *marja'iya*, the collective clerical establishment under Sistani's overall leadership, never wanted to create Shi'a militias that would be beholden to Iran. As Sheikh Bashir al Najafi, one of four grand ayatollahs in Iraq, explained: "We don't take issue with Iranian references in Qom. But the problem occurs when they use it to work against the Iraqi state, such as their support for the Shi'a militias. We live in fear of being accused of being aligned with Iran."[13] Najafi received his religious education in Gujranwala, Punjab. He then moved to Iraq during the 1960s to continue his education. He is one of the few Pakistanis ever to have been elevated to the rank of ayatollah, and he is considered a possible successor to Ayatollah Sistani, who is now 85 years old.

The Popular Mobilization Forces (PMF) soon transcended their original mission; they were no longer just a group of volunteers fighting the Islamic State. Instead, they emerged as a force on an equal footing with the Iraqi Armed Forces, and with matching authority to operate, which creates different scenarios for the future and complicates the political process further, especially after the liberation of Sunni-dominated northern and western regions of Iraq. Sistani's *fatwa* constituted the umbrella under which armed groups were formed, and volunteer fighters from the PMF joined them.[14]

The volunteer fighters helped the Iraqi Armed Forces avoid complete collapse as a result of the rapid advancement of ISIS. As one fighter put it: "The Iraqi Army depends on us a lot, because we are skilled at guerrilla war, and this is what it takes to confront the Islamic State."[15] However, some Iraqi politicians were prescient in fearing that the existence of these armed groups would exacerbate the sectarian nature of the conflict. Some Shi'a politicians believe that the PMF have transcended the role set by Sistani's *fatwa*, especially after their transformation from zealous volunteers to highly organized military structures.

As a result, the *hasdh*, or PMF, has become a leading source for sectarian discontent and conflict—resented by Sunnis and just as fiercely defended by many Shi'a. Already, this has exacerbated regional tensions, also along sectarian lines, and threatens to draw much of the Middle East into the fray. The Iranian media, for example, likes to boast that Soleimani is the true leader of the PMF, whereas al Azhar Mosque, the traditional seat for Sunni learning based in Cairo, has labeled the volunteer fighters of the PMF "sectarian killers."[16] According to many regional analysts and other sources, including the US government, many of the Shi'a militias are now primarily under the control of Iran's Revolutionary Guards and commit violence almost on the scale of ISIS. This was surely not what Sistani or any clerics in Iraq had in mind when they supported the initial idea of a Shi'a mobilization force.

All indications suggest that such fears are justified. In short order, the PMF were committing acts of violence nearly on par with those of ISIS, although there are no reports of the PMF kidnapping women and making them sex slaves, as is the case with ISIS. They entered Sunni-dominated towns taken over by ISIS, such as Tikrit, the hometown of Saddam Hussein and his clan, and they vowed to secure the cities against the Islamic State until the majority of the Sunni communities could return. But in many cases, this did not happen.[17] In October 2014, just months after the new militias formed, Amnesty International issued a report documenting the militias' human rights abuses. "The militias have burned Sunni homes and stole our possessions and refused to allow us to return," said a Sunni religious scholar who fled Iraq and is in hiding in Iraqi Kurdistan. "The goal of this is to change the demographics of Sunni towns," he said in an interview, and did not want to be identified for security reasons.[18]

The Amnesty report confirmed such claims and drew an extremely important conclusion that speaks to the character of the sectarian conflict not only in Iraq, but also in the entire Middle East. Amnesty concluded the militias were making no distinction between Sunni terrorists and ordinary Sunni citizens. In the same way that the Sunnis across the Arab world tend to view Shi'a populations as puppets of Iran—even in a city such as Najaf, where there is fierce opposition to Iran's political and theocratic system—the Shi'a do the same. According to the Amnesty report:

> In recent months, Shi'a militias have been abducting and killing Sunni civilian men in Baghdad and around the country. These militias, often armed and backed by the government of Iraq, continue to operate with varying degrees of cooperation from government forces—ranging from tacit consent to coordinated, or even joint, operations.[19]

Amnesty interviewed Sunnis who were victims of the militias in Samara, Kirkuk, and Tikrit. In Kirkuk, for example, Amnesty's findings concluded that, even in a city where citizens in the past did not distinguish Sunni from Shi'a and where there were intrasectarian marriages, this all changed in 2014. Kirkuk, a city famous for its diversity of Sunni Arabs, Kurds, and Turkmen, has become the frontline, with Peshmerga forces against Shi'a militias, at times backed by Iranian fighters.[20]

After years of deteriorating security, including frequent car bombings and attacks on pilgrims and other religious celebrants, the Shi'a today consider the PMF the only power capable of protecting them. Yet, the Shi'a insist on describing the PMF in nationalist terms, dismissing sectarian affiliations. In general, various PMF elements share its sectarian membership and—at least in theory—the broader struggle against ISIS. However, it does not have a unified political vision or party platform. Moreover, some elements belonging to the PMF do not participate in the fight against ISIS, but are deployed to the cities and towns in southern Iraq to protect those predominantly Shi'a areas from potential threats, according to sources in Najaf.[21]

Private conversations among the Shi'a political leadership focus on turning the PMF into an internal security force in the future, placed under the auspices of the state, with the support of major political groups. As such, the PMF resemble the *Basij* in Iran, which deals with internal security and differs from the Islamic Revolutionary Guards, which tackle national security matters.[22]

There is no precise count of the number of recruits belonging to the PMF, but several conflicting estimates exist. Despite the disparity, the majority of sources confirm the approximate number of recruits is near 120,000 fighters, 60,000 of whom are actively engaged in fighting. The remaining number seems to be a matter of dispute, given that many sources believe leaders of the armed factions have been registering false numbers of fighters with the Iraqi government to receive salaries and money for equipment.

Although the PMF have many branches, some of which follow Sistani, their influence can be traced to four major figures who dominate the movement and its military activity. Their roles are divided essentially along two distinct lines, the first featuring Hadi al Amiri and Qays al Khaz'ali, and the second Shebel al Zaidi and Abu Mahdi al Mohandis. Both groups coordinate with Soleimani, the Iranian commander.[23]

Al Amiri, also known as Abu Hassan al Amiri, a former transport minister and a current member of parliament, is the leader of the Badr Organization and the PMF. Al Amiri's political career started during the early 1980s, when he was a member of the Shi'a opposition, when he left Iraq for Syria following the execution of Ayatollah Mohamad Baqer al Sadr. In Syria, he connected with the Islamic Supreme Council led by Mohamad Baqer al Hakim. He then traveled to Iran and spent the following years cofounding the Badr Brigade, the armed group of the Badr Organization.

Al Amiri won parliamentary elections with the State of Law Coalition headed by former Prime Minister Nouri al Maliki, securing 22 seats for the Badr parliamentary bloc, and only narrowly failed to become Minister of Interior. After that incident, al Amiri quit politics in Baghdad and devoted himself solely to military work in the field as commander of the PMF.[24] He is disliked by many Sunnis for his close Iranian connection, particularly to the Islamic Revolutionary Guards. Amiri told *The New Yorker* magazine in 2013: "I love Qassem Soleimani! He is my dearest friend."[25] Other Shi'a factions are also involved in the fighting against the Islamic State, including the Hezbollah movement (of the Noble/Victorious) led by Akram al Kaabi; the Hezbollah Brigade in Iraq led by Hashem Abu Alaa al Hamadani and comprising 600 fighters; the Master of Martyrs Brigade led by Abu Mustafa al Shibani, with 400 fighters; the True Promise Legion led by Muhamad al Tamimi, with 2,000 fighters; the al Khorasani Forefront Units led by Ali al Yasiri of 200 fighters; the Mohamad Baqer al Sadr Forces led by Abu Mahdi al Mohandis (Jamal Jaafar), with 300 fighters; the Abu al Fadl al Abbas Brigade led by Amjad al Bahadli containing 500 fighters and considered the most famous of the Iraqi fighting factions since the outbreak of the Syrian crisis; and, last, the Imam Hussein Brigade led by Abu Shahd al Jubouri comprising 150 fighters.[26]

The armed faction that has emerged as the most prominent since the Islamic State invaded Mosul is the Imam Ali Brigade, estimated to comprise about 3,000 fighters. Members dress in military uniform with a yellow insignia woven into the costume, no doubt a conscious nod to Hezbollah in Lebanon, whose strong discipline and high level of organization they seek to emulate. The Imam Ali Brigade is prominent in areas such as Amerli, Tuz, and Diyala, fighting alongside other armed groups. Iraqis exchange stories about the strength and severity of these fighters, to the extent that a video clip was released showing what were said to be the severed heads of people presumed to be ISIS, captured by the Brigade. This group is also training Iraqi Christians to form a group called The Spirit of God, Jesus Son of Mary Brigade.

Kata'ib Hezbollah (KH), also known as the Hezbollah Brigade, is another important Shi'a Iraqi insurgent group based in central and southern Iraq. The group is led by Abu Mahdi al Mohandis and receives large amounts of training, logistical support, and weapons from the Iranian al Quds Force, the special military unit of the Iranian Revolutionary Guards Corps. From 2007 to 2011, the KH directed the majority of its attacks against US–Coalition forces in Iraq and often posted recordings of the attacks on their website. The US State Department officially designated the KH as a foreign terrorist organization on July 2, 2009.

After the US withdrawal from Iraq in 2011, the KH sent large numbers of its fighters to Syria to fight alongside Hezbollah and the Assad government. Although it has continued to fight in Syria, since the rise of the Islamic State in 2014, the KH has concentrated on fighting ISIS in Iraq, working closely with the Iraqi government. The KH has played a role in fighting along with Iraqi security forces in Anbar Province since 2014, particularly in the town of Fallujah. The group says it has formed the People's Defense Brigade to "defend the country and holy places" and fight ISIS. It lists among its local enemies Sunni groups.[27]

The Jihad and Construction Brigade was formed in conjunction with Sistani's *fatwa* as the military wing of the political movement known as *Islamic Jihad and Construction*, established in early 2011 through a merger of three Islamic movements: the Hezbollah movement in

Iraq, the Master of Martyrs movement, and the Nahda Party in Iraq.[28] The current secretary general is Hassan al Sari, a member of parliament and a former minister, and one of the leaders of the Iraqi Islamic Supreme Council (led by Sayyed Ammar al Hakim). The Brigade maintains a close relationship to Iran's Khamenei through Secretary General Hakim, who spent years in Iran. The number of members is estimated at about 3,000; they are characterized by their ferocity in fighting and are considered among the most religious fighters. They use light and medium weapons, and are backed by the Iraqi Army's heavy fire through a relationship mediated by the Badr Organization.[29]

The creation of the new Shi'a militias as a response to the Sistani *fatwa* has backfired—and done so precipitously. These new forces have enabled Iran's Revolutionary Guards to spread its ideology and deepen and diversify its roots in Iraq—the exact opposite result the Najafi clerical establishment had sought when the *fatwa* was issued. In an attempt to limit the damage, the clerics of Najaf downplay the violence the Shi'a militias are committing against the Sunnis for several reasons. First, they want to avoid undermining Ayatollah Sistani, whose religious decree instigated the formation of the militias and then endowed them with religious legitimacy. Second, they are reluctant to acknowledge that some of the militias are brutal and are an impediment to displaced Sunnis returning to their homes. Third, although they are most eager to talk about Iran's attempts at religious influence in Iraq that challenges what they consider to be a proper relationship between religion and state in the Shi'a tradition, they are more reluctant to discuss Iran's military intervention.

Finally and most significantly, it is becoming increasingly harder to make the case that Iraq's *marja'iya* are not involved intimately in politics. Although Ayatollah Sistani's political involvement is unusual in the religious tradition, particularly given the fact that there is a Shi'a-led government in power and not a Sunni one, there have been periods in history when Iraqi clerics have intervened. The clerics' political activity increased significantly after the fall of the Ottoman Empire and the clerics rebelled against British forces, which soon thereafter occupied Iraq.

The *ulama* of Najaf staged an uprising in 1920 against British rule and some were forced into exile in 1923—a development that paved the way for the revitalization of the Iranian religious center of Qom, which had long since fallen on hard times. This uprising still looms in the memory of the Iraqi Shi'a, so much so that Sistani is credited for warning the Shi'a after the US invasion to act in moderation, not like 1920, or they would risk forcing the United States to hand power over to the Sunnis.

Militancy among the political Shi'a can be traced to the 1950s with the establishment of the Da'wa Party. During the 1960s and 1970s, Saddam Hussein's Baath Party executed many Shi'a religious leaders in response to intense Islamic activity that tried to counter the secular regime. Since that time, the Shi'a movement—composed of an array of political parties—has maintained different and often conflicting objectives, especially when compared with those of the *marja'iya*.[30]

After years of resistance to Saddam Hussein, the US invasion held out promise for the *marja'iya*, some of whom supported the war and later paid a heavy price as a result. Their aim was to end their marginalization, and that meant the senior clergy had to take a position with regard to the American occupation. Although some clerics cooperated with the United States, others stood in opposition. The most prominent religiously inspired militia that emerged to confront the United States was the Mahdi Army, formed by Muqtada Sadr in June 2003, who claimed political and religious legitimacy because of his father, Mohammed Sadiq Sadr.

Much like Khomeini, the younger Sadr preached about the need for establishing an Islamic State in Iraq. His goal was to oust US forces and install a Shi'a government in Baghdad. In 2004, his fighters battled US troops. For some in the US government, the Sadr militia was considered more dangerous than al Qaeda, then also operating in Iraq. They were accused of carrying out the most gruesome sectarian violence in Iraq. Sadr dissolved his militia in 2008 and fled to Iran.

In interviews with three of four grand ayatollahs in Najaf—Sistani was not meeting any visitors at the time, including the prime minister—and dozens of clerics, they described their recent entry into overt politics, in particular the *fatwa* sanctioning the popular militias, as "a matter of necessity." Significantly, Ayatollah Khomeini frequently invoked a similar argument of "religious expediency," or *maslahat*, whenever the practical needs or interests of the state that he headed clashed with traditional Shi'a principles.

The future of Iraq's *marja'iya* will be determined by tensions with Iran and the political forces Tehran controls inside Iraq. The conflict between Iraq's traditional clergy and Iranian-backed military and political operatives is mounting. And it is likely to come to a head when Sistani dies. Already, the Iranians are promoting as his successor Mahmoud Hashemi al Shaharoudi, the arch-conservative former head of the Iranian judiciary. If this occurs, it will likely end whatever autonomy Iraq's traditional clerics still retain from their historic rivals in Qom.

The problem of authority in Islam has always been particularly acute among the Shi'a, who owe their very existence and identity to fundamental disagreements among the early Muslims over the rightful succession to the religious and political mantle of the Prophet Mohammad. Over time, the Shi'a community came to share a series of ideas, beliefs, and practices distinct from those of the majority Sunnis.

As with so many lasting foundation narratives, the Shi'a historical tradition was forged in battle, amid the last gasps of the fallen, the moans of the fatally wounded, and the mournful prayers for the dead. In this way, it very much resembles the later creation myths that surround the emergence of the European nation state during the 18th century, for the sacred history of the Shi'a, like the nationalist myths of France or Germany for example, transforms "fatality into continuity ... and concerns itself with the links between the dead and the yet unborn."[31]

In the case of the Shi'a, their remarkable communal continuity and self-awareness has been strengthened further by the futile nature of their initial quest, a doomed struggle for political and religious authority

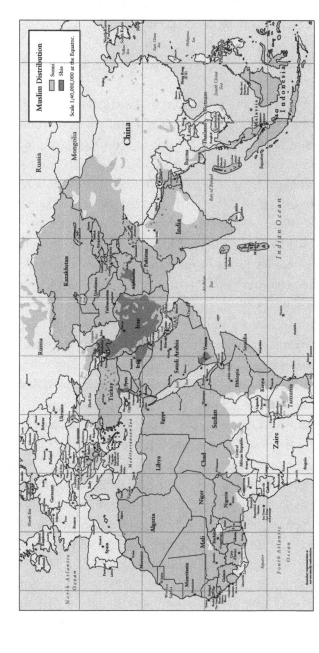

Figure 1.1 Muslim distribution in the world. Courtesy of the University of Texas Libraries.

on the part of their claimant to the office of Caliph—from the Arabic *khalifa*, or successor—Hossein ibn Ali ibn Abi Talib, grandson of the Prophet. The death in 680 of Hossein, hopelessly outnumbered by the forces of his Sunni rival, in the desert at Karbala, in modern-day Iraq, marks the true start of the Shi'a epoch, although it would be a century or so before it would be even possible to speak of a distinct Shi'a identity.

According to tradition, told and retold meticulously to this day, the dying Hossein called out in vain for aid and comfort from any true believer within hearing: "Is there not one professing the oneness of God who would fear God for our sake? Is there no one to come to our help, seeking thereby that which God has in store as a reward for those who would aid us?"[32] Hossein had led his band of rebels into the inhospitable desert, we are told, knowing full well his mission would end in his own death and that of his followers. He even directed his handful of comrades to sneak out of camp before the battle without shame, if they, too, were not prepared to die with him for a righteous but hopeless cause.

The Shi'a consider universally the tragedy at Karbala the greatest act of martyrdom and redemption the world has ever seen. This has endowed them with a tradition of struggle against oppression, tyranny, and injustice that can, under appropriate circumstances, fuel popular rebellion and even revolution. In the eyes of the Sunni majority, the Shi'a represent an untrustworthy, unstable, and dangerous element, one that must, if possible, be kept under control at all times; in more extreme interpretations, it must be eliminated altogether. The conjunction of politics and religion as presented by the suffering of Hossein, as opposed to the passion of the quietist Jesus with which it is often but wrongly compared, is central to Islamic tradition, whether Sunni or Shi'a. As Imam, or leader of the community, Hossein would have commanded both political and religious authority, as did his grandfather, the Prophet Mohammad, and his father, Ali ibn Abi Talib, before him.

The long road to Karbala began two decades earlier during the incipient succession crisis that followed the death of Mohammad—an internal conflict that came to a head in 656 with the election of

Ali, cousin and son-in-law of the Prophet, as the fourth successor, or Caliph. The social, political, and religious tumult that followed the Revelation and the rise of the young Muslim community left in its wake competing claims among the disparate factions, tribes, and economic classes that made up the nascent *ummah*. Mohammad himself had provided no unambiguous guidance or clear identification of an heir—notwithstanding later Shi'a claims that he had proclaimed Ali as his successor. Nor was there another charismatic figure able to step into his mantle, although a number of prophets from various Arab tribes came forward with their own revelations and bids for recognition and authority.[33]

With no designated successor or charismatic leader in sight, the tensions, rivalries, and competing interests of the *ummah*'s emerging constituencies—the early loyalists now centered in Medina, the old Meccan merchant aristocracy that had once bitterly opposed Mohammad's teachings, other nearby Arab tribes, and recent converts among conquered Berbers, Persians, Syrians, and Egyptians—came to the fore. To this might be added a fifth faction: those who demanded the Caliphs maintain a hereditary link to the House of the Prophet, a movement that would coalesce first around the figure of Ali ibn Abi Talib and then around his second son, Hossein.

Soon enough, members of the Meccan elite were able to assert themselves and restore the influence they had lost during their initial and unsuccessful bid to quash Mohammad before his preaching of radical monotheism, which threatened their own religious, economic, and social positions, could gain a foothold in the Arabian peninsula. The first three Caliphs of the Muslim community, Abu Bakr (632–634), Umar (634–644), and Uthman, were all important Meccan figures, and under their rule their kinsmen assumed positions of power, wealth, and influence. Rapid military success helped spread the faith, but also brought into an expanding *ummah* new players, traditions, factions, and ethnic and linguistic groups jostling for recognition and influence of their own. The competing forces unleashed by the succession struggles came to a head with the murder of Uthman, in June 656, and the disputed election of Ali that followed. Many of the new Caliph's opponents, most notably the powerful Banu Umayya of Mecca, saw Ali as complicit in the murder of Uthman, also an Umayyad, and demanded blood vengeance.

Soon the Muslim community found itself caught up in a virtual civil war involving multiple factions, personalities, and groups, and Ali was forced to face down major armed rebellions against his rule. A partisan of one such group, the Kharijites, assassinated Ali in December 656 to avenge the faction's earlier defeat by the Caliph's forces. Ali's death set in motion the events that would ultimately create a specific "Shi'a" identity—the word itself means *party* or *partisan* and refers to the partisans of Ali—and leave the Muslim *ummah* irreversibly splintered. It also created among the Shi'a an extraordinarily durable tradition or "idea" of Ali as the fount of wisdom, piety, supreme eloquence, and bravery in battle. These qualities then redounded to the credit of his second son Hossein, who accepted stoically the burden of his father's cause and sacrificed himself in a one-sided struggle against the Umayyads, now ensconced in the institution of the caliphate and based in Damascus.

Hossein launched his campaign from Medina and marched to the desert of Iraq, south of the city of Kufa, determined to spark a rebellion against the Umayyad Yazid, the first of the Caliphs not to have known Mohammad personally. He also sought to secure the principle of succession to the caliphate for the bloodlines of the Prophet. Earlier, partisans of his father, Ali, from the Iraqi city of Kufa had implored Hossein to lead the struggle to depose the corrupt and illegitimate Yazid. Yet, promised aid from the city, then a hotbed of opposition to the Umayyads, failed to materialize at a decisive moment, leaving Hossein and a handful of supporters to face the Caliph's cavalry on their own.

This brief rebellion, against the Umayyad "usurpers" and in favor of the House of the Prophet, had no military significance and could easily have been lost in the desert sands of time. Instead, it gave birth to a unique communal identity among a vital part of the young Islamic community and launched a religious and social movement that remains a powerful force in world affairs to this day—a result few could have foreseen from the wastelands of seventh-century Karbala. Heinz Halm, a leading scholar of the Shi'a, wrote:

> There was no religious aspect to Shi'ism prior to 680.... For Shi'ites, Karbala represents the central point in their belief, the climax of a divine plan of salvation, the promises of which are offered to all who take the side of the martyred imam [Hossein].[34]

Hossein's martyrdom at Karbala sparked the emergence of an identifiable Shiite consciousness, distinct from clan, personal, and generational interests that drove other rebellions against the acute centralization of power and authority under the early Caliphs. In spiritual and religious terms, it spelled out self-sacrifice and suffering as the true source of redemption for the broader community of believers. It also provided in the figure of Hossein an intercessor at the future Day of Judgment.

Still, the bitter defeat at Karbala provided the necessary impetus for the Shi'a to coalesce around a communal identity and a communal idea of history that stood as something of a rebuke to what would become the ruling Sunni majority, whom the former denounce as "usurpers" of the caliphate.

In time, the Shi'a gradually ritualized the experience of Hossein at Karbala, a sorrowful event commemorated every year as Ashura, named for the tenth day of the month of Moharram when their champion fell in battle. They also began to ritualize their early history as the supreme human tragedy and to draw from it ideals of self-sacrifice, unavoidable suffering for a just cause, capped by inevitable defeat. These notions have provided the core identity around which the Shi'a have defined themselves ever since.

The majority of Shi'a came to see Ali, his sons Hasan and Hossein, and the nine direct descendants who succeeded them as representatives and infallible defenders of the true Islamic ideal, locating them somewhere between the human and the divine. The Sixth Imam, Jafar al Sadeq, a scholarly figure who codified Shi'a holy law and traditions known later as the Jafari School, spelled out the unique status of the

Holy Family—composed of the Prophet, his daughter Fatemeh, his son-in-law Ali, and the 11 Imams: "God created the spirits [of men] two thousand years before their bodies. He made the spirits of Mohammad, Ali, Fatemeh, Hasan, and Hossein and of the other imams the highest and noblest of all."[35]

The men of the Prophet's House are, collectively, the Twelve Imams of what is today the most numerous branch of the Shi'a, known as Twelver or Imami Shi'a. Other subsets of Shi'a follow different lines of succession and recognize different figures, most prominently the Islamailis, or Seveners, whose belief system emphasizes the esoteric and metaphorical meanings hidden inside traditional Islamic teachings rather than the more literalist and legalistic tendencies of the Twelvers. Another significant faction, the Zaydi Shi'a, follow yet another line and do not generally see the early Imams as infallible; they are largely concentrated in Yemen.

Whatever the preferred line from Ali, the Shi'a as a whole present a serious challenge to the majority Sunni by disavowing religious authority on the part of most of the Prophet's earliest supporters and Companions, the so-called First Muslims, on whom the later Sunni project largely rests. It was, after all, these same First Muslims who provided the expanding *ummah* with crucial first-hand accounts of the sayings, or hadiths, and lived example, or Sunna, of the Prophet Mohammad that form much of the basis of Islamic law, religious understanding, and ritual practice. This, then, is the origin of the Sunni charge—still a highly emotive staple of Salafi rhetoric today—that the Shi'a are "rejecters," *rafidha*—or even heretics—for their insistent refusal to recognize the early Muslim leaders and their unswerving loyalty to Ali and his bloodline as the only legitimate heirs to the mantle of the Prophet.

As the revealed word of God, the Koran is the sole text within Islam that is infallible; for the vast majority of Muslims, even its grammar and pronunciation as recorded in the so-called Uthman Codex are perfect and must not be altered or questioned in any way. Yet, in the eyes of many Muslims, it apparently fails—at least within the limits of human understanding—to address key questions and issues faced by the *ummah* on a daily basis, an issue that would become all the more problematic in modern times so far removed from the Arabian peninsula of the seventh century.

The Prophet Mohammad, the repository of both political and religious authority over the community, was able to provide guidance to his followers, but his death left behind a theological and legal void that could not be filled easily. Islam makes no claim that Mohammad, the absolute last in a line of monotheist prophets that stretches through Jesus, Moses, Abraham, and Adam, was himself divine, yet any successor was bound to lack his charismatic authority and fail to satisfy some portion of the broader *ummah*.[36]

In response, the Shi'a gradually developed a highly evolved system of independent legal and religious reasoning, an organized system of theological training, and a complex hierarchical system of scholarly jurists to lead believers through uncertain times and seemingly novel circumstances. Their sources include the Koran, but also rely on the collected and corroborated sayings and actions of the infallible Imams, often at the expense of accounts of the First Muslims outside the line of Ali. Among the Sunni, in contrast, the emphasis has been on the reports of the Prophet's closest aides, Companions, and wives, as well as the comprehensive edifice of Sunni religious law, codified throughout the centuries by several competing legal schools, or *madhabs*. It is this divergence in interpretation and realization of proper Islamic practice, then, that lies at the center of the religious divide between Sunni and Shi'a.

Moreover, the former hold their rivals responsible for splintering the *ummah* and thus weakening the community from the outset. Also flowing from the early divergence between the two communities are a whole series of different traditions, ritual practices, folk beliefs, orientation toward political authority, and such that serve only to exacerbate the sense of difference at the expense of their significant agreement on virtually all key points of Islamic doctrine. In the eyes of the Sunni, conclude Fuller and Francke: "Shi'ite veneration of the twelve Imams; their belief in the power of intercession; and their visits, prayers, and sacrifices at the shrines appear to contradict the principle of . . . [the] oneness of God (*tawhid*) that is cardinal in Islam."[37] Yet, it is difficult to take at face value the zealous Sunni contention—exemplified famously in the writings of Ibn Tamiyyah (1263–1328), the 18th-century Wahhabi movement he later inspired, and today's Salafis, who invoke this shared legacy—that the Shi'a are not Muslims at all but heretics whose very existence poses an existential threat to the faith.

The ongoing problem of Umayyad legitimacy and their aggressive patronage of Syrian Arabs against the interests of other Arab tribes and recent Muslim converts, in particular among the Persians and North Africans, set the stage for the overthrow of the dynasty and its replacement, during the Abbasid Revolution of 750 CE and the shift eastward, to Baghdad, of the locus of Muslim power. At first, the transition to Abbasid rule saw the advancement of the Shi'a, and some held important posts in the new seat of the empire as administrators, advisers, scholars, and religious thinkers—a phenomenon that has led one recent scholar to view the ninth century as very much a Shi'a one. Shi'a figures also played an important part in the remarkable philosophical and scientific achievements of imperial Baghdad. Setting a pattern that would become all too familiar throughout succeeding eras, the rise of the Shi'a during the early Abbasid period helped spark a backlash among the Sunni, pushing them toward traditionalist readings of the faith, with heavy reliance on the reports and opinions of the Prophet's Companions, the very figures rejected by their Shi'a rivals.[38]

Still, the Imami Shi'a hold on influence and respectability was a tenuous one, and it largely remained so for hundreds of years, until the establishment of Twelver Shi'ism as the state-sponsored faith of the Safavid rulers of what is today Iran, Azerbaijan, and beyond during the early 16th century. At the time, Sunni Muslims predominated throughout the Persian-speaking heartland, but conversion, often coerced, as well as official patronage of Twelver ideas, ritual, and institutions, brought about a relatively rapid consolidation of the Shi'a's power and prestige, and a swift increase in their numbers. By the end of the 17th century, the Twelver Shiite clergy had solidified its religious authority and established successfully a uniform reading of the older Jafari School of Law.[39] This, then, effectively gave the Shi'a *ulama* a degree of autonomy and power unmatched among their Sunni counterparts, a phenomenon that has remained to this day one of the distinguishing features of Twelver life and practice.

The Safavid empire collapsed formally in 1722 when Afghan invaders captured the capital Isfahan after a lengthy siege, but Shi'a influence remained intact, and even strengthened further, under the Qajars, Persianized Turks who ruled what is today Iran from 1785 to 1925. In addition to their disciplined and increasingly unified approach to Islamic law, the Shiite *ulama* were able to bolster their social and political autonomy through management of lucrative religious endowments, collection of religious taxes from the faithful, and enforcement of civil regulations in the Sharia courts. They also became increasingly organized in the holy cities of Karbala, the scene of Hossein's martyrdom, and Najaf, the site of Ali's tomb, providing independent power bases at the seminaries and shrines out of reach of Iran's political leaders.

In a very real sense, the Safavid era and, even more so, the Qajar period set the stage for the emergence of today's ruling Shi'a clergy in the Islamic Republic of Iran, although it took a novel and extremely radical approach on the part of Ayatollah Khomeini to the religious jurists' traditional shunning of any direct role in governing society. Among the quietist majority of Iran's senior clerics, the absence of the infallible Twelfth Imam meant that any form of government was impure religiously and association with it was inherently suspect.[40]

Most important for today's widening sectarian conflict, the novel phenomenon of state-sponsored Imami Shi'ism, first under the Safavids and then under the Qajars, established once and for all in the eyes of the Sunni—and those of many Shi'a as well—the notion that the fate and interests of mainstream Shi'ism and those of the nation state of Iran were one and the same. In this connection, it is worth noting that Shi'ism's formative years, from the election of Ali as the Fourth Caliph through the death of Hossein at Karbala and its aftermath, involved purely *Arab* actors and predated the arrival of Islam in any meaningful sense among the region's large and influential Persian speakers.

This same discourse, however, gained additional traction under the Iranian revolutionary leader Khomeini and his successors, all of whom wrapped their own bid for political power successfully in the mantle of Ali and the other Imams. And both sides in the Iran–Iraq War of 1980 to 1988, the ruling Shiite clergy in Iran and Iraq's secularist leader Saddam Hussein and his Sunni Gulf allies, cast the conflict in the apocalyptic terms surrounding the succession struggles of the seventh century—a dynamic not unfamiliar to anyone following the current rivalry for regional leadership between the Sunni Kingdom of Saudi Arabia and the equally strident Shi'a rulers of the Islamic Republic of Iran.

Grand Ayatollah Mohammad Sayyed al Hakim, an elderly cleric with a long white beard, greeted his visitors one day in November 2015 with graciousness, although it was clear he did not want to talk too long. Hakim is a member of one of the most prominent clerical families ever to live in Najaf. His father and grandfather were also ayatollahs and the family led a resistance against Saddam Hussein for years. Shortly after the invasion in 2003, his house in Najaf was bombed. Three people died but he suffered only minor injuries. Among the dead was Hakim's brother, Ayatollah Mohammad Baqir al Hakim, who was assassinated at age 63. He devoted most of his adult years to opposing Hussein's regime. He had just returned from living for decades in exile in Iran, and was warned his life was at risk.

Despite the Hakim family's great exposure to, and no doubt influence from, Iran, family members do not agree with the concept of an Islamic State, nor do they believe fundamentally in a direct role for the clerics in politics. When asked why Ayatollah Sistani took such unprecedented action within the Iraq Shi'a tradition by issuing the *fatwa*, Hakim said:

> We tried to preserve our consultative role but *Daesh* [the word for ISIS in Arabic] was at the gate. After 2003, there was such mistrust in Iraqi society that no one party was able to triumph politically so the *marja'iya* had to step in and give endorsement to the Nuri al Maliki government [the former and first prime minister of Iraq after Saddam's fall]. The greatest risk is when a society is in a state of *fitna* [chaos]. It remains our

position that the *marja'iya's* direct involvement in politics is not in the interest of the state.

What is perplexing about Hakim's remarks is that the *marja'iya* today, fighting against Iranian influence and the incompetent policies of their own Shi'a-led government on the one hand, and ISIS on the other, hold enormous sway in Iraq. In the past, they held influence in Najaf, but had limited access to power nationwide.

Sayyed Mohammad Ali Bahrululum, director of the al Alamein Institute in Najaf, was extremely articulate and clear in explaining what is a seeming contradiction:

> The ideas Sistani has put forth, even in terms of *fiqh* [jurisprudence], are new, including free elections, a constitution, a system of political parties. He has said the main theme is that we do not want a religious state but we want a state that respects religion, a state that does not impose laws that are against the religion. If you want to call this a civil state, okay. So our political project is neither a religious state like Saudi Arabia nor a civil state in the American concept. This is a religious society and we do not want a civil state as it is conceptualized in the West. It is difficult to mix *Sharia* [Islamic law] with civil laws, but it has to happen.[41]

Sitting in an elaborate home, decorated with Islamic-style wooden lattices and Arabic furniture of another prominent clerical family, the Khoeis, relatives tell the story of the late Hojatoleslam Sayyed Muhammad Taghi al Khoei, who was traveling home to Najaf after a weekly visit in 1994 to Karbala. His car was rammed deliberately by a heavy truck and crushed. He was the son of the late Grand Ayatollah al Khoei, the leading Shi'a religious authority in Iraq and much of the Shi'a world until his death in 1992. The three passengers in the car, including a six-year-old nephew of Khoei and the driver, were killed in the fire that followed. He was the most prominent ayatollah for Shi'a until Ruhollah Khomeini came to power in Iran after the 1979 revolution.

43

Despite the family's illustrious history in politics, Jawad Sayyed al Khoei, the assassinated cleric's charismatic son and his fellow scholars, who also gathered on the large and lush sofas in the family home, insists that what Sistani is doing differs from Iranian-style governance. "Sistani does not agree with the Iranians to give clerics executive powers and he does not agree with the concept of an Islamic state," he explained. Jawad had prepared an enormous feast for his visitors, including the traditional Arabic mezze with hummus, kebabs, and an enormous Iraqi fish dish called Maskoof, grilled to perfection. The food served was far better quality than anything foreign visitors generally encounter in Najaf.

Jawad explained further that Sistani's decisions since 2003 fall completely within the Islamic tradition, according to *hisbah*, the Arabic term taken from the Koran and the hadiths, the sayings of the Prophet, which is an obligation placed on every Muslim to call for what is good or right and to prevent evil and wrongdoing. The Koran states: "Let there rise from you a group calling to all that is good, enjoining what is right and forbidding what is wrong" (Koran 3:104). Scholars and leaders have generally interpreted this verse as an obligation to protect the community from disorder and harm.

CHAPTER TWO

THE SUNNI SALAFISTS

In 2012, after the revolution ousted former President Hosni Mubarak and the Muslim Brotherhood took power, a prominent Salafist sitting in a rundown Cairo office proclaimed in an interview: "The Salafists want to redefine how Islam is interpreted and practiced."[1] His words at the time seemed both overstated and improbable. Although Egypt's Salafists had been more politically active than those in other Arab countries and had a role in the official *ulama*'s religious debates within al Azhar, the primary institution for Sunni thought and interpretation, they were generally considered to be on the margins of official orthodoxy and within society itself. But, 4 years later, the Salafists, who changed historically the authority of legal schools, such as al Azhar, have gained traction in nearly every Arab country.

The Arab rebellions that brought down dictatorial rulers in Tunisia, Egypt, and Libya, and threatened a number of others, have been largely seen by the outside world strictly in political and economic terms. Little or no attention has been paid to the pent-up sectarian pressures, grievances, and social unrest they helped unleash. Only with the blossoming of the Syrian conflict into a full-scale civil war between Shi'a and Sunni Muslims and its spillover into parts of Iraq and Lebanon have US policymakers and Western analysts at last begun to examine seriously the ways in which fundamental doctrinal differences, rather than political rivalry and socioeconomic grievances, lie at the heart of this increasingly deadly struggle.

Although the violent jihadists of the Islamic State and similar groups have made headline-grabbing territorial gains and carried out or inspired spectacular terrorist acts around the world, their long-term popular appeal and staying power have yet to be demonstrated. In contrast, it is the established Salafist movement that has carried most effectively the banner of Sunni empowerment at the expense of their Shi'a rivals across the Middle East. The Salafists have shown themselves supremely adroit at exploiting opportunities to advance their rhetorical and theological positions amid the religious reexamination and outright rivalry among subgroups sparked by the Arab uprisings and their successful challenge to existing institutions of power in the region.

At the heart of this resurgent Salafist movement is the emergence of a compelling message of a return to the ideas and morals of the era of the Prophet Mohammad—that is, claimed textual literalism—at the expense of Islam's subsequent rich tradition of religious interpretation, law, and practice. Given that the uprisings occurred on the heels of a surge in Shi'a power in Syria, Iraq, and Lebanon, the Sunnis were predisposed by their own reading of religious history to feel threatened. In Egypt, the Salafists found an opening because they believed the Muslim Brotherhood, for decades considered the religious guides for society, were neglecting their religious duties after they entered politics officially. In addition, the sectarian war in Syria was pivotal in providing a compelling narrative for both Sunni and Shi'a to revisit, once again, the fundamental questions within the world of Islam: Who is a Muslim? And who gets to decide? Although these are age-old questions within the faith, dating back to its earliest days, the violence that has ensued since the Arab uprisings over these very issues threatens to redraw the map of the Middle East and create instability for years to come.

The conflict over resolving these two questions is both a Shi'a–Sunni debate as well as an internal conflict among the different strands within Sunni thought. Although some scholars and specialists argue that the root of today's conflict is the result of weakening or collapsed states in the aftermath of the US–led war in Iraq and the Arab rebellions, one of the fundamental causes—if not *the* fundamental cause—of the violence lies elsewhere; Islam itself is being rethought and revised in the midst of political upheaval in the Middle East. In other words, today's jihadists,

Salafists, members of the hardline Shi'a militias, and other nonstate actors are all caught up in the daunting and difficult enterprise of redefining and remaking Islam in their own image.

A proper understanding of contemporary Salafism requires some initial unpacking of the term, particularly because it is often used in media accounts and other Western discourse. Among the common distortions imposed from without is a reflexive conflation of the Salafists with the Wahhabis, whose integral ties to the Saudi State mark them as one component of a global originalist trend within Islam. Named for scholar and preacher Muhammad Ibn Abd al Wahhab (1703–1792), this religious movement seeks a return to the fundamentals of an idealized notion of early Islam by stripping popular religious practice of what it sees as dangerous accretions, including the worship of saints and the veneration of shrines, which undermines Islam's strict monotheist orientation. A fortuitous alliance with a local tribal leader in what would later become Saudi Arabia established Wahhabism as a significant force in the world of Islam; today, it represents the official doctrine of the Saudi State, which has used its vast petro-dollar wealth to spread Ibn Abd al Wahhab's teachings worldwide.

The charge of "Wahhabism," with its implication of direct association or even subservience to Saudi national or royal interests, is leveled frequently against the Salafists by opponents of the movement. This is particularly the case in those countries where a growing Salafist minority is seen as a potential threat by local Muslim authorities.[2] Yet, it is important to take a more expansive view of contemporary Salafism— one that goes beyond the narrow teachings of Saudi-led Wahhabism— for the former is, in fact, a multidimensional notion that cannot be circumscribed easily by narrow political or national affiliation or allegiance. And after the Arab uprisings, as Salafists from nearly every Arab country enter politics increasingly—in some cases informally and in others through political parties—the notion of Salafism itself has become diversified.

Ahmad Moussalli, of the American University of Beirut, oversimplifies the case only slightly when he noted in a recent study of contemporary trends in Islam, "As a rule, all Wahhabis are Salafists, but not all Salafists are Wahhabis."[3] However, aspects of the Wahhabi legacy within contemporary Salafism are crucial to understanding the movement and its import today across much of the Islamic world. Chief among these is opposition to the Shi'a on two fundamental grounds. First, core Shi'a practice includes the veneration of a series of divine and even messianic figures from the early centuries of Islam, a tendency that, effectively, reduces them in the eyes of the Wahhabis to *mushrikin*, or polytheists—a heretical notion for all Muslims.

Second, the Shi'a staunchly refuse to recognize the righteousness of the Prophet Mohammad's Companions and three immediate successors. For Ibn Abd al Wahhab, as for the modern Salafists, this Shi'a "rejectionism" undermines the supreme importance of the "pious ancestors" and with it the entire Salafist theological enterprise, which rests on the beliefs and practices of these early Muslims. Thus, today's Salafist discourse is characterized by the abiding belief that the Shi'a are not real Muslims and are out to extinguish Sunni believers who, in the Salafist view, are the only legitimate followers of Mohammad's teachings and his Revelation.

The ambivalent relationship between the Salafists and a Saudi religious and political establishment that is, increasingly, the subject of the movement's wrath—even as the kingdom plays host to a large number of influential Salafist clerics and supports their mission both financially and politically—only complicates the picture further. How, the observer might well ask, can a religious movement under the name of Salafism have room for both the violent extremism of al Qaeda and the political conservatism of Saudi religious officialdom?

Analysts have responded generally to these challenges by parsing the Salafist movement into several main tendencies or orientations, under different headings but essentially comprising the following groups: traditionalists, whose quietist approach focuses on spreading the religious call, or *da'wa*; the politically engaged, intent on applying Salafist principles to politics and governance; and the so-called jihadists, who pursue their goals through violence and revolution.[4]

It is important to note at the outset that although violent groups do certainly exist under the rubric of contemporary Salafism, the more common and significant trend is the *salafiyya al dawwiyya*, or evangelizing Salafism. In a seminal essay, "Anatomy of the Salafi Movement," Quintan Wiktorowicz makes an important distinction within the broader tendency of evangelizing Salafists between what he calls the "politicos" and the traditionalists, or purists. Wiktorowicz notes that, in recent years, the politically active have shaken the purists' long-standing grip on authority because the former argue they have a better understanding of modern concerns and are thus better equipped to apply the Salafist creed in today's world.[5]

After the Arab uprisings, the question of authority in Islam has become more salient with the growing influence of the Salafists throughout the Arab world, achieved largely at the expense of their more traditional-minded counterparts. Although they are religious scholars in their own right, these contemporary Salafists are exercising a new-found authority that stems from their willingness to adopt overtly political stances: they fight against the Syrian regime of Bashar al Assad; they oppose actively policies of Western governments; and they warn against Shi'a Iran's excessive interventions and ambition for greater influence in the Sunni Arab world.

In addition, some are critical of the Sunni monarchies in the Gulf, and they present themselves as alternatives to the purists, whom they accuse, often with good cause, of acquiescing blindly to the government line and providing it with religious cover for more narrow state policies. This new, dynamic cohort of Salafists, then, believe calling all Muslims to the true Islam does not exclude engaging in political activity. In fact, some Salafist groups, such as the Ansar al Sunna in the Sudan, the Noor Party in Egypt, and Salafists in northern Lebanon, all of whom could be classified as *da'wa* Salafists, no longer withdraw from current affairs or adopt a fully apolitical stance. In some cases, they feel they are being dragged into politics because of the wars in Syria and Iraq, which in their view necessitate commentary and action.

The important distinctions drawn here between competing quietest and activist tendencies among today's Salafists must not obscure the fact that a single body of religious thought has formed the heart of the movement from the very beginning—one that unites both "politicos" and traditionalists. Here, the central guiding principle rests on a strict reading of Islam's defining notion, the unity of God, or *tawhid*. This central monotheist proposition is captured lyrically in the opening of the *shahadah*, the Muslim profession of faith: "There is no god but God." Among the Salafists, the focus on the primacy of *tawhid* is accompanied by a general rejection of human agency—in particular, reason and legalistic or logical argumentation—in understanding and applying Islam's divine law. Flowing from this is a narrow focus on the Koran and the Sunna, or lived example of the Prophet Mohammad, and a general dismissal of man-made religious law, metaphorical interpretation, or other "innovations" in religious thought and practice.

Thus, the movement seeks a return to an Islam—real or imagined—as practiced at the time of the Prophet and his original followers, the so-called ancestors, *al salaf*, from which the term *Salafists* is derived. The notion of three authoritative generations rests on a popular hadith, or saying of the Prophet Mohammad: "The best of my community are my generation, then those who came after them, and then those who follow them."[6] This exclusive focus on the perceived practices and beliefs of the First Muslims forms the bedrock of Salafist doctrine, whatever their political or social stances. And, it is central to Salafi antagonism toward the Shi'a, who do not recognize the Sunni line of succession to the Prophet Mohammad and, by failing to do so, cast doubt on the religious authority of the Prophet's immediate circle.

Throughout the centuries, the difference between the Sunni and Shi'a has crystallized around the question of who should succeed Mohammad as the head of the political and religious community. Should the new leader be chosen from his Companions or from his direct bloodline only? The Shi'a believe his successor should have stayed within the Prophet's family, whereas the Sunni believe the most qualified person among his Companions was his rightful successor, the view that generally prevailed.

The resulting Salafist claims of authenticity, doctrinal certainty, and distinct unity of purpose, underscored by distinctive modes of dress, personal appearance, and speech, have successfully attracted Muslim believers worldwide. This appeal is all the more compelling in contrast to the dizzying forces of globalization arrayed against traditional religious and social values. Salafism, then, has proved to offer a potent message in a Muslim world deeply affected by the US-led invasions of Afghanistan and Iraq, and then by the Arab popular rebellions, all of which have toppled old certainties and provoked the search for new approaches and new solutions.

As in other faith traditions, including Hinduism, Judaism, and Christianity, such an uncompromising stance naturally increases the likelihood that those who disagree will be pushed beyond the borders of acceptable practice and be labeled *unbelievers*, a process known in Islam as *takfir*. Although legal rulings are generally seen within the broader Islamic tradition to lack absolute certainty and thus have a multiplicity of acceptable answers, there can be no such flexibility in the unyielding Salafist understanding of *tawhid*. In other words, the Salafists have attempted to stake out a monopoly over response to the question: Who is a good Muslim? In this regard, they are following firmly in the footsteps of Ibn Abd al Wahhab, for whom *takfir* was a common weapon in his claim on Islamic purity.

Wiktorowicz writes:

To ensure the purity of Islam as they define it, contemporary Salafists articulate a very demanding interpretation of monotheism, which has the consequence of making unbelief more likely. They also advocate an expansive definition of innovation (*bid'a*), which narrows the scope of acceptable Islamic practice, and they remain wary of extra-scriptural influences and sources of knowledge in religious matters.[7]

To counteract man's natural inclination to further his own interests or fulfill his own base desires in the name of religion and religious rulings, the Salafists place a particular premium on the sayings and actions of the Prophet, as recorded in the hadith, over later and thus fallible interpretation, however learned. Not surprisingly, hadith scholarship plays an important role in Salafist intellectual life, and those who cast doubt on the accepted corpus of hadith are prone to being cast out as nonbelievers.

The same stress on the hadith also reflects the complexities and seeming contradictions in the Koran—a text that, in the Salafist view, remains inherently obscure to human understanding and thus beyond human reason. Among the most significant targets of Salafist suspicion have been the canonical schools of Sunni religious law, established during the centuries after Mohammad's Revelation, and, as far as the Salafists are concerned, far removed from both scripture and the practices and beliefs of his day. In particular, Salafists oppose so-called emulation (*taqlid*), which they believe to be blind following, of these schools of thought and prefer independent religious interpretation, or *ijtihad*, and its application to contemporary conditions and problems, albeit within narrow, literalist limits.[8] Herein lies one particularly important area of difference between the Wahhabis and most Salafists: the former follow the Hanbali School of Religious Law, or *madhhab*, whereas many Salafists reject the practice of *taqlid* altogether in favor of *ijtihad*, or religious interpretation, grounded in a strict reading of the Koran and the accepted Sunni hadith.[9]

Despite a reputation for doctrinaire conservatism, such an approach has given contemporary Salafism a flexibility and openness lacking among many other Muslim traditionalists, who generally remain bound within the confines of one or another of the main schools. This has led some scholars to label them "relatively open, even democratic."[10] Although this might be true for some Salafists, such as those in Egypt who formed political parties and ran in elections shortly after the uprising began in 2011, it is premature to characterize Salafists elsewhere as embracing recognizable democratic principles.

Like the Wahhabis, Salafists also strongly oppose popular religious traditions, such as the worship of saints and spirits, and appeals for their intercession with God; the veneration of tombs of local religious figures; the celebration of the Prophet's birthday; and so on—all of which represent idolatry and a violation of their cardinal principle: *tawhid*.

Many of these practices reflect the integration of folk customs or ethnic traditions into Islam as it spread out from the Arabian heartland. Rooting them out and returning Muslims worldwide to a pristine reading of the faith is central to the Salafist mission. Needless to say, Salafism also rejects the many Western accretions to Islamic thought, chiefly from classical Greek and early Christian influence, as dangerous, alien innovations grounded in necessarily fallible human attempts to understand God's will.

Clearly, the interrelated beliefs that sit at the heart of Salafism—an uncompromising reading of the notion of *tawhid*, an originalist notion of true religious practice, with its inherent historicist approach to the First Muslims, and deep-set suspicion of human agency and reason as applied to religious interpretation—virtually guarantee the movement will target divergent tendencies within Islam. Among the largest and most threatening of such tendencies is Shi'ism, with its notions of history and rich traditions of *ijtihad* that stand in direct opposition to core Salafist ideas.

Anti-Shi'a sentiment, then, has a long and tenacious history among the Sunni forebears of modern Salafism, including the revivalist Wahhabi movement that first arose during the 18th century. Wahhabism remains at the core of the Saudi State, although its rulers have, periodically, had to rein in clerical animosity toward the Shi'a as a result of fear that the kingdom's significant Shi'a minority might rise up in response, as the Shi'a have done periodically in neighboring Bahrain for the past two decades and particularly since 2011, when a popular uprising began that continues today.

A brief look back reveals the extent to which these religious differences remain as relevant as ever. In his 18th-century treatise, *The Refutation of the Rejectionists*, Ibn Abd al Wahhab refers to all those who deny the legitimacy of the first two Caliphs Abu Bakr and Umar while defending Ali's right of succession to the Prophet as rejectionists; this includes the Twelver Shi'a, the largest of the Shi'a subgroups. Ibn Abd al Wahhab, like other like-minded Sunni scholars, has tried to establish that the Shi'a are heretics because of their claims that the Prophet had designated his cousin and brother-in-law, Ali, to replace him, the Shi'a denial of the first three Caliphs as legitimate leaders of the Muslim community, and particularly the Shi'a critical view of the Prophet's Companions, who are considered by the Sunni to be the authenticators of hadith material. As a result, Ibn Abd al Wahhab and others have argued that the Shi'a are opposed to the core principles of Sunni belief.

"This is the destruction of the basis of religion, because its base is the Koran and the hadith," wrote Ibn Abd al Wahhab.[11] Thus, he declared the Shi'a nonbelievers and saw in them a corrosive danger to Islam far greater than any external threat posed by either Christians or Jews.[12] For the Salafists, the Shi'a veneration of their Imams—in the case of the so-called Twelver Shi'a who predominate in Iran, Bahrain, and parts of Lebanon, Ali ibn Abi Talib, the son-in-law of the Prophet, and Ali's 11 successors—smacks of idolatry and offends the all-important notion of *tawhid*.

SYRIA

Salafist thought has a long and illustrious history in Syria. The reformist ideas of Mohammad Ibn Abd al Wahhab, Jamaleddin al Afghani (a prominent religious scholar), and his students, including Mohammad Abdu and Mohammad Rashid Rida, reached Syria through Jamal al din al Kasimi (1866–1914), who brought Salafist thought to the country through his invitation to representatives of the four competing streams of Sunni law—the Hanbali, Shafi'i, Maliki, and Hanafi—to pray together in the same mosque. Kasimi also advocated a purer version of Islam that would unite Muslims. He had several students, including Mohammad Bahjat al Bitar (1894–1976) and Ahmad Monther al Othma (1909–1982), who were Salafists and worked to spread the doctrine.[13]

The Salafist role in sectarian discourse throughout the Levant and Iraq has been evident since the 1950s. In Syria itself, the confessional distinction became more dominant after late president Hafez al Assad took power during the early 1970s, particularly after he convinced

Lebanese Shi'a cleric Musa al Sadr in 1973 to declare Syria's ruling Alawite minority represented an offshoot of mainstream Twelver Shi'ism rather than a heretical sect outside the pale of Islam altogether.[14] Religious identity was so important to Assad that he moved to make religion part of the country's national identity.

This led the Muslim Brotherhood in Syria, a hotbed of Sunni activism, to challenge this designation openly and label Assad and his fellow Alawites "unbelievers." When Assad's regime became the only Arab country to support Shi'a-ruled Iran in the Iran–Iraq War (1980–1988), this only escalated sectarian conflict further in Syria. The Iranian Revolution in 1979 had already produced alarm among Sunnis in the Arab world, and Assad's open alliance with Iran was a critical move in threatening the Sunnis inside the country.

A leader in the Muslim Brotherhood, Sai'd Hawwa, the Syrian group's ideologue, published a booklet titled *Khomeini, Deviation in Doctrines, Deviation in Positions*. In the booklet, he criticizes the Shi'a veneration of the Imams as rightful successors to the Prophet and asserts that the Shi'a teach that the Koran had been altered to accommodate Sunni belief regarding who should succeed the Prophet after his death—in what would be a direct challenge to Salafist (and, in fact, orthodox Sunni) belief. He also denounces their rejection of the Prophet's Companions. Hawwa argues that the Iranian Revolution was an attempt to take over all Arab countries with Shi'a populations— much like the argument being made today about Supreme Leader Ali Khamenei, Syrian President Bashar al Assad, and former Iraqi Prime Minister Nouri al Maliki.

During the 1980s, another influential Syrian, Mohammad Surer Zain al Abidin, in his book *Then Came the Turn of the Fire-Worshippers*, went even further on an anti-Shi'a campaign. Al Abidin, a Salafist, lumped all Shi'a in the same category and accused them of being part of a "Persian conspiracy." By invoking the once-common ritual use of fire by the Zoroastrians in pre-Islamic Persia, Abidin aimed to demonize the Shi'a as pseudo-Muslims. He also charged Iran with trying to take over the Arab world—the same argument the Sunnis have been making since the Arab uprisings began. The late al Qaeda leader Ayman al

Zarqawi was highly influenced by this text, according to references he made in his anti-Shi'a speeches.

Despite these efforts, the initial Salafist *da'wa*, or evangelization, was not successful in penetrating the Syrian community, where the appeal of the more politically active Muslim Brotherhood proved more attractive.[15] Salafism returned under Sheikh Nasir al Din al Albani (1914–1999), who had studied under Mohammad Bahjat Bitar. He also took his Salafist direction from the thinker Mohammad Rashid Rida, who was more of a rationalist than many of today's Salafists.

LEBANON

In Lebanon, the Salafist mainstream was established by Sheikh Salem al Shahhal in 1946. After returning from a visit to Medina in 1964, Shahhal founded a group in Tripoli called *Shabab Muhammad*. It was later disbanded, and he formed another group called *al Jama'a Muslimun*—literally, "The Group Is Composed of Muslims." It was not connected to any other mainstream Islamic group and was focused primarily on charity work and *da'wa*.[16] Salem sent his three sons, Dai, Radi, and Abu Bakr, to study Sharia at the Islamic University in Medina, Saudi Arabia. As Salem grew older, his son Dai took control and this marked the second phase of Salafist work. Instead of focusing merely on the *da'wa*, Dai combined both evangelization and politics, and during the Lebanese civil war in the 1970s he founded the so-called Islamic Army to defend the Sunni community.[17] The Salafist movement in Lebanon took hold during the early 1980s.[18]

After the Taif Agreement in 1989, which ended the Lebanese civil war, the senior al Shahhal went on to resume *da'wa* though religious schools, charity work with orphans, the building of mosques, and creation of the Koran Karim radio station. He also founded Jami'yat al Hidayya wal Ihsan, which was the official face of the movement in 1988. Its work covered traditional *da'wa*, as well as education and social work.[19]

The government disbanded the Jami'yat in 1996 and accused it of inciting sectarianism in some of the books the group distributed.

However, the real motivation of the crackdown appears to have come from the Syrian regime that then exercised considerable control over the Lebanese.[20] The Syrian Army managed to crack down on Islamists in Tripoli in 1985. After the Syrian Army withdrew from Lebanon in 2005, the Jami'yat al Hidayya wal Ihsan was allowed to operate again.[21] Al Shahhal died in 2008, but Dai al Islam al Shahhal has picked up his father's mantle. In 2006, he established an association called the *Zadal Akhira Institute*. This association, along with a multitude of Wahhabi-inspired charities, provides a good foundation for Salafists to mobilize and expand their base.

Among the Salafists in Lebanon, there is a direct connection with their Saudi counterparts, who serve as mentors for some of today's important Salafist leaders. Lebanese Salafists such as Dai al Islam al Shahhal studied theology in Saudi Arabia and are influenced undoubtedly by the traditional Wahhabi antagonism toward the Shi'a. During the late 1970s, when Saudi Arabia's theological schools became an alternative—and serious rival—to Cairo's al Azhar, the university long considered the seat of learning for Sunni Muslims, Salafism took hold in Lebanon. The Saudi influence—and no doubt money—helped endear some Lebanese to the Salafist movement.

When Rafik Hariri was prime minister, his Future movement distanced itself from the Salafists publicly, but a private alliance was maintained behind the scenes. The Future movement believed Salafist support was useful in elections, and both sides believed they had common enemies—Hezbollah and Iran and, by association, the Shi'a in general. Hariri's assassination in February 2005, which, according to a United Nations Special Tribunal, was the work of Syrian-backed agents of the Assad regime and some leaders in Hezbollah, allowed the Salafists to attain greater prominence. Hariri was close to the Saudi royal family and was himself a powerful Sunni leader who posed a threat to Hezbollah. His assassination made him a martyr and a rallying point for all Sunnis because they had a common target: Shi'a Hezbollah.

In 2006, Hezbollah's war with Israel also mobilized the Sunnis, who feared the Shi'a militia's victory against Israel would make the movement too powerful and thus upset Lebanon's precarious religious-based balance of power. In addition, the 2008 Hezbollah takeover of parts of Beirut gave credibility to the anti-Shi'a rhetoric and warnings from Sunnis, including Salafists. During these years, some Sunni political leaders found the Salafists useful, but since that time they have generally parted ways.

Now, in part because of the absence in Lebanon of a strong Sunni leadership, Salafist power in the north is again on the rise. This is particularly the case as the Syrian war continues to simmer across the border. The moderate Salafists are forming a movement that bears resemblance to Hezbollah during the 1980s, when it began mobilizing support in Lebanon. But even so, they are quick not to exaggerate their influence. One Salafist leader in Tripoli told me in June 2014 that he estimates their support in Lebanon to be only 5% to 6% of the population.

IRAQ

According to Yehya al Kobeissi, one of the few authorities on Salafism in Iraq, the religious tendency did not take hold there in significant ways until the 1960s, when it began to spread through individuals or small mosques but failed to create an intellectual party or movement. Sheikh Abdel Hamid Nader states that the first attempt to form a Salafist movement was during the 1960s by a group who studied under Sheikh Abdel Karim al Sa'eka. They succeeded in founding Jama'at al Mowahidin, a group that produced an attempt at the Islamic Party in 1960.[22]

During the mid-1970s, there was another attempt to forge a Salafist identity that was more political in nature and deviated from the strict proselytizing agenda that once lay at the movement's roots. When the Iraqi State authorities discovered these Salafists, they were arrested in Mosul and Baghdad. As a result, there was no organized and politically self-conscious Salafist movement in Iraq in any meaningful sense until 2003, according to al Kobeissi.[23]

Of course, the situation in Iraq today is very different because the violence and disruption from the US-led invasion continues a brutal refashioning of what was once an authoritarian Sunni-dominated regime, under Saddam Hussein, into a complex quilt of competing tendencies, religious identities, and political orientations. Among the beneficiaries of this free-for-all are the Salafists, who can be classified into three main streams, according to al Kobeissi and other analysts. The first trend is traditional Salafism that is not ideological and is close to the Muslim Brotherhood in thought. This trend is still present in Iraqi Salafism today, as represented by Jami'yat al Aadab al Islamiyya (founded during the mid-1940s) and such figures as Sheikh Sobhi Badri Samer'ee, who died in 2013, and Sheikh Abdel Hamid Nader.[24]

The second trend is al Salafiyya al Jameeya, which came into the spotlight after the US invasion of Iraq. This group encouraged Iraqi citizens to join the army and police, and participate in the political process. In a book published in 2004, the group asserted the religious legitimacy of Iraqis taking positions in the occupied state, even if the appointment had come at the hands of the "infidel" occupying power, meaning the United States. Members of this group follow traditional Salafist thought in that they do not believe in challenging the political authorities of the state, and in December 2012 issued a *fatwa* prohibiting protests against Iraqi Prime Minister al Maliki, a prominent Shi'a leader.[25]

The third trend is jihadi Salafism, which evolved as a direct response to the US invasion. Among the most prominent local jihadi Salafist groups is al Jaysh al Islami, which was founded immediately after the invasion. This organization joined with two others, Jaysh Ansar al Sunna and Jaysh al Mujahideen, on May 2, 2007, and formed Jabhat al Jihad wal Islah to counter al Qaeda in Iraq.

The recent fear of Iranian Shi'itization of the Sunni Arab world did not begin with the Syrian war. Rather, in 2003 this simmering animosity was transformed into a virtual Sunni–Shi'a civil war by the US invasion and its many knock-off effects, chiefly the rise of Shi'a power—until then, a numerical minority with little political, social, or economic power—in what had been the Sunni political stronghold of

Iraq. The emergence of the Islamic State is a perfect example of a sectarian, extremist group that evolved in the aftermath of the US-led invasion to oust Saddam Hussein from power. At that time, it was called al Qaeda in Iraq (AQI) and was led by Abu Musab al Zarqawi, who was killed in 2006 by a US airstrike. One of al Zarqawi's central aims was to target the Iraqi Shi'a. The militant group found fertile ground to wage their sectarian war. Some Iraqi politicians who favored the US invasion deliberately resisted building an inclusive political system in part because there was no real incentive; there was little outside pressure and it was an opportunity for them to take advantage of the embryonic, weak state.

One of AQI's strongest bases during the US invasion was in the town of Fallujah, scene in 2004 of one of the most decisive battles in the Iraq War. Once a stronghold of Saddam Hussein, where the Sunni elite enjoyed a privileged life, now the Sunnis of Fallujah and the rest of the surrounding Anbar Province believe they have been marginalized by years of a US-backed Shi'a government.

For many Sunnis, the arrival of Western forces, with the connivance of Shi'a Iran, posed a direct threat to the Muslim community of believers, and even more so when US-backed Iraqi Prime Minister Maliki, a Shi'a leader, marginalized the Sunnis, leading to the chaos of war and the emergence of competent and well-armed resistance leaders. Iraqi Shi'a proved willing and able to fight back. In other words, all the necessary ingredients were now present for a full-scale sectarian conflict.

After a US counterterrorism campaign against AQI in 2006 and 2007, the group's power and activity decreased, and it is believed to have put down new roots in Syria, setting the stage for the militant group's takeover in 2014 of territory in Syria and Iraq as the newly constituted Islamic State. Much is written about the Islamic State, but what is less known is that its adherents consider themselves Salafists—a designation most Salafists refute in strong terms. Most Salafists in the Arab world disown ISIS and condemn their ideology and violence.

By 2010, when the Arab uprisings started, religious identity, although significant, did not appear to be the central cause of this new polarization in the Arab world. Instead, the immediate mobilizing issue was the removal of dictators from power and an accompanying demand for greater social justice. In Egypt, liberals worked alongside the Muslim Brotherhood to end the authoritarian rule of President Hosni Mubarak. In Iraq, a country with a long history of discrimination against the majority Shi'a population, many Sunni and Shi'a shared the common objective of deposing Saddam Hussein, long before the Arab uprisings began in other countries and even though sectarian differences were simmering largely unabated. The determination on the Arab streets was driven by demands for human dignity, social justice for all, and a better standard of living. Even in Bahrain, where the majority Shi'a population had been at odds with the Sunni monarchy, their Sunni fellow citizens were initially sympathetic to their socioeconomic grievances.

However, by 2012, the uprisings began to take on a far more overtly sectarian tone. In nearly every Arab country, even in Egypt, where the Shi'a represent less than 1% of the population, religious difference is center stage, causing the social contracts by which these societies once adhered to break under the weight of sectarian tension for the first time since the 1980–1988 war between Shi'a Iran and Sunni-ruled Iraq. Although the Sunni and Shi'a identity is shaped by modern-day experiences, it draws heavily on past religious conflicts.

Accompanying the complex question of religion's direct role in today's divide is another, equally important query: Why now? The peaks and valleys of sectarian identity in Arab societies have always depended on the social and political context. Sectarian identity has the potential to go from being latent or largely ignored to being inflamed in a short period of time—as was the case with the Arab uprisings. In the modern nation state, it is always present, perhaps not in the romanticized memories of many who will argue that Shi'a and Sunni existed peacefully until the Arab uprisings; but, because of its perpetual presence. It is ignited easily with such developments as the US invasion and the subsequent Arab uprisings that opened the gates to deepening the Shi'a–Sunni divide.

In Iraq and Syria, the Sunnis believe they are facing an existential threat—with the Shi'a contributing materially to this danger. The perception among Sunnis today in nearly every Arab society is that the Shi'a, backed by Iran and Hezbollah, are determined to expand their religious influence and power in the region. This is the result of a Shi'a-led government in Iraq that enforced highly discriminatory policies against the Sunnis; Assad's survival, at least for now, over the opposition, with heavy material support from Hezbollah and Iran; and of warming relations between Iran and world powers, including the United States. The rise of violent Shi'a militias has also led the Sunnis to believe their community is at risk.

As one Iraqi religious scholar explained, the US invasion in 2003 allowed the Shi'a in Iraq to gain political supremacy, which they then used to marginalize the Sunnis. "The Shi'a objective in Iraq was to force the Sunnis to leave the country," Muthanna Harith al Dari, a leader in the Muslim Association of Scholars in Iraq, said in an interview. "Iraq was the gateway because it encouraged the people to say no and stand up for their faith. The dominance of the Shi'a in Iraq and the increasing sectarianism encouraged sectarianism in other countries."[26]

In nearly every Arab country, Shi'a and Sunni remember the days before the Arab uprisings, when religious sect was not a marker of identity. Whether these memories are simply versions of a glorified past or grounded in reality is hard to assess; but, in some cases, such as Iraq, the lack of sectarian identity was the result of repression by the ruling power of Saddam Hussein. For example, Hussein banned the Shi'a from practicing their religious traditions publicly, such as the mourning ceremony of Ashura, although he allowed the Shi'a to hold high posts in the government.

A former Iraqi ambassador to Jordan, Sabbah Yassin, blames the United States for creating the conditions that allowed for a Shi'a-led government, which ultimately marginalized the Sunni population. And, after years of abuse in the aftermath of the US-led invasion, he explained, the Sunnis had no recourse except to welcome the invasion of the Islamic State (ISIS) into parts of Iraq. "Support for ISIS is simply to get revenge on the Shi'a after years of abuse," Yassin said in an interview.[27]

The rivalry between Iran and Saudi Arabia, with the Saudis using sectarianism to advance their own agenda, certainly has affected public perceptions, particularly through the media. Although Ayatollah Ali Khamenei often speaks publicly about the need to unite all Muslims, the Sunnis believe Iran has expansionist ambitions based on its activity in Iraq and Syria, where Tehran is involved directly in keeping Assad in power. All these conditions came together around the time of the Arab uprisings, causing the Shi'a–Sunni divide to deepen and, eventually, to rupture into outright conflict.

At a conference on Salafism in January 2014 organized by the Al Jazeera Center for Studies, Syrian researcher Marwan Kabalan observed: "Salafist movements have historically formed in response to one of two things: the state fails to address internal societal needs or the state fails to address external threats to protect its people."[28] The uprisings created both of these conditions in many Arab states.

CHAPTER THREE

THE SALAFI POLITICOS

As the son of the founder of the Salafist movement in northern Lebanon, Dai al Islam al Shahhal was an active figure, particularly around the Tripoli area, but more importantly he had made a mark on Twitter through his sectarian rhetoric. Although his tweets denouncing the Shi'a brought him fame among his Sunni followers, they also made him a target. During a visit in June 2014, armed bodyguards insisted no cars should drive near his house. Shahhal's visitors were forced to leave their car on a rocky road and be escorted in an SUV, driven by Shahhal's handlers.

Like many Salafists in northern Lebanon, Shahhal feared that Hezbollah or Syrian intelligence, which often operates undercover in Lebanon to keep Assad in power, would take revenge because of his active support for the Syrian rebels. "Today, many foes of the Assad regime have waned, but not the Salafists," Shahhal, an elderly man with a long white beard, said in his darkened living room. Although the Salafists in Lebanon were becoming less significant, he was correct in referring to the Salafists across the Middle East more broadly.

A year later, Shahhal's fears for his safety increased after the Lebanese army arrested his son on charges that he battled the Lebanese security forces in October 2014 during 4 days of clashes. Two months later, Shahhal fled to Saudi Arabia, where he is believed to be in hiding.

For years, Shahhal focused on protecting the Sunnis in Lebanon as opposed to the Sunni *ummah* region-wide, particularly since the war began in Syria. He very much sees Hezbollah as an Iranian project aimed at igniting a Shi'a–Sunni civil war. His intolerance for the Shi'a is more in response to events on the ground, and does not represent the kind of proactive sectarian campaign conducted by other Salafist clerics in Saudi Arabia. He blames the United States for what he says is support for the Shi'a because of the historic nuclear deal the United States and world powers signed with the Islamic Republic in 2015:

> The Americans have committed a historical scandal because they are willing to support the minority—the Shi'a—to create a balance in the face of growing Sunni influence. If the Sunnis had been able to prove themselves as a world power, the Americans, who act on their own self-interests, would have let go of Iran and built power with the Sunnis.

The visit with Shahhal revealed the influence and also the dangers inherent to social media platforms such as Twitter, which have seen explosive growth across much of the Muslim world. When probed about many of his most partisan, even bigoted, tweets during the preceding months, he tried to distance himself from his own writings. And when asked about one tweet in particular, in which he declared the Shi'a were not real Muslims, he told me someone else had written it for him and posted it under his Twitter account. But, when pressed, he stopped just short of acknowledging his earlier views of the Shi'a as nonbelievers: "I don't want to say [whether they are Muslims]. Ideologically, their ideas are corrupt. Their beliefs are not based on proof. They are not on the right track. They are misled." When referring to the Shi'a, he often tweeted that they wave the "Oh Hussein" banner to "burn, rape, and kill [Sunnis]."

For much of his life, al Shahhal has embraced Salafism, beginning in 1977 when he began *da'wa* work. Born in Tripoli, Lebanon, in 1960, he studied in the Sharia department of the Institute of Education and Teaching in Tripoli, and furthered his studies at the Islamic University in Medina where he graduated in 1984.[1] Having been forced to leave Tripoli in 1986 following the massacre of Sunnis at the hands of the Syrian army in Bab al Tabbaneh, a nearby Alawite district, Shahhal continued preaching in Beirut and Sidon. He returned to Tripoli after the end of the Lebanese civil war in 1990.

Although his Twitter followers numbered little more than 14,000 in early 2016—some other Salafists have millions—Shahhal is identified regularly as one of the most influential members of the Salafist movement in Lebanon, in part because of his family history. As mentioned in Chapter 2, his father, Salem, founded Lebanon's Salafist movement during the late 1940s and 1950s. Salem al Shahhal is still seen as one of the "spiritual icons" of the Salafist movement.[2] For his part, the son has been active politically for many years in response to the demands of the times. Recently, he said the Sunnis "see their political leaders as weak.... Today, the pulse of the street in Lebanon is with the Salafists."[3] However, since the Syrian war began, some Sunnis in the Tripoli area believe his ideas have become too extreme.

Much popular attention in the Western media, on the Internet, and in political speeches is devoted to radical jihadists whose claims on territory in parts of Iraq and Syria, and acts of terrorist violence have captured public imagination. Yet, those Salafists, such as Shahhal, who are more pragmatic—the politicos—are playing an increasingly important role in destabilizing and remaking the face of the Middle East today. Uncovering and understanding Salafist subculture, and in particular the power and influence of their public discourse, is crucial to understanding this complex and restive region. Absent such an approach, the prevailing result has been a litany of confusion, misunderstandings, and misinterpretations about this important religious and social movement.

Now, however, new social media technologies taking hold around the world—in particular, the widespread use of Twitter as a communication or broadcast platform—have provided a window through which we can gain valuable insight into Salafist ideas and practices, uncover important interrelationships, and reveal significant discursive trends in what has, until recently, been an obscure and largely inaccessible phenomenon.

These technologies also help identify significant personalities and players, long before they come to the attention—if they ever do—of traditional media, policymakers, or academic experts. "Social media has revolutionized the way that the world has understood the Syrian conflict and how that conflict has been waged," asserted a study published by the United States Institute of Peace, a Washington, DC–based think tank. "Syria has been at the cutting edge of the evolution of new uses of social media and the Internet by political actors, insurgent groups, journalists and researchers."[4]

I tracked the Salafists' sectarian discourse—both political and religious—through social media, primarily Arabic Twitter feeds. This discourse, unrestrained and unregulated even in countries such as Saudi Arabia, where free speech is minimal, is an important window into Sunni attitudes toward the Shi'a. Through an examination of selected Twitter feeds in Arabic in 2013, 2014, and 2015, the perceptions, fears, and overreactions are on full display among Salafists, who are far more moderate than other Sunni political actors but who fear the survival of the ways they practice the faith are at risk of Shi'a domination.

I chose to study Twitter—a form of social media that is, arguably, flawed in terms of what it tells us about life on the ground—as a reflection of contemporary Salafist thought. To date, there is no scientific methodology to assess whether someone with more than 14 million Twitter followers—as is in the case with one of the Salafists profiled in this chapter—can affect directly the killing fields in Iraq and Syria or political rivalries across the Middle East. Nonetheless, the Arab uprisings demonstrated the power of social media and it has to be taken into account.

As skeptics of the power of social media have noted, Twitter cannot inspire revolutions and certainly did not create the Arab uprisings. Yet, as many studies have established, Twitter provided a tool that allowed millions of people during the uprisings to coordinate strategies and spread immediate news, announcements, and rumors about events unfolding on the streets, although it must be noted that the political and social conditions for revolution or other political unrest did not emerge from cyberspace on their own accord. In the end, it is still individuals who are responsible for creating the Arab protest movements, not the tools available to them that allowed them to get there.

A major battle in the Syrian war or the arrest of a Sunni leader provides fodder for religious intolerance in the Twitter-sphere, which then can exacerbate religious strife. Any doubts about the power of social media, including Twitter and YouTube, to engage and mobilize forces for religious struggle should have been dispelled by the recent recruitment and propaganda successes of the militant Sunnis of the Islamic State.

Twitter and other social media channels have also been dismissed in some circles as little more than "echo chambers," repeating endlessly the ideas and rhetorical claims of a handful of established figures rather than generating much significant new content. This attribute, however, makes the Twitter universe particularly attractive to quantitative study and analysis. At the same time, the changing tools and patterns of communication that shape our world today must be acknowledged, and it has become clear that Arabic Twitter feeds provide a much wider lens through which to examine Salafist views than more traditional one-on-one interviews between researcher and subject. Although clerics during the 1990s issued traditional religious rulings, or *fatwas,* as well as Koranic commentary, today's leading clerics have gone virtual, using Twitter, Facebook, and other forms of social media as their main platforms.

Thus, the Salafists profiled in these pages were chosen largely on account of their discourse on Twitter, taking into account the scope and depth of sectarianism among key figures through shared sentiments, words, and opinions. Some in Lebanon, for example, were selected because they disseminate the opinions of their mentors and their participation in the Twitter-sphere shows the transnational nature of sectarianism, which is not restricted to political borders and is not characterized by national identities. Geographic location also matters. Salafists in northern Lebanon were selected despite a relatively low number of followers because of their close proximity to Syria and their demonstrated influence on Lebanese involvement in the Syrian war. It is worth noting, too, that the featured Lebanese Salafists are highly influenced by leading Salafists in Saudi Arabia, which demonstrates the transnational nature of messaging via social media.

What emerges from a thorough examination of the tweets under review is the importance of the centuries-old rift between the Sunnis and the Shi'a, only now set in a contemporary context. In fact, sectarian conflict and its associated historical grievances frame and even determine Sunni discourse in almost all its guises, whether the topic at hand is political, economic, or social.

Clearly, this phenomenon has very real implications for any attempt by outside players to understand, react to, and influence events on the ground. Specifically, the analysis of tweets from 2013 to 2015 shows several consistent messages. First, the Salafists conflate Iran's political and military activities in the Arab world with all Shi'a. It is rare that they made a distinction between, for example, the Arab Shi'a in Najaf, Iraq, who oppose Iran's policies and system of religious government, and those who favor Iran. Second, the driving force behind much of the inflammatory rhetoric is a feeling that Sunni Islam is at risk of being overtaken by Iranian conquests and, by extension, Shi'a expansionism. The changing political dynamics in the region, which have made Iran more powerful in the aftermath of the Arab uprisings, creates feelings of an existential struggle for survival of the Sunni community. And third, with the exception of one self-declared Salafist in Lebanon, who was silenced after his arrest in summer 2015, no Salafist who is part of this analysis supports ISIS. In fact, in condemning ISIS' violence, they compare it with the violence Hezbollah has committed while fighting in Syria against the Sunnis to keep Assad in power. They also compare the ISIS atrocities with those being carried out by Shi'a militias in Iraq.

Language is also an important and consistent tool. The terms the Salafists use to describe the Shi'a are almost invariably sectarian in nature, describing their foes as infidels—that is, non-Muslims. For example, Hezbollah is referred to regularly as *Hezb al Shaytan*, or Party of the Devil. The Salafists use this phrase to posit the Shi'a as evil devil worshipers and the Sunnis as righteous worshipers of God. The Salafists believe Hezbollah has monopolized maliciously a claim on the name of God by calling themselves "the Party of God"—a particular affront given Salafist opinion that the Shi'a are, in fact, nonbelievers.

Thus, the Salafists also refer to Hezbollah as *Hezb al Lat*—a reference to a pre-Islamic Arabian goddess who was one of the three main female pagan deities of the city of Mecca. She is mentioned in the Koran (53:19), and pre-Islamic Arabs considered her one of the daughters of Allah, along with Manat and al Uzza. In pre-Islamic Arabia, Allah was like the other polytheistic deities. Therefore, in this way, the Salafists are refuting Hezbollah's Islamic legitimacy as a religious party and movement. The Salafists also refer to the Shi'a as *rafidha*, or the rejectionists, because of their rejection of Sunni beliefs about who were the rightful successors to the Prophet.

Such references demonstrate clearly that although the conflict has been reignited in the context of the recent transformations in the Middle East, set in motion first by the 2003 US invasion and then by the Arab uprisings, these disputes are grounded ultimately in unresolved doctrinal difference and in related events dating back many, many centuries. Seen in this way, the Shi'a are nonbelievers, *kuffar*, and more dangerous than Jews or Christians because they pose an existential threat from within the faith.[5]

Such views toward the Shi'a drive today's Salafist Twitter discourse.[6] The relevant tweets generally fall under four categories: rehashing ancient religious differences; fear that the Shi'a will become the majority Muslim sect in the Arab world; links between violence on the ground and contested religious beliefs; and calls for practical action, such as donations of aid and money for the Syrian rebels, who are seen as fighting for the Sunni cause against the pro-Shi'a Syrian and other members of the Alawite elite.

For example, this tweet falls into the first category: "The Shi'a say Hussein (may God be pleased with him) knows the unknown, so we tell them if he knew the unknown why did he go to his fate? So they remain silent with the answer," tweeted Adnan al Arour, an influential cleric in Saudi Arabia with nearly three million followers as of February 2016.[7] Al Arour makes repeated references to Hussein and other Shi'a Imams in relation to the events during the decisive May 2013 battle for Qusayr in Syria, often in a mocking and sarcastic manner. The battle, which the Syrian Sunni opposition lost to Hezbollah and Assad forces, was decisive in securing the strategic city of Homs.

This sarcasm often evokes anger and hostility toward the Shi'a among his followers. Al Arour asked if the Shi'a were killing the children of Qusayr to avenge Hussein's death at the battle of Karbala. One follower responded to al Arour on June 9, 2012, when he tweeted: "What is funny and sad is that the people who are killing our Sunni brothers in the name of Hussein in Syria and Iraq are also the grandchildren of those who betrayed Hussein and participated in his killing under the leadership of Ibn Marjana."[8]

The following tweet falls into the first category of rehashing religious differences: "Where are the Twelve Imams who are present and know the unknown that you so desperately look towards?" tweeted Abdul Rahman Mohammad Said Dimashqiah, a cleric based in the United Kingdom, who very much demonstrates the rift as being a war of opposing doctrines.[9] He also uses sarcasm and mocks the Shi'a for believing that the Twelfth Imam—the Hidden Imam, or *Mahdi*—will return to earth one day to make Islam the triumphant religion around the world. Similarly, Salem al Rafei, a Salafist in northern Lebanon, asked: "Is it really [the Iranian] revolution that has shown them in their true light, hypocrites who claim to belong to Islam when they kill Muslims? They claim to defend holy places and they bomb mosques."[10]

Mohammad al Arefe, a cleric in Saudi Arabia, has often focused his rhetorical wrath on Hezbollah. Many of his tweets fall into the second category because he fears Iran and Hezbollah will take over the Sunni world. He also conflates repeatedly the interests of Iran with those of all Shi'a. "The relationship between Hezbollah and Khomeini is one of body and soul, and the party has used it to spread Shi'ism in the Arab world," he tweeted on June 6, 2013.[11] Similarly, he tweeted one day earlier: "After the victory of the Safavid [i.e., Iranian Shi'a] order in Syria, God forbid, Iran will fight to occupy the Gulf. They see us as *kuffar* [infidels] anyway!"[12]

Arab regimes reacted differently to the development of the explosion of the Twitter-sphere as a platform for sectarian discourse, depending on each state's particular domestic and regional political agendas. In Saudi Arabia, for example, some Salafists who developed millions of followers by 2015 were, for the most part, allowed free expression because their anti-Shi'a sentiment was an asset to the Saudis' regional rivalry with Iran. For others, Twitter is a tool to express direct support for Saudi regional policies.

For example, some Salafists took to Twitter to praise the Saudi-led invasion, equipped with ground troops, tanks, and air raids, into Yemen in summer 2015. The Saudi-led coalition targeted Houthi rebels, who are backed by Iran in their fight against the Yemeni State. Arefe provided support for the invasion and Saudi Arabia's policy of trying to counter Iranian influence in the Arab world by sending out on his Twitter feed a declaration signed on January 17, 2016, by Saudi Islamic scholars warning of the threat Iran poses in Iraq, Yemen, Lebanon, and Syria. In Lebanon, however, where the Shi'a movement Hezbollah controls parts of the government and has huge influence over the security apparatus, the Salafists have faced mounting pressure and even arrest, forcing something of a retreat from the positions of relative strength they had commanded since 2012.

In contrast to recent events in Lebanon, Saudi Arabia has embraced Salafism after the Arab uprisings in an attempt to shield the state from the unrest across the entire region. In addition, when the Muslim Brotherhood came to power in Egypt, some Saudis saw the Salafists, who were often at odds with the Brotherhood, as a counterweight to the latter's influence. Leading the cause in Saudi Arabia was Crown Prince Nayef bin Abdul Aziz, also a former interior minister. He declared that Saudi Arabia would continue to follow the Salafist ideology and criticized those who connect Salafism with extremism. "Salafism is rooted in the Koran and the Sunna and calls for peaceful co-existence with other faith communities and for respecting their rights," the crown prince said at a conference on the subject in the Kingdom. "We have to stand united against those who launch smear campaigns on Salafism."[13]

In late 2011, Sheikh Abdulaziz al Shaikh, a descendant of Ibn Abd al Wahhab, gave a keynote speech at a conference convened under the title "Salafism: Legal Path, National Demand":

My brothers, you know that true Salafism is the path whose rules derive from the book of God and the path of the Prophet. This blessed state

[Saudi Arabia] has been established along correct Salafi lines since its inception by Imam bin Saud and his pact with Imam ibn Abdul Wahhab. Saudi Arabia will continue on the upright Salafi path and not flinch from it or back down.

As a result, the most influential Salafists, with millions of Twitter followers, thrive in Saudi Arabia. Some are mentors to lesser-known colleagues, such as those in Lebanon. The Salafists are given free rein, even as the Saudi government restricts freedom of expression in general, tightens press laws, and has executed a prominent Shi'a cleric the government accused of threatening the stability of the state.

Saudi tolerance of the Salafists is related directly to how the latter serve as echo chambers in support of the rivalry with Iran. When the Saudis carried out airstrikes against the Houthi rebels in Yemen, who are aided materially and verbally by Iran and who are an offshoot of Shi'ism, support poured out among the Salafists. Arefe, the popular Saudi Salafist, endorsed the campaign and sent a message to the Yemenis fighting with the Houthis and ordered them to abandon the fight so as not to be used by the "Safavid"—that is, Iranian—State. One Salafist, Awad al Qarni, who is part of the Sahwa movement historically opposed to the state and supported the Saudi campaign, although not as forcefully as Arefe.

The Saudi marginalization of the Shi'a in the country as well as those Shi'a across the causeway in Bahrain, where the Kingdom sent troops in 2011 to quell the start of a Shi'a-led uprising in the capital Manama, has also been part of a broad response to Iran's intervention in the Arab world. The Sunni Bahraini government and the Saudis accused the mainstream Shi'a opposition movement, al Wefaq, of being Iranian funded, although there is no such evidence of a connection. Al Wefaq, along with other groups, led the uprising that the Bahraini royal family claimed was aimed at overthrowing the government, although the Shi'a demands were reasonable and called for their inclusion in a more democratic political system.

The following religious scholars are presented as leading examples of how Salafist religious and political discourse fuels anti-Shi'a sentiment.

MOHAMMAD AL AREFE

Mohammad al Arefe is a well-known Saudi cleric who enjoys a popular base that includes 14 million Twitter followers as of February 2016. He is particularly notable for controversial statements that have been perceived widely as increasing sectarian tensions in the region. Al Arefe is a professor at King Saud University in Riyadh and is also cited as being the Imam of the King Fahd Academy of the Saudi Navy and a preacher at al Bawardy Mosque in Riyadh. He hosts a weekly television show on the Iqraa channel in which he emphasizes the importance of individual and collective charity work.[14]

Al Arefe is well known for incendiary comments toward the Shi'a across the Middle East, even before the Syrian war began. In a sermon in 2009, Arefe claimed the Shi'a murdered Sunnis in Iraq in gruesome ways, saying:

> They would use the most severe torture methods against them. They would kidnap a child, boil him in water, skin him like a sheep, and then, they would bring him on a platter, wrapped in a cloth, and when his family uncovered the platter, they would find this 7- to 10-year-old boy.[15]

In an interview on May 15, 2011, al Arefe said:

> Shi'ism is a heresy. It did not exist at the time of the Prophet or [the first and third Caliphs] Abu Bakr or Uthman. They have an issue with making Ali (peace be upon him) greater than he is. Then they started with other heretical things like building shrines on graves, praying to others than God, claiming that Ali knows the unknown and that he brought the dead back to life.

Asked during the same interview if it is the role of religious scholars to deescalate sectarian tension, al Arefe answered: "I say that we need both types of scholars. Those who keep the situation calm and others who also say the truth as long as it is wisdom that guides them."[16]

Al Arefe often criticizes the Shi'a-led government in Iraq and connects events there directly with the war in Syria. On December 31, 2013, for example, he tweeted: "The Shi'a Council in Najaf supports the military operation on the Sunni people in Anbar [Iraq].... Then they say 'We are not sectarian.'" Al Arefe then went so far as to criticize Iraq's highest Shi'a authority, Grand Ayatollah Ali al Sistani, saying that he was an "infidel and debauched."[17]

Born in Saudi Arabia in 1970, al Arefe has a PhD in the fundamentals of religion.[18] At times, he has been in trouble with the Saudi authorities, who believe his anti-Shi'ism serves a useful purpose but who also arrested him for traveling to Egypt in 2013 and denouncing the coup that ousted former president Mohammad Morsi from power. Al Arefe's ideas and beliefs are closer to Salafism, but also bear some similarity to the Muslim Brotherhood in Egypt. However, although he might at times be at odds with the Saudi government, he provides a prime example of how the Salafists view the Shi'a negatively.

Al Arefe is a Salafist by birth although he has been criticized repeatedly by colleagues for deviating from the mainstream of Salafist thought. They also criticize him for supporting Egypt's Muslim Brotherhood and claim he is a follower of Mohammad Qutb, the brother of the movement's intellectual and chief ideologue Sayyed Qutb. Salafists generally do not support the Muslim Brotherhood because of the movement's long history of involvement in state politics.

An ardent supporter of the Syrian revolution, al Arefe has often encouraged young men to fight in the civil war, and in a meeting with prominent Muslim scholars in Cairo last year, he called for jihad in Syria "in every possible way."[19] In summer 2013, he traveled to the United Kingdom, where critics pointed to the cleric's sectarian rhetoric that had already led to him being banned from Switzerland. It was suggested similar measures should be undertaken to ensure al Arefe's sectarian diatribe did not provoke any further discord in an already tense Middle East.[20] Al Arefe defended his trip, saying his mission was to raise awareness of the Syrian conflict and to encourage the engagement of the British Muslim community to aid with refugees fleeing the ongoing civil war. And he dismissed allegations that he was visiting the United Kingdom to "whip up sectarian tensions" as "nonsense."[21]

Al Arefe is no stranger to controversial statements about social issues, and he has been lambasted for some such remarks. Among them, he has instructed believers on the correct way to beat one's wife, not in excess or near her face, but just enough to tell her that one is fed up.[22] He has said that the hot temperatures in the Gulf cause girls to reach puberty faster, making child marriages permissible.[23] In addition, he has said that girls should not sit alone with their fathers, lest she provoke their lust.[24]

Official Saudi wariness toward social media has, so far, not extended to any move against Twitter stars such as al Arefe. Grand Mufti Sheikh Abdul-Aziz al Sheikh, Saudi's top religious cleric, has denounced Twitter as a tool for spreading unjust and incorrect messages.[25] Yet, many of the Kingdom's most popular clerics continue to use it as a powerful vehicle for spreading their views and messages. His rise to Internet stardom has been rapid; al Arefe had one million followers in 2013; but, by early 2016, that figure had reached an impressive 14 million, with thousands signing up each day.

ADNAN AL AROUR

The meteoric rise of Salafist scholar and religious activist Adnan al Arour reflects the radicalization and escalation of sectarian sentiment across the Levant. Al Arour has emerged from obscurity in Hama, Syria, to become a powerful force shaping the direction of the war in Syria and influencing negative Sunni attitudes against the Shi'a of the region. The Syrian war provided him with a powerful platform.

At first, al Arour's uncompromising stand against the Shi'a—he once publicly vowed to "grind the flesh" of pro-regime Alawites and "feed it to the dogs"—attracted few followers, and it allowed the Assad regime to paint him and, by association, the Sunni-led opposition, as dangerous extremists who must be crushed. However, as the conflict in Syria escalated and overheated sectarian rhetoric became more acceptable on all sides, al Arour found his public voice, aided by the increasing marginalization of mainstream opposition forces and his own flamboyant populist style.

Al Arour plays multiple roles to leverage his power and influence broader audiences, including Islamic scholar; televangelist; philanthropist through his Al Salam Group for Relief and Development, which raises food and money online for the Syrian rebels; and his very formidable activism on social media through his Twitter and Facebook accounts. For example, one of his most effective tweets of 2013—which was retweeted 8,843 times and "liked" 1,558 times—said: "Whoever wants to support Qusayr and the others with aid and rice and sugar and other things ... you can connect with us by phone.... For after God, we have only you."[26] This tweet was one of many al Arour used to help mobilize military support for the rebels, as they tried unsuccessfully to defeat Assad's forces at Qusayr, one of the most important battles of the war.

In satellite channels broadcast from Saudi Arabia and through his astute use of social media, al Arour's discourse deftly anticipated the seismic shifts in Sunni public opinion. From his base in Saudi Arabia, al Arour has collected almost 1.6 million Twitter followers, the vast majority of whom are men. Around 50% of his followers are between 18 to 24 years of age. An analysis of al Arour's Twitter activity in 2013 shows that each of his tweets is, on average, retweeted around 300 times, and he receives an average of 15 replies for each one he posts. The importance of his views on the Syrian war can also be gleaned from his Twitter data; his most retweeted posts, some repeated as many as 10,000 times, all concern the conflict there.

His tweets appear to peak in response to significant events in Syria, such as the intervention of the Hezbollah militia, who joined forces with Assad's forces to expel the Sunni rebels outside Qusayr in May 2013. In fact, one of al Arour's most popular and most retweeted posts is related to that very battle, when he sought to mobilize military support to help the rebels defeat Assad and the Hezbollah militia.[27]

Such tweets attract the attention of his supporters, especially second-tier Salafist leaders such as Ahmad al Assir, who was once active in

Lebanon, and Salem al Rafei, who follows al Arour from Lebanon. These tweets are then turned into commands to be executed on the ground, hence the brief rebellion by al Assir's militia against Hezbollah forces in June 2013 and during the battle of Qusayr in Syria in late May and early June 2013.

Al Arour relies on his Twitter feeds to promote his satellite television program on Shada TV called *With Syria Until Victory*, which he devotes almost exclusively to events in Syria and to the role of Hezbollah and Iran in support of the Assad government against the Sunni opposition. As part of another one of his television programs, *Laa'lahom Yahtadun* (May They Be Guided), he created a platform through which he could debate with Shi'a callers on religious issues in an attempt to guide them back to the correct path—that is, to Sunni Islam. His sarcastic style and readiness to antagonize his opponents in televised sectarian debates has helped al Arour gain a broad audience among those Sunni eager to confront the Shi'a.[28] Further bolstering al Arour's popular appeal is his personal charisma and a marked ability to speak the language of the street, in contrast to other sheikhs who use a more rigid and outmoded style.

He also uses his television program to send signals to the rebels to follow certain strategies, and to the Syrian people to perform specific nonviolent protest actions. In the early days of the uprising, al Arour called on Syrians to chant *Allah-u Akbar* ("God is greatest") from their rooftops as a peaceful tactic to keep the momentum of the rebellion going and to signal disobedience, despite the Assad regime's violent response to such symbolic protests.

In general, an examination of his tweets shows his vitriol against Iran, Hezbollah, and the Shi'a in general. In one tweet on August 31, 2013, the sheikh asks how the Sunnis can fail to respond to an invasion by the Shi'a into Sunni lands.[29] In another, al Arour writes: "Hezb al Shaytan [Hezbollah] penetrates borders and kills and slaughters and supports the falling army and the Safavids come from Isfahan through Iraq.... Then you want us to remain silent?"[30]

Part of al Arour's success stems from the effective way in which he plays on time-honored sectarian themes to convince his followers the

Shi'a aim to eradicate the Sunnis. Two tweets from May 26, 2013, typify his religious intolerance. "The Shi'a are the most *takfiri* [those who excommunicate other Muslims] of sects for they cast out anyone who doesn't believe in their Imams or who doubts one of their sect or who allies with one of their enemies."[31] In another tweet that day, al Arour wrote: "The Mahdi, according to the Shi'a doctrine, is thirsty in the basement, hiding and quenching his thirst with the blood of the Sunnis, and they say in their books that there is nothing between the Mahdi and the Arabs except slaughter."[32]

Al Arour does not confine his remarks exclusively to events in Lebanon and Syria, for his sectarian views are regional and often take aim at the Shi'a-dominated government in Iraq under then-Prime Minister Nouri al Maliki. On January 1, 2014, he tweeted: "Nobody is hidden from the injustices of the Maliki government, for he killed them [the Sunnis] on account of their identity and Iraq has never seen sectarianism like it has seen it under Maliki's term."[33] As with the other active Salafist clerics, his followers increase the longer the conflicts continue. In March 2014, he had 1.6 million followers and by September, 1.8 million. In February 2016, his followers had increased to 2.7 million.

SALMAN AL ODAH

Unlike Arour and Arefe, Salam al Odah, once a hardline conservative activist, claims in the media he does not advance most government policies to appease the state. He had eight million Twitter followers in February 2016. He does agree with the Saudi government that Iran has expansionist aims. From 2013 to 2015, he warned his followers consistently about Iranian activity and questioned why Sunni governments were not doing enough to combat Tehran's intervention. For example, on February 26, 2015, he tweeted: "What is happening in Syria, Iraq and Yemen is sectarian mobilization which has exposed the claims of moderation!"[34]

Much of Odah's appeal lies with his penchant for taking positions critical of Saudi government policies. In 2013, he posted an open letter on Facebook and Twitter demanding the government acknowledge the growing calls for reform or face "disintegration of the Kingdom." After the Arab uprisings, he became an advocate for tolerance and democracy. In an interview with the *New York Times*, he said: "The Gulf governments are fighting Arab democracy because they fear it will come here."[35] However, some question his sincerity as a government critic.

Odah was born in 1955 or 1956 near Burayda, in central Saudi Arabia, and holds a PhD in Islamic jurisprudence. During the 1990s, he was part of a group of clerics in Saudi Arabia who criticized the government for allowing American troops to enter the Kingdom during the 1991 Persian Gulf War. As a result, he was sentenced for his dissident behavior and served 5 years in prison. In the years since the Arab uprisings, he has also complained on Twitter of Arab governments' inability to provide jobs and services for the youth in their societies. This conversation on Twitter has earned him great popularity and distinguishes him from other Salafists who focus largely on regional conflicts.

NABIL AL AWADHY

Nabil al Awadhy is a Salafist cleric known for his televised sermons on shows hosted by Al Watan Channel, Risala Channel, and MBC.[36] In 2016 he had seven million Twitter followers. In recent years, the Kuwaiti-born cleric has become particularly well known for bellicose rhetoric regarding the wars in Syria and Iraq. Like many other Kuwaitis, al Awadhy has been an extremely vocal supporter of the rebel opposition seeking the overthrow of Bashar al Assad and his Alawite-dominated government. Indeed, widespread support from Kuwaiti Sunnis for the Syrian opposition has propelled a financial campaign that has raised millions for the rebels.[37] Perhaps as a reflection of Kuwait's troubled history with Iraq, al Awadhy often connects the suffering of the Sunnis in Iraq with those in Syria as a way to demonstrate the Shi'a in both countries are out to kill Sunnis. For example, on June 22, 2013, when Shi'a Prime Minister Nouri al Malaki was still in power, he tweeted: "To the men of Iraq and its heroes: Maliki is still sending his Safavid soldiers to Syria to kill children and violate women and destroy the country."[38]

Comments from clerics like al Awadhy stoke the fires of sectarianism, which play out on the battlefields in Syria and have the potential to direct a stream of weapons, fighters, and money to the war. Al Awadhy has said that the leaders of other Muslim countries must "send out the armies to help out the people in Syria and arm the Free Syrian Army, or [they] are traitors."[39] Furthermore, al Awadhy makes it clear that he sees the Syrian war as part of a wider sectarian—even millenarian—struggle between Sunni and Shi'a, and that Shi'a Iran is the driving force in this conflict. In addition, al Awadhy has demonstrated he believes the war to be a holy one—that it is mentioned in the Koran and the hadith as the battle at the end of days, blessed and chosen by Allah.[40]

Al Awadhy, born in Kuwait in 1970, is said to be a Bedouin who was granted Kuwaiti citizenship.[41] Al Awadhy graduated from the College of Basic Education with a bachelor of arts degree in mathematics, and went on to receive a master's of arts degree and PhD from universities in the United Kingdom. Sheikh al Awadhy also studied *fiqh*, or the knowledge and understanding of the body of Islamic law, at the University of Kuwait. He is a preacher at the Mostashfa Mubarak al Kabri Mosque; a speaker and Imam in the Ministry of Awqaf, the ministry in charge of religious endowments; a journalist for the Kuwaiti *al Watan* newspaper; and the general supervisor for the Center of New Converts in the United Kingdom.[42] He is frequently the subject of scrutiny by anti-Islam websites such as Islam-Watch.org and yourdailymuslim.com.[43] These websites lambaste al Awadhy because he often finishes many of his sermons by praying for Allah to infect nonbelievers with AIDS or strike them with a terrible catastrophe.

Al Awadhy is an active Twitter user and holds accounts in Arabic and English. In March 2012, al Awadhy had 3.9 million followers; by February 2016, this figure had increased to seven million, more than 10,000 of them English speakers. Al Awadhy uses his large Twitter platform for his preaching, and he tweets often about Syria, Iran, and the Shi'a. On June 5, 2013, for example, he tweeted, "Qusayr will remain a thorn in their beards. Their doctrinal war will burn them," discussing the then ongoing battle for Qusayr in Syria.[44]

In related tweets, al Awadhy declared that Iran now controlled Iraq, and he further condemned Western criticism of the Sunnis for the fighting when, according to him, the Shi'a were the ones responsible for the violence: "Since the invasion by America of Iraq and it being given to the followers of Iran ... they have been killing Sunnis! And if Sunni people defend themselves, they accuse them of sectarianism and terrorism!!"[45] On June 24, 2013, he tweeted: "Iran wants to take attention away from Syria and shift it to Lebanon. The head of the snake does not know that Muslims will not give up on Iraq, or Syria, or Lebanon. And Iran will be returned to the [true] Muslims!"[46]

These tweets are particularly interesting because not only do they demonstrate al Awadhy's support for the Syrian opposition, but also they show he clearly views the fighting as a division between the Sunnis and the Iran-backed Shi'a. Al Awadhy calls particular attention to the Iranian role in Iraq, implying the Shi'a government now in control of the country is, in effect, an arm of the Iranian State. This reflects a feeling of marginalization common among Iraqi Sunnis that has been growing since the handover to the new Shi'a-led government. Furthermore, al Awadhy implicates the United States directly and says it has given Iraq to Iran and the Shi'a.

Al Awadhy's commentaries on the war reflect both political and religious angles. Although he calls on political leaders to aid the rebels, he also makes a plea for all Muslims—by which he means orthodox Sunnis—to follow the call and join the fight, either through picking up arms themselves or by funneling financial contributions to opposition groups. Al Awadhy uses both hadith and scripture to back up his demands, making it clear to all able-bodied Muslim men that the fight in Syria is a holy war and will determine the future of the entire Islamic community of believers: the *ummah*.

Although some more mainstream Sunni clerics share such views, the difference between them and a Salafist such as al Awadhy is that the former do not call for joining the fighting in Syria. In fact, many have called for an end to the conflict. However, analysis of the Twitter feeds of within the Salafist tendency show that those most active in inciting direct support for the Sunni in Iraq and Syria are increasing steadily.

SHEIKH DAI AL ISLAM AL SHAHHAL

Al Shahhal, the son of the founder of the movement in Lebanon, describes Salafism as the "one true face of Islam" and has declared that its goal is "a call to go back to the basics" of the religion, primarily through the spread of religious education.[47] He frequently uses language that characterizes the Salafist movement as the defenders of the entire Sunni community, especially in Lebanon, against a Shi'a-led conspiracy—a clear reference to Hezbollah and its powerful backer, Iran. Al Shahhal also spreads his ideas through media outlets he has established. He founded the Holy Koran radio station in 1992, the Good Word radio station in 2005, and the Echo of Islam television channel in 2008.

As with many clerics in the Tripoli area, al Shahhal believes he has a great stake in the Syrian conflict—more so than some Saudi or Kuwaiti religious scholars who are further removed from the fighting. As a result, he has taken an active role in the deteriorating security situation in Tripoli and wider Lebanon, primarily as a result of the spillover of the Syrian war across the nearby border. After the dual bombings of Sunni Mosques in Tripoli in August 2013, he declared the Sunnis of Tripoli would be taking matters into their own hands, and he blamed the Syrian regime and Hezbollah for the attacks.[48] In the midst of an ongoing security crackdown in Tripoli, al Shahhal has been a vocal critic of the Lebanese military and has led several protests against the Army.[49]

Al Shahhal has voiced his criticism frequently, not only of the Lebanese government, but also against all those he sees as being involved with the "conspiracy ... targeting the Sunni sect to make way for the Iranian project."[50] Furthermore, al Shahhal has continued to maintain that the Sunnis of Lebanon are being targeted specifically: "Lebanon is held hostage and [its] army is treating its people as the Syrian army treats its people."[51]

In April 2014, Lebanese security reportedly confiscated two cars from al Shahhal's convoy during a protest condemning army raids in Tripoli. Two people, who media reports said belonged to al Shahhal's entourage, were arrested. Al Shahhal also announced after a meeting with Interior Minister Nouhad Machnouk that any "violations" during the implementation of a security plan in Tripoli could ignite civil strife in the fragile region, and warned him against taking any action that would qualify as "injustice toward Tripoli and its sons."[52]

An active supporter of the Syrian rebels, al Shahhal has voiced unwavering backing for the opposition in the media and on Twitter. "To the oppressed [Syrian people] we say: We are with you and beside you and feel your pain."[53] He has pledged the support of the Salafists, saying that they "express rage at what is happening to the Sunnis in Syria at the hands of the criminal regime," and that "as Sunni people, we cannot distance ourselves [or] turn a blind eye to the oppressor and neglect the oppressed." In March 2014, al Shahhal had 3,300 Twitter followers and, by February 2016, the number had increased to more than 14,000.

Al Shahhal has encouraged young men in Tripoli and elsewhere in Lebanon to support the Syrian uprising and to "sacrifice blood and life" to prevent a Shi'a-backed plot to take over the region. In fact, his own son Zayed fought with the Syrian rebels in the battle of Qusayr.[54] Al Shahhal has denied, however, that he has called explicitly for a jihad in Syria and has maintained that he only would issue a *fatwa* encouraging support for Syria against the Shi'a-led government and its allies. He denies specifically that the Salafist movement poses any sort of violent threat against the people of Lebanon or the civilians of Syria.[55]

Al Shahhal has often been noted for his firebrand rhetoric against Hezbollah, and has reportedly led protests at which Hezbollah flags have been burned. Shahhal also was a leading force in organizing a meeting of Salafists from rival factions, and has expressed interest in developing a Sunni front that would also include Islamists and secularists.[56] Al Shahhal is reportedly still very well connected with Saudi charitable organizations that have donated large amounts of money to his organizations and movements.[57] According to American University of

Beirut Professor Ahmad Moussalli, in 2008 the new Salafist movement in Lebanon was attempting to "break down the new relations between Lebanon and Syria in the interests of Saudi Arabia and its supporters."[58]

Al Shahhal maintained close ties to the late Saudi Grand Mufti Bin Baz, who made it possible for hundreds of students from Lebanon and Palestine to study Islamic theology at Saudi universities during the Lebanese civil war, among them al Shahhal himself.[59]

SALEM AL RAFEI

Through sermons in his Al Taqwa Mosque in Tripoli, an active Twitter feed, and his membership in the Association of Muslim Scholars—a group of clerics in Lebanon that participates in political and religious activities—Salem al Rafei advances a narrative of Sunni martyrdom at the hands of the Shi'a. Al Rafei also uses this narrative for domestic political purposes, condemning Hezbollah and accusing the Lebanese Armed Forces of collaborating with the armed Shi'a-dominated movement. He argues that, because of this collaboration, the state does not provide adequate security for non-Shi'a Lebanese civilians, particularly those in the predominantly Sunni north of the country.

Although al Rafei has fewer Twitter followers than other Salafists discussed here, his Tweets are retweeted consistently—an indication that his followers engage actively with the content of his posts and then disseminate the information to their own networks of friends and followers, thus applying a powerful multiplier effect. In March 2014, al Rafei had 3,600 followers and, by September, that figure had increased to 4,000. Al Rafei studied in the Sudan, where he received his PhD in Islamic law. He has published dozens of books and keeps a large library in the basement of his house. He lived in Germany for about 10 years until he was deported in 2005 for the radical content of his sermons. Now, he teaches in mosques and Sharia institutes, and serves as Imam of the Al Taqwa Mosque.

Al Rafei is an example of how mainstream Salafism has left behind its strictly theological roots and taken on much more of a political hue. "We were dragged into politics over Syria," according to al Rafei. "Most Shi'a—and I am not saying all Shi'a— have decided to take part in the Iranian project," al Rafei told me in June 2014. In more recent published comments, al Rafei has become increasingly direct about his views on sectarianism. In his eyes, the so-called Iranian project is Tehran's attempt to take over all Muslim lands—that is, to put the Muslim world under Shi'a domination. In a YouTube video, al Rafei strikes a notably more strident tone. "Look at the Iranian project and how they treat Muslims in the Arab world. They denied the importance of the prophets and cursed them. They also allied with the enemies of the *ummah* to control Islamic and Arab lands."[60]

On first meeting al Rafei in 2012, he said the Salafists in the Tripoli area were creating a political party, but, as a result of internal differences and the lack of support across the country, this never happened. Those who are quietest and part of the *da'wa*, the Salafist trend that keeps out of politics meticulously, remain steadfast against it. Al Rafei is considered the leader in the politicization of the Salafist movement in Lebanon, which began after the Syrian withdrawal from the country in 2005. The Syrians had conducted a harsh crackdown on the Salafists in northern Lebanon for many years.

Since the start of Syrian war, the most important event in Lebanon to mobilize the Salafists against Hezbollah, and in fact all Shi'a, was an attack on June 5, 2013, against Sheikh Ahmad al Assir, who is considered a Salafist and who was the former Imam at the Bilal Bin Rabah Mosque in the city of Sidon. Assir had become perhaps the most inflammatory Salafist voice against Hezbollah, Iran, Assad, and the Shi'a and their Alawite allies in general. On that day in the suburb of Abra, outside Sidon, the Lebanese Armed Forces pushed for a decisive conclusion to the threat posed by al Assir, after at least 10 soldiers and two gunmen loyal to the anti-Hezbollah sheikh were killed the previous Sunday when al Assir supporters attacked a military base.

During the clash on June 5, fierce fighting broke out between the military and al Assir and his followers. Hezbollah apparently aided the Lebanese army in its attack in Abra, according to many reports. This caused not just the Salafists but also many Sunni clerics to join in the public campaign to denounce the violence against al Assir. Al Rafei, who defended al Assir, was at the forefront, and he volunteered to mediate between the sheikh and the Lebanese army. Rafei kept the battle alive and has framed it as stark evidence of Shi'a aggression against the Sunnis. He told *An Nahar*, a leading Lebanese newspaper, that the army's attack against al Assir was not against the Salafists, but against all Sunnis.[61]

A year later, al Rafei's Mosque in Tripoli was bombed and, a few minutes after that, there was an attack on Bilal Baroudi, another Salafist Imam, and his al Salam Mosque in what is known as *the double Tripoli bombing*. The apparently coordinated blasts—the biggest and deadliest in Tripoli since the end of Lebanon's own civil war—struck as locals were finishing Friday prayers. The explosions came a week after a huge car bomb killed at least 24 people in a part of Beirut controlled by Hezbollah, and it was clear, according to al Rafei, that he had been targeted because of his campaign against Hezbollah and the Shi'a in general. Al Rafei blamed Syrian intelligence agencies and said he had received threats beforehand. "I received threats from the Syrian intelligence and I told them I will stop my sermons [against Assad] if they stop the killings. They tried to assassinate me even before the bombing," he told me.

BILAL BAROUDI

Bilal Baroudi is a notable anti-Syrian regime Salafist cleric from Tripoli, Lebanon, who has also been the target of a failed assassination attempt because of his views on Iran, the Shi'a, and Hezbollah. Like many of his fellow Salafist preachers, Baroudi proselytizes against the threat Iran poses to the Sunni. "Shi'a-ruled Iran is trying to take over the Sunni world," he told me in an interview in June 2014.

Baroudi considers himself a Salafist, but like most Salafists, he is not part of any organized movement. In an earlier interview, in October 2013, he explained

> What we believe is Salafism, not formal Salafist organizations. We count ourselves as part of the Salafist School in the sense of it teaching

us how to live in the world. For Muslims to progress, they need to clean their religious channels of all toxic things that are distorting the original Salafist view. The danger to the idea of Salafism in the way that I see it is that there is no immediate source [for religious interpretation] that can tie people down. It's loose. Because of this it will face a lot of dangers.

Baroudi was born into a religious family and attended al Azhar University in Cairo, where he studied the Koran and the Koranic sciences from 1987 to 1996. In particular, Baroudi specialized in Koran recitation rather than Islamic jurisprudence. He returned to Tripoli after his graduation from al Azhar and became known as one of the most skilled reciters in northern Lebanon. As part of the ongoing debate among Lebanon's Salafists over whether they should enter politics formally, Baroudi weighs in against the formation of a political party because it is "unnatural" for the Salafists to do so. "But I do consider my role as showing the good and bad things about the leader, whoever is in power at the time," he said in an interview with this author.

When the bomb exploded outside the Salam Mosque in August 2013, Baroudi said it was in retaliation for his sermons and beliefs. "I had issued a *fatwa* prohibiting young men from taking part in the conflict in Syria," adding that he called "on the state to remove the weapons of strife from Lebanon as well as the rockets that targeted Qusayr," a reference to that important victory claimed by the Assad regime.[62] Many commentators linked the motivation for the bombings to both Baroudi and al Rafei's harsh condemnations of the Syrian regime and Hezbollah's support for it. Baroudi had told worshippers previously, before the bombing, "Hezbollah is responsible for the consequences of this jihad invasion against Sunnis in Qusayr," adding, "the response that is coming will be harsh."[63]

Baroudi gave me a tour of all that remained of his mosque—a brick shell that had also served as his home. He said the extremists tried to plant the explosives directly underneath the area of the mosque where he was preaching that Friday, but a parked car obstructed their access. Instead, the explosives were set off farther away. All the same, the entire mosque was destroyed. Baroudi was struck near his heart by shrapnel, but a pen in his shirt pocket apparently prevented the flying debris from penetrating his skin. He blames the attacks on a lack of security provided by the state, and he thinks this is intentional.

> Our religion commands us in the Koran not to burn a garden, or cut a tree, or burn a church. It is forbidden and it is not religion. But they [the Western world] have the nerve to accuse us of these things when they have the blood of two million Iraqi children on their hands. The Alawites should take a stance against the people from their communities who were behind the blasts. The government—the Lebanese president and the head of the army—did not make a statement of condemnation. They were nowhere to be found.... They [the Shi'a and Hezbollah] want to kill us because they cannot handle people who tell the truth, and the Syrian people are oppressed.[64]

After the bombings, Baroudi announced that if the government was unable to protect the city from violence, then the people would take up arms themselves to defend it. The warning proved unneeded as security forces quickly swooped in.

Baroudi, as well as many other pragmatic Salafists, does not condone violence:

> Islamism, and Salafism in particular, are against all actions targeting innocent people, whatever the justifications and reasons. Courage is in confrontation and not in bombings in safe areas. We strongly condemn all the bombings and we consider that this has nothing to do with our Islam ... We are at loggerheads with Hezbollah over its positions, but we feel that what is happening in the southern Beirut suburbs [Hezbollah strongholds bombed periodically, presumably by Sunni extremists] is unacceptable.

Warning that Sunni–Shi'a strife in Lebanon will affect everyone, Baroudi noted:

> We said following the blasts that rocked Al Taqwa and Al Salam mosques that the Tripoli blasts and the southern suburbs bombings are carried out by the same entity. We are keen to use a unified vocabulary that unites and heals. . . . We have received no cooperation from Hezbollah. To the contrary, the party accuses us of harboring terrorism and, through its media, it threatens us, provokes us and allows our bloodshed.

CHAPTER FOUR

LEBANON

Sectarianism and the Modern State

In August 2014, Sheikh Salem Rafei and Nabil Halabi, a human rights lawyer, set out for Arsal, a town in the north along the border with Syria on the slopes of the Anti-Lebanon Mountains, which constitutes much of the Lebanese border with Syria. The city is famous for benches carved out of solid rock and an ancient fortification. Since war in Syria broke out 4 years ago, Arsal has also become known as a gateway for the many by-products of the conflict spilling over across the border into Lebanon: Syrian refugees and rebels fleeing the violence, fighters from the Islamic State crossing into Lebanon to extend the group's reach and establish a foothold in the country, and Hezbollah fighters along with the Lebanese Armed Forces trying to prevent any Sunni militants—from ISIS or other groups—making their imprint on Lebanese soil. In the face of this crisis, Rafei and Halabi, along with other Sunni clerics from the Association of Muslim Scholars of Tripoli, hoped, perhaps naively, that they could secure a cease-fire.

At first, they negotiated with a leader from the ISIS unit charged with entering Arsal, where Sunni residents in the center of town lie surrounded by Shi'a communities effectively under Hezbollah control. The pretext for the ISIS intrusion was that the Lebanese army had arrested a leader from al Nusra Front, Abu Ahmad Jomaa. At the time, al Nusra Front, an extremist but less violent group than ISIS, was cooperating closely with the Islamic State, still a budding movement set on taking territory in Lebanon and Syria after their great victory in capturing Mosul, Iraq, in summer 2014.

Halabi had another mission as well: he wanted to secure passage for trucks carrying aid to the Syrian refugees in the area from

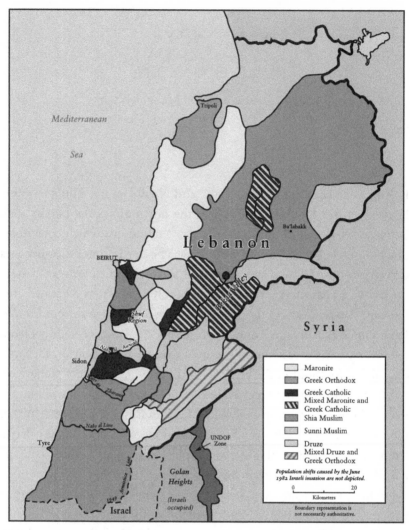

Map 4.1 Distribution of religions in Lebanon. Courtesy of the University of Texas Libraries.

the human rights organization he founded and directs, LIFE, which is based in central Beirut. However, Hezbollah blocked his trucks, he explained, 2 years after the Arsal battle. While Rafei, the other clerics, and Halabi were leaving Arsal, what was believed to be an airborne regiment from Hezbollah attacked their car. According to Halabi and Rafei, everyone in the car was wounded in their upper body—a possible sign the attackers were shooting to kill. Rafei was also severely wounded in the leg. Halabi told me the incident was a turning point for Lebanon: "Hezbollah showed in the battle of Arsal that it would encourage instability in order to make it more powerful in the region. The [Lebanese Armed Forces] began cooperating in a big way with Hezbollah." [1]

Perhaps more than any other event in three decades, the revolution and subsequent war in Syria are a primary determinant in Lebanon's foreseeable future. As Halabi pointed out, the battle of Arsal—small in the broader scheme of the Syrian war—is nonetheless an important window into the spillover effect of the conflict there. It was further evidence that Hezbollah was transitioning from a movement based primarily on fighting Israel in Lebanon into a regional Shi'a militia that would fight ISIS and other Sunni militants. The battle would work to keep Assad in power and to maintain its own grip on the Lebanese State. It also demonstrated that Hezbollah had the support of the Lebanese Armed Forces.

On May 24, 2013, more than a year after Hezbollah became involved intimately in the war in Syria, Hassan Nasrallah, the movement's leader and religious guide, gave a rambling speech in his stronghold to thousands of his supporters, declaring, "This battle is ours." Although the media and the world interpreted this speech as Hezbollah's resolve to fight to the end in Syria until Assad's enemies were defeated, the speech marked another, and perhaps more significant, turning point. Nasrallah was acknowledging that Hezbollah was departing from its historical role since its inception in 1982 as a movement dedicated strictly to Lebanese resistance to Israel.

Instead, Hezbollah was now transforming itself into a militia devoted to the defense of Shi'a interests across the Arab world. By the start of 2016, this transformation was in full operation, with Hezbollah having all but declared victory in Syria, its proxies in Iraq taking on the Islamic State, its direct or indirect support for Shi'a youth groups in Bahrain, and its aid in helping the Shi'a Houthi rebels in Yemen oust a Sunni government.

Much like its patron to the east, Nasrallah in 2013 was adopting Iran's style of rhetoric in emphasizing the need to avoid sectarian *fitna* (chaos) while doing the opposite militarily and deepening Shi'a–Sunni strife. Demonstrating this duplicitous strategy, Nasrallah said at the time: "Accusing us on sectarian basis has no purpose, and our history bears witness of that whether in Lebanon, Palestine, Bosnia and Herzegovina.... We were defending Sunni Muslims in Bosnia." On March 2, 2011, Iran's Supreme Leader Ayatollah Ali Khamenei made similar claims when speaking of the Arab uprisings as a pan-Islamic awakening: "We do not distinguish among Gaza, Palestine, Tunisia, Libya, Egypt, Bahrain and Yemen.... It is not an issue of Shi'a or Sunni. It is the protest of a nation against oppression."

At the time of this writing in February 2016, neither ISIS nor its sympathizers have yet to enter Lebanon in any meaningful way. The Syrian war has spilled across the border into Lebanon only on the margins—aside from the two million Syrian refugees who fled their homeland and are now scattered across Lebanon. In addition, there remains a general and accepted social contract within Lebanese society that civil war must be avoided at all cost. A founder of the Lebanese Armed Forces, who does not support Hezbollah's emergence as a Shi'a militia, explains the movement is a necessary evil for Lebanon:

> Hezbollah had to go and fight in Syria. If this had not happened, the Syrian war would have come to Lebanon. But one day all guns [Hezbollah's arsenal] must be with the Lebanese army. This is the only way Lebanon will have a functioning government. The key to our crisis is this political solution. There is no military solution.[2]

However, the war in Syria next door combined with the regional sectarian conflicts after the Arab uprisings exacerbated the sectarian conflict in Lebanon. The Syrian war empowered Hezbollah in Lebanon and across the region. It is common to hear complaints from Lebanese that "Hezbollah controls the country." On appearances, at least in Beirut, there is scant evidence Hezbollah is imposing religious restrictions on Lebanese society, as is the case in Iran. However, the movement holds great sway in many key institutions, not only the Lebanese

Armed Forces, but in the intelligence ministry. As Lebanese scholar Bassel F. Salloukh and other authors wrote in 2015:

> Hezbollah's actions tell a story different from the one often portrayed in its official discourse. The party actively sought to infiltrate and/or appropriate causes and institutions that did not initially advocate for narrow sectarian interests, created partisan institutions to shadow and rival those of the state and civil society, and turned co-opted individuals and institutions into mouthpieces of sectarian party politics.[3]

No one group controls Lebanon. The Sunnis lack real leadership, there is no functioning government, and there has been no agreement in the appointment of a president (who must be a Christian according to Lebanon's confessional political system) for 2 years as a result of a conflict between Hezbollah and the Future movement, the mainstream Sunni party established by Rafik Hariri and then inherited by his son, Saad, who splits his time between Saudi Arabia and Paris.

The lack of a strong Sunni leadership has contributed greatly to Hezbollah's growing power in Lebanon, and also that of the Salafists in the Tripoli area, at least between 2012 and 2015, before many were either arrested or driven out of the country. Rafei and other Salafists encouraged young Sunni men during those years to cross over to fight in Syria. "The Salafists were given weapons and money," explained Misbah Ahdab, a former parliamentarian from Tripoli whose prominent and wealthy family has had roots in northern Lebanon for generations.[4]

According to many sources, Saudi funding, whether from the government or individuals, kept Lebanese Sunni political and religious leadership influential until the funds dwindled significantly. In February 2016, the Saudis announced they were ending payments on $4 billion worth of military and other support to Lebanon because the country did not condemn attacks on the Saudi embassy in Beirut after Riyadh executed a Shi'a sheikh who had called for the Kingdom's downfall.[5] The execution in late 2015 sparked protests among the Shi'a all over the Arab world, including in Lebanon. The Saudi decision was targeted at Hezbollah—another sign in the continuing geopolitical sectarian rivalry between states and nonstate actors.

Perhaps nowhere is the lack of funding, the absence of Sunni leadership, and the power of Hezbollah more apparent than in Tripoli, a city in the north that has become the echo chamber inside Lebanon for the developments in the Syrian war. It is here that local and regional conflicts are intertwined, and where the outcomes of these disputes have long-term effects all over Lebanon. As clashes erupt routinely in Tripoli, they are echoed up the road in Jabal Mohsen and Bab al Tabbaneh—villages separated by a small road, evocatively known as Syria Street. Bab al Tabbaneh, home base of many of the Sunni militias, is a neighborhood situated beneath the steep hill where Jabal Mohsen is located.

Both districts are impoverished. The pictures of Bashar al Assad in Jabal Mohsen and the flags of the Free Syrian Army, once a formidable force opposing Assad's rule, in Bab al Tabbaneh replicate the story of the Syrian conflict in Lebanon. Suspicion runs deep all around; the Alawites of the region suspect the Sunni are provided safe passage for Syrian rebels fighting against Assad's government whereas the Sunni suspect the Shi'a of smuggling arms into Damascus to help Assad's army. The Alawites of Jabal Mohsen support Syria's Alawite government and are allies of Hezbollah. The Sunnis of Bab al Tabbaneh support the Syrian opposition.

"Over the last six months, the on-going turmoil in the Syrian Arab republic has further affected Lebanon, increasing political polarization and concern that the unrest in Syria could have negative consequences or Lebanon's stability," the United Nations secretary-general stated in his semiannual report, issued on October 18, 2012. "In particular, domestic tensions have significantly increased across Lebanon among groups with diverging positions vis-à-vis the Syrian crisis, leading to armed clashes that resulted in death and injury in the north of the country."[6]

The message from Shi'a circles that support Hezbollah was generally that the violence was being instigated by the growing Salafist movement in the Tripoli area. The pro-Hezbollah *Al Akbar* newspaper reported:

The equation is clear. The security in Tripoli depends on the security in Homs [Syria] and vice versa. For the "revolutionaries" in Homs, Tripoli is the important city. It provides them with arms, supplies, and possibly even fighters. The Salafists and Islamists do not say so openly, but this can be deduced from what is being said in their circles.... Transforming the city into a backyard for the fighters in Homs requires a lot of energy from the Salafists.[7]

According to Ahmed Fatfat, a member of the Lebanese parliament who has represented Tripoli for many years, the Shi'a–Sunni conflict before 2000 was restricted to Beirut. But, after the 2005 Syrian withdrawal from Lebanon, the Syrians left behind a militia in Jabal Mohsen, which then encouraged Lebanese Sunni militias to take up a presence nearby to defend their territory.[8]

Conflict in this area has been exacerbated, no doubt, by the fact that tens of thousands of Syrian refugees are now in and around Tripoli. There are at least two hospitals in Tripoli for treating Syrians injured in the fighting across the border. The presence of the Syrian refugees, many of whom side with the Syrian opposition, is bound to unsettle the local Alawite population. Many interviews in Lebanon start off with declarations that the violence in and around Tripoli has nothing to do with sectarianism, but invariably the conversation comes down to criticism of the other sect.

Sitting in his men's clothing shop along a road separating Shi'a and Sunni neighborhoods, Ali Faddah, the spokesman for the pro-Assad Alawite party in Lebanon, the Arab Democratic Party, did not hide his views of Sunni Islam. "We think the Wahhabis are the main causes for the problems in the Middle East," said Faddah. "They reject what other sects believe and they created a new religion far from Islam. This resulted in *takfir* [apostasy]." He also said that Sunni sheikhs, particularly the Salafists, stir sectarian strife from their pulpits during Friday prayers.[9]

As with many Shi'a, Faddah associates all Sunnis with Wahhabism, the socially conservative form of Islam practiced primarily in Saudi Arabia. But, as much as the sectarian conflict represents a continuum within the history of Islam, Faddah also said the West was to blame. He said he believes the West benefits when Sunni are battling Shi'a. "The Sunnis are instruments of the West, and serve to eliminate the Shi'a."[10]

The assassination on October 19, 2012, of Brig. General Wissam al Hassan, a respected Sunni security chief and Rafik Hariri loyalist who was aiding the Syrian opposition, made a lasting impression on Shi'a–Sunni relations in Lebanon. It is one of the most significant examples to date of the spillover effects of the Syrian conflict. The assassination exposed the lawlessness and dysfunction of the Lebanese State to an embarrassing degree. It also showed that if, indeed, Assad was behind the assassination, Syria still carries a big stick in Lebanon and has little regard for Lebanon's sovereignty. And it convinced many Sunni that Hezbollah carried out the attack on orders from Iran and the Assad regime.

Not only had al Hassan been highly successful in supporting the Syrian opposition, but he was instrumental in the investigation into the assassination of Hariri, which led to indictments of members of Hezbollah. Some Lebanese also believe that Syrian support for the strike against Hassan was designed to exacerbate the sectarian conflict in general and to destabilize the country further.

The assassination is widely seen as direct retaliation for Hassan's part in the Hariri investigation and, more recently, for the uncovering of a pro-Syrian subversion campaign in August 2012. Lebanon's Internal Security Forces arrested a former cabinet minister, Michel Samaha, who is close to Bashar al Assad, for transporting Syrian-assembled bombs to attack rival targets inside Lebanon.[11]

Samaha's arrest, along with that of two Syrian officers, was a major blow to Syrian interests because it confirmed the Assad regime's determination to escalate sectarian divisions, and revealed that Syrian officials would even use a high-ranking Lebanese politician to achieve their goals. On August 11, a Lebanese judge charged Samaha and the Syrian army officers with setting up an armed group to incite sectarian strife.

Immediately after Hassan's murder, deadly violence broke out in Tripoli, and in Jabal Mohsen and Bab al Tabbaneh along Syria Street, between pro- and anti-Assad forces. Clashes also erupted in Beirut.

"This time we began the fighting," said Abu Mohammad, a Sunni fighter from Bab al Tabbaneh. "Following the news of Wissam al Hassan's assassination, we fired toward Jabal Mohsen in anger.... After the funeral [of Hassan] the clashes became really violent."[12]

The political fallout from the assassination has also been significant. The March 14 movement, which was established as a Sunni, pro-Hariri bloc, demanded the ruling Hezbollah coalition at the time, including Prime Minister Najib Mikati, step down. Hezbollah blamed Israel for the assassination, and Mikati declared he was staying in power.[13]

Indeed, for Lebanon, there is seemingly no way to avoid being caught up in the Syrian conflict. Mikati, who is from Tripoli, warned the Lebanese "not to allow anyone to drag them into battles. We have frequently warned of the need for Lebanon not to slip into the smoldering around Lebanon, but it is clear that there are several parties who want to implicate Lebanon in this conflict."[14] The prime minister's words ring hollow when events on the ground are taken into account.

In Lebanon, where sectarianism has openly defined the modern state, bouts of conflict since independence from France in 1943 were centered traditionally on the Christian–Muslim divide. A system of power-sharing among various sects was created, specifically in the form of the National Pact of 1943 and the Taif Agreement that ended the civil war in 1989.

But, between the signing of the Taif Agreement and the assassination 16 years later of Prime Minister Hariri, Lebanon experienced the rise in power of the Shi'a, led by Hezbollah. As a result, the historical divide between Muslims and Christians has been supplanted largely by Sunni–Shi'a cleavage with some Christians, under the leadership of former military commander Michel Aoun, cooperating with Hezbollah.

The nature of sectarianism in Lebanon has changed because the political context has changed. The shifting regional dynamics as a result of the Arab uprisings were destined to work in Hezbollah's favor because Lebanon, perhaps unlike any other country in the Middle East, is most susceptible to regional change. As Imad Salamey, a political scientist at Lebanese American University, wrote:

> Lebanon's political track is dictated by a double-leveled power dynamic: domestic, which pits sectarian groups vying for political control against one another; and regional, which positions proxy sectarian groups at the ends of a polarized ideological spectrum. Therefore, as regional politics evolve, so do the dynamics of Lebanese sectarianism and its corresponding confessional power-sharing arrangements.[15]

Four events in particular have increased tensions between Lebanon's Sunni and Shi'a, and all have their origins well before the start of the Syrian uprising. One is the assassination of Prime Minister Rafik Hariri and the subsequent findings of the Lebanon Special Tribunal in July 2011, which issued arrest warrants for four members of Hezbollah. To this day, no arrests have been made and Hassan Nasrallah, Hezbollah's leader, has vowed that no one will find the men. When the tribunal told the Lebanese government the men must be arrested, Nasrallah responded: "They cannot find them or arrest them in thirty days, or sixty days, or in a year, two years, thirty years, or three hundred years."[16] The rulings implicating Hezbollah are a reaffirmation for many Sunnis that this faction is determined to triumph over all sects in Lebanon. "Hezbollah concluded that Hariri represented a threat to be eliminated, a view shared by Tehran and its Syrian henchmen," wrote Hilal Khashan, a professor at American University in Beirut and an expert on the armed Shi'a movement.[17]

Also fueling renewed sectarianism was the 33-day war in 2006 between Hezbollah and Israel, which most Lebanese, regardless of their religious affiliation, saw as a triumph for the Shi'a militia, but also as a source of national pride. Hezbollah's ability to rain hundreds of rockets a day onto Israel's north as far as Haifa had huge political repercussions back home in Lebanon. It not only showed the military strength of the Shi'a fighters, but also it cast the armed Shi'a movement as the only Lebanese force able to stand up to the Israeli army—something Arab governments have failed singularly to do for the past 60 years. As a result, Hezbollah emerged heroic in the eyes of many Lebanese. This view was strengthened by the way it quickly rebuilt parts of the country badly damaged by Israeli bombing, particularly in South Beirut.

Over time, however, shared triumphalism began to give way to old communal suspicions. After the Lebanese army relieved Hezbollah positions south of the Litani River during the aftermath of the war, many began to question why Hezbollah should remain an armed faction, as provided for in the Taif Accord. The pro-Hariri member of parliament from Tripoli, Ahmad Fatfat, voiced fear that Hezbollah's goals would shift from fighting Israel to controlling Lebanon and "transforming it into a forward base on the Mediterranean for Iran."[18]

The war with Israel also lifted Hezbollah's self-confidence to such heights that, in 2008, when former Prime Minister Fouad Siniora shut down the militia's private telecommunications network—seen as vital to its command and control infrastructure—Nasrallah called the move "a declaration of war." Hezbollah, joined by the Amal Movement (The Movement of the Deprived) and the Syrian Nationalist Party, moved through the streets of West Beirut, a Sunni stronghold, fighting and overwhelming the government-supported forces.

The fact that Hezbollah fought against fellow Lebanese—something the party said it would never do, vowing instead to restrict its armed struggle to the fight against Israel—caused many in Lebanon to accuse Hezbollah of the "Persianization" of Beirut. "The day Hezbollah took over the streets in Beirut in 2008 is now like Karbala for the Sunnis. We were humiliated. May 7 created a wall between the Shi'a and Sunni," said Mohammad Kabbani, a former Future movement member of parliament who was close to Hariri.[19] Three years later, however, in January 2011, a new government dominated by Hezbollah and its allies was announced. Najib Mikati, a Hezbollah-backed billionaire businessman, was tapped to replace Saad Hariri as prime minister. Since Hezbollah effectively won control over the government, Lebanese society has become increasingly fragmented along sectarian lines. The war in Syria put the final seal on this divide. As of 2016, Ahmad Fatfat's fear that Hezbollah's goals would shift from fighting Israel to controlling Lebanon and "transforming it into a forward base on the Mediterranean for Iran" seemed to have come true.

Lebanon's unique standing as a "house of many mansions"[20] serves to multiply exponentially the complexities of its own confessional and sectarian politics. It is also particularly vulnerable to cross-currents issuing forth from local and regional players, and to its uneasy, but still binding, history as a once-integral part of Greater Syria, to which its own fate remains so closely intertwined. The hard-won gains of the Lebanese Shi'a and the accompanying emergence of Hezbollah as a major force in the country's affairs highlight just how much is at stake for the community, and for relations in general between the Shi'a and the Sunni, in the raging civil war just across its northern and western borders.

Before Lebanon was established as a nation state in 1920, sectarianism there had a long and sordid history, with a consistent narrative of the Shi'a as backward, regardless of their accomplishments. More recently, the Shi'a have no doubt become a dominant part of Lebanese heritage and have won a hard-earned place within Lebanon's historiographical landscape. Since the mid-19th century, the political system has been structured formally by proportional representation among the main religious groups.

In contrast to other Arab states, such as Bahrain, Kuwait, and Iraq under Saddam Hussein, the Shi'a of Lebanon were the first in the Arab world to achieve a recognized identity. This came about first when the Ottomans imposed a proportional confessional system in 1843. The French later carved out Jabal Amil in the north and the Beqaa Valley in the south as formal Shi'a districts, although they had been Shi'a unofficially for centuries.

Under the French mandate, the Jafari School of Law was accorded official state recognition, allowing Shi'a clerics and scholars to issue rulings on religious practices particular to the Shi'a, including a heavy reliance on independent religious interpretation, or *ijtihad*, and such rituals as self-flagellation during Ashura.[21] The Jafari courts were also empowered to adjudicate matters of personal status, including marriage, divorce, inheritance, and other property issues, which allowed the courts to become the "official face" of the Lebanese Shi'a community. "The court's power to integrate Lebanese Shi'a was significant.... The Shi'a community was increasingly inclined to consider itself a key player in Lebanon's fledgling sectarian democracy."[22]

Although the Jafari courts helped establish a Shi'a identity, the National Pact, agreed on in 1943 to grant Lebanon independence from French colonial rule, failed to recognize the Shi'a, although the 1932 census had recorded them as the third largest communal group.[23] The Pact also gave the presidency and the post of army commander to the Maronite Christians, and the premiership to the Sunni.

The Shi'a were shut out of high office and the community remained, throughout the 20th century, the most economically disadvantaged of all major Lebanese sects. In Jabal Amil and the Beqaa Valley, the Shi'a paid more taxes but received little in the way of government services. Jabal Amil had few paved roads and most of its 300 predominantly Shi'a villages had no electricity.[24] Until the 1960s, the Shi'a in Lebanon were mostly peasants and there was no sizable middle class. The Shi'a constituted about 80% to 90% of the workforce in Beirut's factories, and 50% to 60% of the service workers in the predominantly Christian eastern section of Beirut.[25]

Real improvement in the standing of the Lebanese Shi'a can be traced in large measure to the emergence of Imam Musa al Sadr, the Iranian cleric born in Qom, who arrived in Lebanon in 1960 to shepherd the Shi'a community. He founded the movement called Battalions of the Resistance, which became known by the acronym Amal, which also means *hope* in Arabic.[26]

Much like Hezbollah, which came onto the Lebanese scene 23 years later, Sadr's Amal was able to bring a sense of unity to the community, and to increase social and political cohesion by building schools and hospitals and by providing other services. But unlike Hezbollah, Sadr relied on local resources to support the movement, not Iranian funding. At the time, Sadr's presence was welcomed by the small but wealthy Shi'a merchant elite, who had made vast sums in Africa before returning to Lebanon.[27]

Iran, however, was dissatisfied with Sadr's moderate political stance. It is believed that Ayatollah Khomeini was at odds with the Lebanese cleric over Sadr's opposition to the notion of *velayat-e faqih*, which Khomeini used to establish himself as both head of the state and supreme religious authority, and therefore beyond all reproach. With the victory of the Islamic Revolution, Iran's answer to Sadr's lingering influence was the creation of Hezbollah, in 1982. Making it easy for Iran to start a rival movement in Lebanon was Sadr's disappearance in August 1978, along with his two companions and a journalist. They had departed for Libya to meet with government officials and were never heard from again. It is widely believed that the former Libyan leader Muammar Gaddafi ordered Sadr's killing, but differing motivations existed from other corners as well.

By the time of the signing in October 1989 of the Taif Accord among the warring Lebanese factions, the Shi'a had gained enough power to secure their place within the Lebanese confessional system. For the first time since independence from the French, who had given their fellow Christians, the Maronites, power disproportionate to their actual numbers, the Taif Agreement established overall Muslim parity. Despite these gains, the political influence of Lebanon's Shi'a community still lagged behind its true demographic strength.

Still, before Taif, the Sunni Muslim prime minister was appointed by the Maronite president. Now, the prime minister answered directly to the elected legislature. The Agreement increased the power of the Sunni and changed the power-sharing arrangement, and thus the political dynamic, among Lebanon's competing sects and faiths. This redistribution of power opened up what had been a deliberately closed political world—a development that also benefited the Shi'a.

Given the Shi'a's long and arduous history of acquiring power in Lebanon, as well as the precarious balance of sectarian and regional power, it is not surprising the Syrian war looms large over the future of Lebanese domestic politics. For Hezbollah and the Shi'a in general, any possibility that President Bashar al Assad's regime might fall from power is a terrifying prospect, according to sources close to the movement.[28] Assad as a leader is certainly dispensable in the eyes of Iran and Hezbollah, as long as key remnants of the regime, such as the security apparatus, remain intact.

Meanwhile, Hezbollah's popularity in Lebanon has suffered among the Sunnis who had supported the party since its success in the war with Israel, and among Shi'a families who lost relatives fighting the war in Syria. The Sunni now are quick to denounce Hezbollah for its continued public support for Assad, whose government has killed tens of thousands of civilians, chiefly Sunni, in cold blood. Although no statistics are available, private interviews with political sources suggest, at least anecdotally, that there is little doubt Hezbollah has lost support from other communal groups in Lebanon, including some Shi'a and Christians.

An Imam in the Beqaa, who describes himself as a Salafist, reflects the views of many Sunni whose favorable attitudes toward Hezbollah's fight against Israel have now been overshadowed by disapproval over the party's position on Syria. He rejects Hezbollah's explanation that it backs Assad because he supports the "resistance" against Israel. Sheikh Adnan Imama noted:

> If a Sunni were committing these massacres in Syria, we would call for him to be killed, even if he were killing Alawites, Christians, and Shi'a. We are not against Shi'a as Shi'a, but we are against political Shi'ism.... Nobody supports the Syrian regime except the Shi'a of Iraq, Iran, and Lebanon.... If the Syrian regime considers itself secular, then why has it become sectarian in the eyes of political Shi'ism and Hezbollah?[29]

Political Shi'ism, as Imama calls it, is an apt description for the support Shi'a have expressed for Assad and his loyalists. According to mainstream Muslim opinion, the Alawites represent a heterodox trend of Shi'ism, and some leaders in the Muslim Brotherhood, the oldest Sunni Islamist movement in the region, have even denounced the Alawites as pagans. It was just such a danger that the late Syrian leader Hafez al Assad sought religious sanction in 1970 for the notion that the Alawites were, in fact, a legitimate subset of Shi'a Islam.

Today, Shi'a support for Assad's son and successor, and for Alawite rule in general, is based not so much on religious orientation as on cool political calculation: the fear that a Sunni-led government in Damascus would be a threat to all Shi'a in the region. As a result of the Syrian conflict, "for the Lebanese Sunnis, the Shi'a have replaced Israel as the number one enemy," said a newspaper editor and founder whose publication reflects the views of Hezbollah.[30] As the civil war in Syria takes on ever more religious and sectarian characteristics, so, too, does the strife in Lebanon. "Sectarianism is worse than the bombings and the shelling," said Sheikh Afif Nabulsi, one of the founders of Hezbollah. "A small child now learns to hate the other sect. I never needed bodyguards. I used to walk in the market alone. But now I need bodyguards. This sectarianism is a sin."[31]

Today, Lebanon's Salafist movement, which burned brightly during the early years of the Syrian civil war, faces something of an uncertain future. Many had abandoned the movement's traditional quietism, stirred into action by the threat to their Syrian Sunni brethren. However, their inflammatory Twitter rhetoric, their street protests, and direct confrontation with Hezbollah led to their decline. The days when the Salafis preached impassioned sermons against the Shi'a regularly in their mosques have come to an end—at least for now—and plans to form a political party have been quietly abandoned, largely for lack of a coherent and shared political agenda or program. Some leading figures have been arrested, chased into exile, and even found themselves the targets of violent attacks.

"Unfortunately, the activities among the Salafists in Lebanon have declined," Nabil Rahim, a Salafist leader in the Tripoli area, who was on trial and accused of aiding extremists, said in an interview in 2015. "The reason is that people are occupied with their daily lives and [another reason] is fear. We are afraid of the Lebanese security and, of course, of Hezbollah." Rahim also said that the crackdown on the Salafists and other Sunni Islamists is leading young Sunni men to become more sympathetic with armed extremist groups, such as ISIS.[32]

Bilal Baroudi, whose mosque was bombed in 2013 (an Alawite leader in Lebanon was charged with the crime), agrees that the weakness of Sunni political leadership is driving some Sunni activists to move in a more radical direction. He also defended the Salafists' past activism in aiding the Syrian opposition. "We helped the Syrian revolution, but we never wanted to revolt against the Lebanese authorities," he said. Although there is a perception in the West that Hezbollah—which is stretched militarily and financially by fighting in Syria to keep Assad in power—has lost influence, the party remains a formidable force in Lebanese politics.

Given the vicissitudes of the Syrian conflict and the complex political and religious dynamics of Lebanon, it is difficult to assess the movement's prospects over the coming years. However, it is important to recognize the degree to which the emergence of individual Salafi Imams was an added effect of the Arab uprisings—in particular, that in Syria against the Shi'a-backed Alawite regime of Bashar al Assad. The increasingly confessional nature of that conflict worked to the advantage of these Salafist activists, who advanced the notion successfully that a Shi'a–Alawite–Iran axis presented the single greatest threat to the Sunni *ummah*—a claim that resonates well with mainstream Sunni opinion across the region. Just as the Shi'a of Hezbollah have exploited the threat to the region of Israel and their ability to resist, the Salafists positioned their movement as a counterweight to the Shi'a and their backers in Iran, which by implication is even more ominous to all Sunnis than the danger posed by Israel and the West.[33]

The Salafists' rise and direct involvement in Lebanese politics are significant for a number of reasons. First, they introduced sectarian discourse into the national debate on television and in other forms of the media that is far more confrontational than in the past. Second, they used the violence being committed by the Syrian government to generalize about the potential for anti-Sunni violence among all Shi'a, regardless of whether they are Alawite.[34] Third, they formed influential transnational networks with other Salafist preachers, particularly those in Saudi Arabia, a country that has funded Sunni groups in Lebanon.

A timeline of the most significant events surrounding their appearance on the scene is helpful in understanding the role of the Salafists in Lebanon. In 2003, Lebanese Salafists began to grow in numbers in response to the US invasion of Iraq. Dozens headed to Iraq, via Syria, to join the insurgency against the United States and allied forces. Shaker al Abssi, a Palestinian refugee from Lebanon, was leading the campaign to send militants to Iraq. He founded the group Fatah al Islam in Lebanon in 2006.

In the wake of the Syrian withdrawal that followed the assassination of Hariri, Salafists who had earlier fled Lebanon for fear of repression began to return to the Tripoli area. The Salafists had been at odds with Assad's government and Hezbollah, but now they faced a new obstacle—the Lebanese Armed Forces. "After the Syrian withdrawal in 2005, the Syrians left an Alawite militia in Jabal Mohsen. The representative of this militia, Rifaat Eid, says he is aligned with Syria's Assad and Hezbollah," said Ahmed Fatfat, member of parliament from Tripoli.[35]

In 2011, when the Syrian uprising began and Sunni refugees fled to Tripoli, the Salafists were positioned uniquely to provide shelter and to use the uprising to enhance their influence in northern Lebanon. They aided the refugees along with the Jami'yat Islamiyya, which was aligned with the now-banned Muslim Brotherhood of Egypt. The Salafists' backing of the Syrians was a direct challenge to the Alawites in nearby Jabal Mohsen, who support Assad's government.

Among these notable figures in the movement was Selim al Rafei, who was intimidated into silence by Hezbollah, the Lebanese Armed Forces, or both. One day in June 2012, he told his all-male worshippers:

> The Syrian Army is killing the people and is supported by Iran, China, and Russia, and the US did not intervene to help the Syrian people. Why are they not supporting the Syrians? Because they are Muslims. The West and America are liars. Their lies are exposed and are a lesson to our people. The only thing that is helpful for Islam is jihad. Jihad will give us back our dignity.

In September 2012, I first spoke with Rafei at his sprawling home overlooking the Tripoli hills. He recounted his life, including 20 years in Germany until he was deported for sermons in which he denounced the

United States for "killing Iraqis," and the "Jews" for killing Palestinians. On that day, Rafei announced that the Salafists in Lebanon, and especially those in the Tripoli area, would form a political party to run candidates in Lebanon's next parliamentary elections, scheduled for summer 2013, but that failed to materialize. Reflecting the historical reluctance of Salafists to participate in politics, he explained:

> The group of Salafists who have wanted to be politically active have believed in elections. But until the Arab uprisings they were against electoral politics because they were not fair. They were corrupt. Now, things have changed. There is more freedom. The party will not be confined to Tripoli and will include Salafists from all over Lebanon, and it will make alliances with other political coalitions just like in any normal political process.[36]

Efforts on the part of the Lebanese Salafists toward public engagement benefited considerably from support for just such a move from leading figures in the worldwide movement, in particular in the charismatic person of Sheikh al Odah, the Saudi preacher who has been gaining influence across the Middle East with his open encouragement of the role of Salafism in politics. Other Saudi-based Salafists also left their mark on the Lebanese scene. For example, Rafei and other like-minded Imams have found a mentor in Sheikh al Arour, the televangelist based in Riyadh who has used the Syrian conflict to expand his own influence in many Arab countries, from Lebanon to Tunisia.

Adding to al Arour's credibility in the region is the fact that he was born in Hama, Syria, the city razed by the late president Hafez al Assad—the current president's father—in 1982 to quell an uprising by the Muslim Brotherhood. An estimated 20,000 to 40,000 people were killed, and the city's grim fate has served as a poignant reference and rallying cry for the current uprising. Like many Salafists, al Arour frames the Syrian uprising as a battle with the Shi'a for Sunni dominance in the Middle East. His argument resonates with many, considering the Syrian regime's reliance on the violent *shabiha*, the pro-Assad mercenaries, and the help that Hezbollah and Iran are giving the Syrian regime.

Al Arour has used his videos to insert himself directly into Lebanese affairs. In May 2012, he posted a YouTube message to Hezbollah leader Hassan Nasrallah:

> The Syrian people no longer respect you because of your support of the Syrian regime that is based on sectarian interest only. Your stance from the Syrian uprising is sectarian. Your ... support for the Bahraini uprising is without a doubt sectarian. Your stance from the Syrian uprising is you are siding with the regime against the Syrian people. Why? Because you ... only abide by Iran's demands.[37]

Using the power and influence of an effective social media presence, al Arour has also sought to discredit Hezbollah over its 2008 takeover of parts of Beirut, a move that cost the Shi'a militia much of its general support within Lebanon, and he has denounced Nasrallah as a "whore" for supporting the Syrian regime.[38] In these and many other videos, al Arour frames the Syrian uprising as a struggle of all Sunnis against the Shi'a and—by extension—against Iranian domination.

One of al Arour's protégés who once made headlines in Lebanon was Ahmad al Assir, the sheikh in a mosque in Sidon. Al Assir said he does not consider himself a Salafist, but he is widely viewed as one by others. A self-proclaimed religious authority with a long, bushy beard, al Assir was no stranger on the Lebanese scene; he has been the Imam of the mosque since 1997. However, his notoriety in 2012 and 2013 stemmed from his statements about the Syrian war.

"For years, the Shi'a have been controlling and insulting us [the Sunni]," al Assir said when I visited him at the Bilal bin Rabah Mosque in Sidon. He went on to say:

> They control the security, the government, and politics. They pay Sunnis to back them to try to create fragmentation among us and they threaten us with a sectarian war. We support the Syrian rebels. Here in the Sidon mosque, we raise money for those who come to pray for the Syrian rebels.[39]

Since the Syrian uprising began, al Assir has become steadily more radical, and his rhetoric has marked a new departure for Lebanon, where, after decades of conflict among the multiple sects, the Lebanese reached a general consensus on the need to speak in euphemisms and to refer to sectarian feeling as *fitna*, or social disorder. But, in the eyes of al Assir, the Syrian war changed everything. "One of the features of the Arab Spring was Sunni power, and some Islamist forces feel that they don't have to deal with Iran and Hezbollah on an indirect level any longer. They can face them directly," said Ali Amir, a reporter for the Lebanese newspaper, *al Balad*, who specializes in Sunni–Shi'a relations.[40]

At first, al Assir was staging protests from Sidon to Beirut amid calls for Hezbollah to disarm. Al Assir also led his followers in summer 2012 to close a 200-yard stretch of the main highway connecting Sidon to Beirut. Dozens of men, most with long beards—the signature style of male Salafists—wandered along the road. However, by November 2012 he was calling for a Lebanese uprising against Hezbollah and vowing to form a Sunni militia to combat the militia's vast arsenal. He also blamed what he called the "Iran project" for the Hariri assassination, as mentioned previously.

Violent clashes erupted in Sidon on November 11, after al Assir tried to force Hezbollah supporters in the town to remove all banners and posters backing the Shi'a party. Two of al Assir's bodyguards were killed in the violence, according to foreign news reports. A day later, al Assir claimed Hezbollah supporters had tried to assassinate him. Emergency meetings were called by Lebanese officials to declare Sidon "a military zone" to quash the unrest. Thus, the radicalization of some Sunnis has gone beyond the control of the Lebanese security, political, and religious authorities. Alarmed Hezbollah leaders responded with charges that Lebanese Sunni officials were supporting al Assir with the intent of diminishing their faction's power.[41]

In June 2012, al Assir was splashed all over the media because he brandished, as a symbol of his grievances, a toy rifle, which he said a Shi'a businessman had mass produced in China and then distributed in Iraq, Jordan, and Lebanon. There is an audio tape inside the toy; after sounds of gunfire—"rat-a-tat-tat"—a voice could be interpreted as saying, "Kill Saida Aisha." Aisha was one of the wives of the Prophet Mohammad. According to the Sunni, Aisha had an important role in early Islamic history, both during Mohammad's life and after his death. Regarded by many as his favorite wife, she was an active figure who was involved in continuing his message.

Although Hezbollah, in coordination with the Lebanese Armed Forces, arrested Assir in summer 2015 as he tried to flee the country at the Beirut airport after years in hiding, the damage he produced contributed to the sectarian sentiment that still remains. In a Friday sermon on October 26, 2012, al Assir told worshipers that Iran and Hezbollah deceive people, and their aim is to establish supreme clerical rule, the *velayat-e faqih*, across the region:

> We have been warning against the Iranian project in the region for years, ever since so many cheered for Palestine under grand slogans as "resistance." We warned that this project means harm against the Sunnis more than it does for the Zionists. These slogans are all lies, all with the aim of executing the Iranian project. They have announced this. They tell us that they are more than honored to be soldiers in the army of the *velayat-e faqih*. They deceive the Muslims with slogans of support for Palestine and uniting the Muslims as they kill and slaughter our children and women and rape our women and destroy our mosques in Syria, and assassinate politicians in Lebanon.

In this one passage, al Assir managed to achieve several objectives of the Salafists: he linked Iran and Hezbollah to the killings of Sunni in Syria, he made the argument that Hezbollah–Iranian–Syrian support for the Palestinian cause is merely a pretext for the larger objective of creating an Islamic State in Lebanon, and he accused implicitly Iran and Hezbollah of un-Islamic behavior through the violence in Syria.

His message bears much resemblance to the ideas that Rafei conveyed through his mosque sermons. "What is taking place today is the extermination of the Syrian people and it is all managed and overseen by Iranian intelligence," Rafei said at Friday prayers on February 24, 2012. "This means they have resentment for religion. Following the events in Syria, it is clear that [the Iranians'] hatred toward the [Sunni] *ummah* is even more than that of Israel."

Such animosity has greatly complicated Iran's broader strategic aim in Lebanon and other countries to influence, if not intervene directly in, the rise of Sunni movements in the region. With every major conflict that has erupted since the Arab uprisings began, Iran has looked for windows of opportunity to embrace Sunni populations, even at times when there was clearly no receptivity to Iran's overtures.

Iran's attempted embrace of the Sunni began shortly after the Islamic Revolution. In an early effort to influence the Sunni, Iran and its local allies created a network of preachers responsible for spreading a revolutionary version of Islam in the areas of Sidon. Sympathetic Lebanese and Palestinians were co-opted to form the Congregation of Muslim Ulama. The Congregation was set up in 1982 by the Iranian ambassador to Lebanon with multiple objectives: to weaken Lebanon's traditional clerics, to give the clergy a direct say in political matters, and to unify the religious communities to reduce sectarianism, which at the time at least threatened to undermine the relatively weak Shi'a community.[42]

Today, a few of the clerics who were involved in this effort still preach in Lebanon. Sheikh Maher Hammoud, a Sunni cleric who was one of founders of the Congregation of Muslim Ulama, denounces the United States routinely from his mosque in Sidon. Hammoud, a white-haired cleric well versed in Iranian politics, was suspicious at first on meeting me, an American visitor, but he quickly became eager to convey his views. In keeping with Khomeini's vision, Hammoud explained that the concept of *velayat-e faqih* was designed to bring Shi'a and Sunni Muslims together because it abandoned the long-held Shi'a belief that no legitimate government could exist on earth until the return of the so-called Hidden Imam, who broke off all contact with the faithful in 941 CE. "Khomeini changed that and brought Sunni and Shi'a together," said Hammoud, who supports Hezbollah.[43]

Where does Hezbollah stand as the sectarian crisis in Syria and Lebanon deepens? The Shi'a movement has tried to balance its need for the Assad regime to stay in power with the sentiments of its constituents at home, some of whom are appalled at the Syrian regime's willingness to kill its own citizens. If at one time Hezbollah was torn between defending its military and strategic interests—keeping Assad in power, which also is in Iran's interest—and maintaining the support of its base, both Shi'a and Sunni, at home, this is no longer the case in 2016. Hezbollah along with its allies, Russia and Iran, have secured the Assad regime's survival for the foreseeable future while also cementing its own hold on Lebanon.

Yet, although no credible opinion polls have been conducted, many experts who have followed Hezbollah for years believe the movement has lost significant Sunni support. And, although the Shi'a might still back the movement, some are clearly uneasy with Hezbollah's continued support for the Assad regime as the death toll mounts across the border. Hezbollah has now become a movement and a party almost exclusively for the Shi'a. Ali al Amin, an *Al Balad* correspondent who follows the movement closely, said in an interview:

> After losing its Sunni popular base and its Sunni political allies, it has become clear to Hezbollah that the Shi'a community is its only support. . . . For that matter, it is necessary for Hezbollah to maintain its position as the only supporter and defender of the Shi'a community . . . and Hezbollah continuously seeks to convince the Shi'a community that it is under threat and that it is targeted, and that Hezbollah is the only party capable of defending it.[44]

Aside from the Salafists and other public figures who have not been afraid to discuss Hezbollah's standing in Lebanon, most ordinary Lebanese are loath to give a candid opinion. One vegetable vendor in South Beirut, Hezbollah's stronghold, reflected the views of many ordinary Shi'a:

> You will not get a clear answer from anyone about how they really feel. Here, everyone is under surveillance and they fear speaking the truth; they fear speaking otherwise of Hezbollah because they believe that they have the power to do as they please, so they prefer either saying nothing or boldly supporting Hezbollah so they can score with them.

CHAPTER FIVE

BAHRAIN AND THE SHI'A QUESTION

Two years after the start of the Shi'a-led uprising against widespread inequities under Sunni rule, the University of Bahrain held a conference in Manama intended to show the great strides the government was making toward addressing the grievances of the majority Shi'a population. Invited guests at the sessions, held in April 2013, included US Congressmen and former American diplomats, on hand to testify to the government's progress toward a more inclusive government and an improvement in human rights, including more freedom of expression.

For their part, government officials took pains to assure their American guests, worried about a US naval base located in Bahrain, that the country was stable. As a participant at the conference, I asked several officials to describe in detail the progress to which they were referring between the government and the opposition. None provided substantive answers. The Bahraini political elites did not want to be perceived to be presiding over a repressive state, but the facts speak for themselves.

According to a US State Department report in 2014, as well as reports issued by Bahraini and Western human rights organizations, there is less freedom in Bahrain than before the uprising began, and the majority Shi'a population is being marginalized increasingly. The US State Department report documented accelerating reprisals against human rights defenders and members of the opposition; greater harassment of political groups, including the moderate and mainstream Al Wefaq National Islamic Society; and severe torture and abuse against dissenters by the security forces. The report also documented a lack of an independent judiciary and the ongoing political and economic discrimination against Shi'a citizens.[1] The main Shi'a opposition group, al Wefaq, has refused to participate in the proposed "national dialogue" with the government because of the state's unwillingness to compromise.

As with other modern Arab states, ethnic and religious identity has come to define Bahrain increasingly today. The underlying causes for the uprising in 2011 have festered and affected how the Sunni and Shi'a perceive one another, not only at home but around the region as well. Thus, the Shi'a-dominated uprising in Bahrain stands as a struggle, not just for the Bahrainis, but for the standing of the collective Shi'a in the Middle East.

For months into the uprising, which began in February 2011, some Bahrainis, Western scholars, and analysts continued to argue that, unlike a war-torn country such as Lebanon, Bahrain did not suffer from deep sectarian divisions. Clearly, this assessment was misguided. Although Bahrain did not endure a protracted civil war, as was the case with Lebanon, the country has a long history of institutionalized discrimination against its Shi'a majority.

Among the nation states in the Persian Gulf that developed during the 20th century on a foundation of oil wealth, Bahrain stands out with its particularly rich and ancient heritage, along with a long history of Shi'ism. The Shi'a of Bahrain were strengthened by Iran's adoption of Shi'ism as the state religion during the early 16th century, and then by Iran's direct control over Bahraini territory beginning in 1602.[2]

At the time, Bahrain was an important center for the Arab Shi'a, along with Jabal Amil in Lebanon and Kufa and Najaf in Iraq. All these places became centers of learning for the newly formed Safavid state in Iran, which needed to educate its Shi'a clerics. In fact, the first Safavid shah cleared his rulings with clerics in Najaf and Bahrain to ensure their theological validity.[3] It is this history that the Sunni government and its loyalists use today when they brand the Shi'a opposition as "Safavid loyalists of Iran."

The Shi'a domination of Bahrain came to end with the conquest by the al Khalifa tribe in 1782. The invasion came from the east from Qatar, and many Shi'a living in that part of the island were killed or expelled; others fled north and west, which remain Shi'a strongholds today. In a precursor of things to come nearly 300 years later, the al Khalifas during the 1820s called on the Dawasir tribes in Saudi Arabia to send troops to Bahrain to displace the Shi'a further.⁴ The Bahraini Shi'a had adopted Shi'ism from the early days of the split within Islam and consider themselves to be the real natives of the land. They called themselves *Baharna*. A minority of Shi'a at the time of Persian descent were known as *Ajam*.

Grievances within the Bahraini population are not new: the modern demand for greater political power in Bahrain can be traced to 1938, when groups of Sunnis and Shi'a presented demands for local autonomy to the British governor.⁵ The British had sought to bring an end to the persecution and killing of the Shi'a. The movement, however, was not successful. During the pan-Arab period during the 1950s and 1960s, as in many other Arab states, Bahrain's opposition groups tended to be left-leaning and nationalistic. Their goal was an end to the British occupation of Bahrain and the Gulf. Compared with today, religion had far less of a role to play in articulating the grievances of the opposition to the state.

The country has undergone rebellions since the 1920s, with significant protests occurring every 10 years or so. However, the latest protests are arguably being taken more seriously by all sides for a number of reasons. First, the successful uprisings that have occurred in Iraq, Egypt, Yemen, and Tunisia have fueled fears within the al Khalifa government that they may not be able to control the opposition much longer. Second, there is an intensified fear among Gulf monarchies of Iran's attempts to exploit the Arab uprisings, sensitivities heightened by Iranian state propaganda, its successful nuclear deal with the major world powers, and its direct intervention in Syria. Third, the Shi'a of Bahrain are no longer willing to wait patiently for reforms that may never be implemented, and even the moderate al Wefaq began to defy government bans on protest in September 2012.

Fears of Iran's potential for interference are supported, at least to some degree, by historical precedent. The 1979 Islamic Revolution made a significant mark on the Shi'a in Bahrain and in other Gulf states. Radical Shi'a groups emerged in Bahrain, Kuwait, and Saudi Arabia. Iranian clerics came to preach in Bahrain, and members of a Bahraini Shi'a movement—the Islamic Front for the Liberation of Bahrain—visited Tehran.

In 1981, the Bahraini government announced it had uncovered a plot to stage a coup, directed by the Islamic Front for the Liberation of Bahrain. The government said the conspirators were trained in Tehran, and even moderate Shi'a were suspected as part of an alleged fifth column.[6] The complaint of the opposition was to address the discriminatory practices against the Shi'a, although different groups had different aims. The Islamic Freedom Movement, another opposition group based in London, for example, did not advocate an Islamic state in Bahrain, but rather wanted a more equitable distribution of wealth. One leader of the group was the cleric Sheikh Abdel Amir al Jamri, a renowned religious scholar, whose son by the same name is now a moderate leader in the opposition and editor of the newspaper *Al Wasat*.

Until the 1979 Islamic Revolution in Iran, the Bahraini opposition was dominated by secular-minded Bahrainis—both Shi'a and Sunni. But, after the revolution, Islamist movements began leading the opposition.[7] Contributing to this new religious character was the fact that, slowly, more Shi'a began attending seminaries in Qom, Iran's holy city and home to much of the Iranian clerical establishment. For the first time, Friday prayer sermons in Bahrain were used in the mosque to discuss the grievances among Bahrainis, such as unemployment and a general lack of social justice.[8]

The Shi'a of Bahrain follow a range of spiritual leaders, as is common within Shi'a Islam. In political terms, this means their allegiances are divided. Some Bahrainis consider Ayatollah Khamenei, Iran's Supreme Leader, their religious guide; others follow Ayatollah Sistani in Iraq whereas others remain admirers of the late Ayatollah Fadlallah, who spent a great deal of his life in Lebanon. It is extremely difficult to determine the exact numbers of Shi'a who follow a particular ayatollah, but it is widely believed that most Shi'a in Bahrain follow Sistani. Just as these spiritual guides hold differing views on the issue of *velayat-e faqih*, so do their followers. Sistani and Fadlallah oppose direct clerical intervention in politics and are considered quietest clerics. Khamenei, of course, favors supreme clerical rule.

Much is made of the fact that the Bahraini Shi'a are attached to their Arab identity, and thus are less inclined to be lured into Iran's embrace. This argument has more credibility when assessing whether Bahrainis would want to be ruled by the Islamic Republic or a similar theocracy, but has less validity when discussing Iran's religious influence over the Shi'a in Arab countries. When it comes to choosing a spiritual exemplar, or *marja*, for example, the teachings of a particular religious scholar—Arab or Persian—seem to trump ethnicity.

During the 1990s, the Shi'a in Bahrain began to unify more than in the past. Between 1994 and 1998, a series of clashes and street protests broke out in Bahrain's Shi'a villages. The root causes behind the unrest were said to include state authoritarianism, the absence of civil and political rights, a stagnant economy, and extensive anti-Shi'a discrimination.[9] The Bahraini government was viewed largely by the Shi'a community as a corrupt regime that favored the loyal factions close to it and utterly ignored the impoverished Shi'a areas of the country.

Although the Shi'a formed the majority of the protestors, a number of Sunni sought a return to relatively liberal 1973 Constitution and helped the cause by collecting pro-reform petitions, signed by thousands.[10] The uprising also brought about a rare union among leftist, liberal, and Islamist factions, who joined forces to demand democratic reforms.

For 4 years, large demonstrations and street clashes became the norm. This period of unrest in Bahrain is referred to as the *1994–1998 Intifada*. And as a result of this uprising, "religious symbolism as a political tool" became one of the characteristics of the protest movement.[11] The government's response to the street protests was brutal. Thousands of demonstrators and activists were arrested and some of the opposition leaders were exiled.[12]

In 1996, the Bahraini government accused Iran of funding an organization called the *Bahraini Hezbollah*, which had allegedly carried out
a number of violent attacks inside the Kingdom. In June of that year, 51
Bahrainis were arrested and charged with plotting against the government.[13] Some Shi'a have questioned whether this plot ever existed and
accuse the government of greatly exaggerating any threat.

The most recent drive among the Shi'a for political and social
reform began when Sheikh Hamad al Khalifa, Bahrain's current king,
took the helm. He released hundreds of prisoners who had been put
in jail, including Sheikh Jamri. He announced a pledge in December
1999 to hold municipal elections, when for the first time women would
be allowed to vote. In 2000, he issued a decree revising the composition of the Majlis al Shura, a special advisory council whose members
were appointed by the king, increasing the number of Shi'a members.
Perhaps his most significant reform was to appoint a committee to create a National Action Charter that would bring in constitutional, judi-
cial, and political reform.

The National Action Charter was approved in a referendum, but
trouble followed. In 2002, King Hamad's unilateral revision of the
Constitution without putting the revisions to a popular referendum
provoked opposition among Shi'a and Sunni alike. The amendments
gave great power to the executive branch over the legislature. For
example, legislation could not be passed without the approval of the
Majlis al Shura.

The broad demands of today's mainstream opposition were outlined
in a proposed plan that emerged in July 2011. It is unclear, however,
whether the main Shi'a opposition will continue to make the demands
it had in the past. These include an elected parliament with expanded
powers, including the power to confirm or reject a nominated cabinet;
direct election of the prime minister by the largest coalition within the
elected parliament; monitoring of elections by an independent electoral
commission; "fairly" demarcated electoral boundaries to prevent the
government from gerrymandering to ensure a Sunni majority in the
lower house; efforts to reduce sectarian divisions; and new mechanisms

to provide food subsidies to the most needy citizens, many of whom are Shi'a.

When the latest protests began as part of the wave of revolutions in the Arab world, the majority of young protestors marching to the Pearl Roundabout, a landmark in downtown Manama that served as the proverbial square for revolution, were Shi'a. The protests started immediately after President Hosni Mubarak had been driven from power in Cairo, and the Bahrainis chose a symbolic day: February 14. On this day 10 years earlier, King Hamad bin Isa al Khalifa had declared that his National Action Charter, the major reform project, would be enforced and proclaimed Bahrain a constitutional monarchy with a bicameral parliament and an elected lower chamber.

Yet, power still remains primarily in the hands of the king and the appointed prime minister since 1970, Sheikh Khalifa bin Salman al Khalifa, who is the king's uncle and has held the post for more than 40 years. The king has the power to appoint and dismiss the prime minister, to appoint and dismiss half the legislative assembly represented by a Shura Council, to appoint judges to the Constitutional Court, and to impose martial law, which he did shortly after the uprising began. The protesters were demanding the removal of the prime minister (who is widely unpopular even within governmental circles), new elections, and a new constitution.

The Bahraini government was clearly determined not to go the way of Egypt and Tunisia, which both saw the overthrow of long-entrenched authoritarian rulers. On March 14, the government welcomed 1,200 troops from Saudi Arabia and 800 from the United Arab Emirates, operating under the aegis of the Gulf Cooperation Council (GCC). King Hamad wrote that his government was forced to use the military option and enforce a crackdown because "the legitimate demands of the opposition were hijacked by extremists with ties to foreign governments in the region"—a clear and direct reference to Iran.[14]

The troop deployment, called "Peninsular Shield," was the first time the GCC used collective military action to suppress a popular revolt.

Iran's government and even moderate clerics expressed outrage over the Saudi military presence in Bahrain. The uprising was not instigated by Iran. However, Iranian officials complicated the picture by handing the Bahraini and Saudi governments the chance to assert that Tehran was, in fact, behind the revolt. As soon as the uprising began, Supreme Leader Khamenei referred to it with elation, and he offered public and moral support for the Shi'a against the repressive Sunni government.

Khamenei continued to express his enthusiasm. At a meeting of the Islamic Awakening and Youth Conference on January 30, 2012, he told the audience: "What you did in Egypt, what you did in Tunisia, what you did in Libya, what you are doing in Yemen, what you are doing in Bahrain ... is part of a battle against this dangerous and harmful dictatorship that has been pressuring humanity for two centuries."[15]

Grand Ayatollah Saafi Gulpaygani, based in Qom, took up the Bahrain uprising as a personal cause. In staunch defense of the Shi'a in Bahrain, he admonished the Saudi government in harsh terms for sending troops to crush the uprising. As the guardians of the two holiest shrines in Islam, he declared, the Saudis owed an explanation of their behavior to the entire Muslim world:

> It is unfortunate that the Muslims' revolutions against American domination and influence causes the ruler of the two holy mosques anger. . . .
> It is questionable for every Muslim that the rulers of the two holy mosques, who should make no distinction [between Shi'a and Sunni] yet in Bahrain support subjugation, dictatorship, [and] vice. . . . No Muslim expects anything like this from the rulers of the two holy mosques.[16]

Factions within the Kuwaiti government, convinced that the Bahraini uprising would provide an opening for Iran, considered sending forces to join the troop deployment, but Prime Minister Sheikh Jaber al Mubarak al Sabah overruled the idea, fearing such a move could prompt an uprising among Kuwait's Shi'a, who make up about 20% to 30% of the population. In a bid to appease calls from anti-Iranian forces within his government while also attempting not to incite the local Shi'a population, the prime minister instead sent a naval force to protect the waters around Bahrain.[17] Sunni members of the Kuwaiti Parliament still criticize the prime minister for not sending ground troops. King Hamad, welcoming the Peninsular Shield force and the Kuwaiti naval presence, declared in March 2011 that "a foreign plot" had been foiled, a direct reference to Iran.[18]

At the start of the Bahraini uprising, Sunnis joined Shi'a protestors in Manama's Pearl Roundabout. Moderate Sunnis generally supported the uprising in the interest of all Bahrainis. Protestors wore badges with the slogan, "No Sunni, No Shi'a, Just Bahraini." But, cross-sectarian cooperation against the government failed to materialize in the long term, as the Sunnis became increasingly reluctant to work with Shi'a oppositionist factions.

Instead, the uprising soon put the Shi'a and the Sunni at loggerheads. And even those Sunni who were critical of the government's policies, when forced to choose, sided with the state over the Shi'a. This appeared to give credence to the government's claims that the uprising stemmed from a strictly sectarian conflict, and it became more visible when the protests gained momentum. There are some exceptions to the deepening Shi'a–Sunni divide. The National Democratic Action Society, or Wa'ad, which is the largest leftist political faction in Bahrain and critical of the government, claims to include an equal number of Shi'a and Sunni in its ranks. According to one Wa'ad leader, 50% of the society's Central Committee is composed of Shi'a and the other half Sunni.[19]

The views of one women's rights activist who went to the Pearl Roundabout reflects the skepticism of many Bahrainis toward al Wefaq, even among those who oppose government policies. "I was in the Roundabout along with all the protestors. And when I listened to [al Wefaq], I felt some wanted to create an Islamic State," said Maryam, a middle-aged Sunni women's rights leader who lives in Manama on the edge of the Shi'a villages, where rioting breaks out frequently at night. "Many women came to the Roundabout because the *maraji* told them to. We all agree the government is corrupt, but we are afraid of [al Wefaq's] religious thinking." Throughout the early weeks of the uprising, the government skillfully pushed its own narrative of the tumultuous events and effectively shaped public opinion among the ruling minority Sunni. This was, it asserted, the long-expected Shi'a revolt, backed by Iran. Saqer al Khalifa, a former media advisor for the Bahraini embassy in Washington, DC, said:

> Since 1979, when the Islamic Revolution occurred in Iran, the Bahraini intelligence has always known there is a Shi'a ideology. . . . After Saddam went, sectarianism rose in Iraq. [The Shi'a] were targeting scientists, religious leaders. . . . Then, all of a sudden, this happened in Bahrain.

Al Khalifa went on to say the government had anticipated the uprising for years and had developed a well-trained security apparatus to fight any unrest. "If the Shi'a opposition had weapons, they would have used them."[20]

Soon, the political divide in the street spilled over into all aspects of everyday life. Ali Fakhro, a former education minister who tried to form a national dialogue among groups in the opposition and the government, noted an upsurge in identity politics:

> People started boycotting restaurants. If a Shi'a merchant owns one place, the Sunni won't go there. School children are not getting along. For the first time, they identify themselves as Shi'a or Sunni. With the Saudis swearing at the Shi'a all day, I have no doubt the Saudis are playing a role to fuel propaganda against the Shi'a.[21]

Some Bahrainis have boycotted convenience stores owned by prominent Bahraini businessman Faisal Jawad, who is accused of giving free food to the protestors during the height of the uprising. Jawad has denied the allegations. Nonetheless, he has been forced to close some of his stores and restaurants as a result of a Sunni-led boycott.

A young Bahraini whose mother is Sunni and father is Shi'a started a loosely formed debate forum, with the specific aim of addressing the rise of sectarianism. "My parents never had a problem, and growing up I was never cognizant of the differences in the sects. Today, things are very different," the young man said over coffee in a Manama hotel.[22]

Ali al Khalifa, a young Bahraini who worked in the foreign ministry after graduating from American University in Washington, and who is a member of the royal family, recalls how the Sunni–Shi'a relationship has changed since he was a boy:

> In the 1990s, I was 7 or 8 years old. I knew there was animosity, but not hatred. I attended public school and there were some Shi'a, but not many. I went to an Islamic school which was Salafist and there were no Shi'a. Since last year, we are not on speaking terms with a lot of Shi'a. They will say it is my fault, even though I am trying to bridge the gap.
>
> In the 1940s, my grandmother ate with the Shi'a until 1979, when the Islamic revolution in Iran broke out. With Khomeini and the religious revival in Saudi Arabia at the same time, both sides became more fundamentalist.[23]

As the government capitalized on escalating unease between Shi'a and Sunni, its sectarian narrative took hold. A protest movement inspired by other Arab uprisings and a desire for political and economic reform for all Bahrainis quickly pitted Sunni against Shi'a. Iran seized the moment and unleashed its media machine in both Persian and Arabic, loudly championing the Shi'a cause. With Iran supporting the uprising and Saudi-led troops intervening in support of the Sunni al Khalifa tribe, the Bahraini protest movement was transformed swiftly into a proxy battle between the leading regional powers.

It provided fertile ground for the notion that political opposition in Bahrain was tantamount to a Shi'a revolt to wrest power from the minority Sunni. To date, there is no hard evidence to indicate Iran has given material support to factions within the Bahraini opposition, but there is circumstantial evidence that some young and human rights groups are receiving direct or indirect funding from Iranian sources to operate outside Bahrain. US officials, who wished to remain anonymous, stated in an interviews that the United States was beginning to see signs of Iranian connections to opposition groups.

Moreover, the Saudis view the Shi'a-dominated uprising as a direct threat to their own domestic security; a victory for the Shi'a of Bahrain

would certainly inspire Saudi Arabia's own disaffected Shi'a population in the eastern provinces, home to much of the Kingdom's great
oil wealth, to mobilize behind similar demands for economic, political, and social equality. In fact, the Bahrain uprising did spark protests
among the Saudi Shi'a, who expressed solidarity with their co-religion-
ists across the Causeway, a bridge that unites the two countries.[24]

The direct involvement of Saudi Arabia, Bahrain's powerful neighbor, ensured that calls from moderates within the Bahraini government
for negotiation or dialogue with the protesters were marginalized.
Instead, the Saudis were able to bolster hardline elements in Manama
to support their harsh approach to the uprising. Bahrain's economic
dependence on Saudi Arabia certainly was a factor. A treaty between
the two countries states that Saudi Arabia is the operator of the shared
offshore oil field Abu Safah, which produces nearly 70% of Bahrain's
oil revenue and 80% of its total oil production.[25]

The Bahraini hardliners did not have to overreach to build their
case that Iran was behind the uprising. Iran has stated for years that it
considers part of Bahrain its rightful territory, and Tehran is believed
to be behind at least two attempted coups to unseat the government
in Bahrain, in 1981 and 1996. The Bahraini government alleged that
the 1996 plot was carried out by Hezbollah and masterminded by Isa
Qassem, now the leading cleric in Bahrain's Shi'a opposition, who
spent many years in Qom.[26] Some US officials also warned of the Iran
factor in the uprising. Former Defense Secretary Gates said in an interview with the Arabic network al Arabiya on March 24, 2011, that
although he believed Iran did not instigate the protest, there was no
doubt Tehran was starting to spread its influence.[27]

Even if Iran was not intervening in the uprising directly, its extensive
Arabic-language media outlet al Alam, Hezbollah's al Manar TV, and
the Iraq-based Ahl al Bayt television were hard at work to convince
the Shi'a, not only in Bahrain, but more importantly throughout the
region, that the conflict was a fight to resolve longstanding political
and religious differences between the sects. In an al Manar broadcast
of March 21, 2011, Supreme Leader Khamenei emphasized his support
for the revolution in Bahrain.

Such broadcasts have continued. On May 17, 2012, a report on al Manar described a meeting of the Union of Muslim Ulema in Lebanon, an organization established by Iran and Lebanese Shi'a clerics shortly after the 1979 Islamic Revolution. The report states the Union was concerned about Bahraini people who are "victims of the politics of sectarian conflict and the provocation of hate as is the case in many countries in the Arab and Islamic world." The report quotes the Union's leader, Judge Ahmed Shaikh Ahmed al Zain, as blaming the United States and Israel for rising sectarianism: "The Zionist enemy and its American ally have succeeded in spreading hatred between the sons and daughters of Islam." Through its tactics, Iran gave credence to the Bahraini government's claims that the Islamic Republic was the driving force behind the uprising.

Just days before GCC troops entered Bahrain, Secretary of Defense Gates and his team were in Manama trying to find a compromise between the government and al Wefaq. But, the day after the Gates delegation left, a huge protest occurred, and the government and the Saudis used this as a pretext to send in the troops, according to US officials. The Saudis discouraged the Bahraini government from making a deal with the opposition, according to US and Bahraini sources. They argued that Iran was backing the opposition and, therefore, it must be crushed. When the talks ended without resolution, Secretary of State Hillary Clinton expressed her frustration with the Saudis and said the United States had only limited leverage.[28]

The Saudi position was, and still remains, that no steps should be taken to weaken Bahrain's Sunni monarchy. Stability in Bahrain is also of great importance to the United States. Manama is the home to the US Navy's Fifth Fleet, the presence of which in the Gulf ensures the flow of oil and other energy exports through the Strait of Hormuz, the waterway connecting the Gulf to the Arabian Sea and the Indian Ocean. Iran threatens periodically to block the Strait, which would disrupt oil supplies severely, although to date it has shown no real sign of making good on its bellicose rhetoric.

Because of significant US strategic and economic interests in a stable Bahrain, the Obama administration has declined to adopt a hard line on the Bahraini government's human rights abuses and institutionalized discrimination. Yet, some US officials believe the administration's criticism is clear—a view Bahraini opposition figures do not share.²⁹ The general feeling among many factions within the Shi'a opposition is that the United States is unwilling to jeopardize its own security interests to try to extract necessary compromises from the Bahraini government

In mid-March 2011, the protest movement intensified among the Shi'a in the Pearl Roundabout. Even more worrying to the government, protestors began a strategy of disrupting daily life in Manama by venturing out from the Pearl to set up barricades in the financial district, hindering business and traffic. In response, the government heightened its rhetorical denunciation of the protests—in particular, its charges of Iranian meddling. Some within the government argued the protestors' tactics indicated they had been schooled in Hezbollah training camps in Lebanon. Staff Field Marshal Khalifa bin Ahmad al Khalifa, Bahraini Commander-in-Chief, was quoted as saying in *Asharq Alawsat* on June 1, 2011:

> The stands and statements of the Iranian officials, the remarks of the secretary general of the Lebanese Hezbollah, the meddling in Bahraini affairs by their satellite [TV] channels, ... the incidents that took place in Pearl Square—expose the training techniques of Hezbollah.³⁰

Although the running proxy contest between regional rivals Saudi Arabia and Iran fed sectarian tensions, political events on the ground in Bahrain enhanced the Shi'a-versus-Sunni narrative further. On February 21, 1 week after a large Shi'a mobilization in the streets, a reported 120,000 Sunnis assembled in the Al Fateh Mosque, the largest Sunni Mosque in Bahrain, although this number is disputed as being inflated. There, a university professor announced the birth of *Tajamma al Wihdat al Watani*, which came to be known as the National Unity Gathering, TGONU, a pan-Sunni bloc supporting the ruling family—at least initially—and designed to curb Shi'a-dominated protest. Sunni Islamist political societies, including the Muslim Brotherhood, Minbar, and the Salafist faction Asala al Islamiya, joined the group.

This development served to reaffirm the government line that Iran and its proxies were behind the unrest.

TGONU never succeeded in articulating a clear agenda for this new coalition. The group's central demand was simply that the government make no concessions to al Wefaq, which it said ought to be banned outright. Interviews carried out in Bahrain reveal that the central Sunni struggle is not based on a desire for religious domination over the Shi'a. Rather, the minority Sunni fear that Shi'a protests could topple the existing government and lead to the creation of an Iranian-style theocracy.

The Bahraini government gave a stamp of approval to TGONU. But what the government failed to foresee in giving a role to TGONU and its constituents was that the more the national drumbeat warned of the Shi'a–Iranian threat, the more pressure came to bear on the government to take harsher action against the opposition, even the peaceful al Wefaq. Soon, the "loyal citizens" of Bahrain, as the government commonly refers to its Sunni supporters, were criticizing the government for not doing enough to protect them and crack down on the Shi'a-dominated opposition.

As the anti-Shi'a—and anti-Iran—rhetoric ramped up among the Sunni population, the National Unity Gathering gave birth to a radical splinter group, al Fatih Youth Union, the Friday rallies of which attract thousands of supporters regularly. This development made it even more difficult for reformist-minded figures in the government, including the crown prince and even King Hamad, to extend any significant concessions to the Shi'a opposition. Heightened sectarianism both altered the dynamics of popular mobilization and gave hardliners within the government, chiefly the prime minister and his faction, a cover for dismissing any calls for reform.

In such an atmosphere, the government unleashed a brutal campaign to crush the uprising. The ensuing human rights violations, including the torture and even the deaths of activists in detention; the dismissal of Shi'a from government positions; the suspension of Shi'a students from universities; and the discriminatory treatment of injured protestors in the hospitals, have been documented extensively by the Bahrain

Independent Commission of Inquiry (BICI), commissioned by the king. [31]

By spring 2012, King Hamad, who appeared interested in reform in 2011, decided it was too costly politically to implement many of the BICI's recommendations. "I told the king in March 2012 what I had previously said in 2011," said lead author Mahmoud Bassiouni in an interview with me. "You have a choice between the unity of the country and the unity of the family." Bassiouni added: "Many in the [Bahraini] cabinet fell back on the Saudis as a justification for not carrying out the needed social, political, and economic reforms." [32]

The BICI issued its 503-page report on November 23, 2011. The document was critical of the government's response to the unrest and noted in great detail extensive human rights violations committed against demonstrators and activists, most of whom were Shi'a. At the time, amid the great fanfare of the report's release, the king promised to implement many of the recommendations Bassiouni and his team had drafted; but, to date, this has not happened. As a result, many factions involved in the conflict have become more radicalized. Bassiouni said he feared the crisis would produce a hardening of positions on all sides, and now this concern has been realized.

To listen to young Shi'a university students is to understand that, although the protest movement might no longer pose an immediate threat to the state's survival, the status quo is not viable over the long term. Many such students, who demonstrate when they can, have pledged not to give up until their demands are met. Few have been deterred by a government crackdown, which includes financial and other institutional pressures as well as physical punishment.

"My sister was called in by the university dean and he asked her, 'Were you in the protests? Do you support the government?' Then they showed her photos of her demonstrating and they suspended her scholarship to study abroad," said one student. Another student explained, "Sixty-three students in our university were suspended because they were accused of being loyal to Iran." [33]

The BICI, in its review of Bahrain Polytechnic University and the University of Bahrain, concluded: "The expulsions by the University of Bahrain and Bahrain Polytechnic as related to the events of February/March 2011 were of such an extreme nature that some of the students are ostensibly prevented from ever again attending an institution of higher education in Bahrain."[34]

Among some university students, there are also feelings of isolation. "We are alone," said one young man. "The US is doing nothing, and anyway they are busy with Iran. The US might pay attention to us at times because of the Fifth Fleet, but we don't need the Fleet. We need to find our own solutions."[35] Even before the uprising began, young Bahraini Shi'a were turning away from al Wefaq, established in November 2001 and today the country's largest and most influential Shi'a political society. Al Wefaq has engaged frequently in negotiations with the government and is recognized by the United States as a legitimate opposition group.[36] Al Wefaq leaders also meet regularly with US officials at the embassy in Manama.

One significant result of the uprising is that unofficial Shi'a factions have increasingly gone their own way, believing that events demand more extreme measures than the moderate al Wefaq is willing to take. For example, some al Wefaq leaders are quick to downplay any sectarian polarization in Bahraini society. "The whole issue is political, not sectarian," one leader said. But, during the same conversation, he said the Salafists in Bahrain think the Shi'a are *kafir*, or infidels.[37]

Since the creation of al Wefaq, some Bahraini Shi'a have moved well beyond the group's call for reforms that would turn Bahrain into a constitutional monarchy. Shortly after the 2006 parliamentary elections in which al Wefaq ran candidates, a number of Shi'a activists dismissed participation in the polls as a sellout to the state and founded al Haqq, a movement that favored an electoral boycott. In March 2011, al Haqq then joined other Shi'a groups to form the Coalition for a Bahraini Republic. The Coalition rejects any political resolution to the conflict and calls for the toppling of the al Khalifa family.

Such a Bahraini republic obviously would not have a role for the al Khalifa dynasty. Nor would it be a constitutional monarchy, which al

Wefaq still favors. The leader of the Coalition of a Bahraini Republic is Hasan Mushaima, who has been accused by the government of being an Iranian operative.

A more significant faction spawned by the uprising is the Coalition of February 14 Youth, which is composed of young activists who took to the streets to demand nothing short of regime change. They, too, are critical of al Wefaq and dismiss all notions of settling for a constitutional monarchy. Some within the movement adhere to a more religiously conservative school of thought within Shi'ism Islam. The February 14 Coalition was named not only for the start date of the uprising in 2011, but also for promises made by King Hamad to create a constitutional monarchy, approved in a national referendum in 2001. When he first came to power, the king did initiate reforms, including the reinstatement of the parliament; but, he also revised unilaterally the Constitution to install the so-called Shura Council under his direct command, which has more power than the democratically elected parliament, as mentioned earlier. This allows him to control the workings of the state, although there were outward appearances of reform. Some Shi'a and Sunni alike gave up on the king ever delivering on his promised reforms.

The February 14 Coalition has no identifiable leadership, does not speak with one voice, and appears to reject conventional political formations. Unlike al Wefaq, which is committed to peaceful protest, February 14's activists first became known for burning tires at night in the Shi'a villages on the island and for battling with the police. The movement, which articulates the desires of many young Bahrainis (particularly the Shi'a), weakened al Wefaq in several respects. First, it appeared to lend credibility to government claims that there is no point in making concessions to al Wefaq because it cannot control the street. Second, the government has used the presence of the February 14 Coalition to claim that Iran is behind the protests. In fact, there is evidence that some radical youth are now seeking help from Hezbollah in Beirut. They have opened offices there and appear to be conducting their operations in Bahrain from Lebanon.[38]

An activist from February 14, who wished to remain anonymous for security reasons, offered this explanation of the group in an interview in December 2012:

> The main differences between the Youth of February 14 and al Wefaq are concentrated around the issue of a dialogue with the regime. While al Wefaq stated many times that they are open to dialogue, the Youth of February 14 believe that this regime is not trustworthy and any dialogue with it is a betrayal to the people. . . . The February 14 Youth believe that there is a need to escalate things to put pressure on the government, which is why they are supportive of burning tires and throwing Molotov cocktails. They genuinely believe that these acts put pressure on the government and change the rules of the game. They believe those actions are defense mechanisms rather than attacks. In the Middle East, you have to use a little violence to change a regime. Pure nonviolent actions do not work in this region, and our actions are not purely violent. By using those actions, we aim to stop the regime from attacking our villages, not to kill anybody, and it works.[39]

The more militant factions within the opposition have provided Sunnis, who may themselves oppose the government, with a reason not to support the opposition. "Our main difference with the opposition is the manner with which we believe political reform can be achieved," said Abdul Hakim al Subhi, head of the political circle for the TGONU. He went on to say:

> We demand reform but we disagree with the opposition's violent ways of achieving it. In fact, we agree with the opposition in all of their demands for political reform and democracy—minus, of course, the demands for the fall of the regime. However, we think that should be achieved gradually. To impose it right now is to impose the views of one sect over the other. Sectarianism should be resolved first.[40]

The dominant presence of the state-run media is, at least in part, responsible for the radicalization of the Shi'a, according to the BICI report:

The lack of access to mainstream media creates frustration within opposition groups and results in these groups resorting to other media such as social media. This can have a destabilizing effect because social media outlets are both untraceable and unaccountable, characteristics which present problems when such media is used to promulgate hate speech and incitement to violence.

The BICI also concluded "there was a tendency in the Bahraini media to defame protestors, both during and after the events of February/March 2011."[41]

As some Shi'a become more radicalized with no hope of a political settlement or an end to religiously based discrimination, the potential for Iran's involvement grows. But, even if ties between Iran and some domestic groups are developed, there is little evidence so far that the outcome would be a push to create an Islamic state in Bahrain; simply, there appears to be little support for theocratic governance. Al Wefaq's position is that society is opposed to an Islamic state and to the institution of the Iranian system of *velayat-e faqih*, according to Khalil Marzooq, a leader in al Wefaq who had participated in the failed national dialogue in 2011.[42]

A majority of Shi'a do appear to reject a religiously based government, but this could change depending on the degree to which Shi'a youth become radicalized and the degree to which they are able to influence the broader Shi'a population. In a 2009 poll of 435 households conducted by Justin Gengler, who has conducted authoritative research in Bahrain, about one quarter of all Shi'a and Sunni respondents opposed a system of government based on religion. Only one quarter of the Shi'a interviewed said Sharia was "a suitable" or "very suitable" form of governance, and 63% said it was "not at all suitable." According to Gengler, even those who said their political views were close to the radical al Haqq movement were no more likely to support an Islamist-only parliamentary system or a Sharia-based state than those who said their views were close to those of al Wefaq.[43]

The protests have also left their social imprint on Bahrain. In the wake of the protests and the accompanying polarization along sectarian lines, some Sunni have become less inhibited in exposing their derogatory views of the Shi'a, which are driven in part by persistent fears that the Shi'a want to turn the country into a theocracy. For Sunni government loyalists, the state-run media have provided a formidable mechanism to express their views. They have also turned enthusiastically to social media—in particular, to Twitter. Two of the topics dominating the state media coverage are Iran's intentions in Bahrain and the Shi'a opposition. Appearing in the popular *Al Watan*, a newspaper reflecting hardliner views, Faisal al Shaikh, a well-known columnist, wrote on September, 9, 2012:

> Every time the revolutionary followers of Iran try to separate their religious and political affiliations from Iran and every time they respond to our fears concerning Iran's interests in Bahrain by shouting "leave Iran out of this," Iran comes in and publicly demonstrates how it considers the "invasion of Bahrain" one of its top priorities.

Online discussion forums also reflect the deepening sectarian difference, with familiar Sunni-backed claims of Iranian involvement in the troubles, as well as the more troubling question of whether the Shi'a are true Muslims. What is striking about the social media forums is that even those Sunni who criticize the government and might be expected to share common ground with some pro-reform Shi'a are still anti-Shi'a in principle. Although difficult to quantify empirically, the monitoring of Twitter feeds during the height of the crisis showed a startling degree of animosity among the Sunni toward their Shi'a countrymen. And a snapshot of Twitter traffic after the crown prince, on December 8, 2012, called for a renewed national dialogue with the opposition indicates that for both sides the scars from the recent uprising may pose too great of an obstacle, at least for now. Nor does this bode well for the prospects of any future national reconciliation.

Despite such indicators of mounting extremism, there are signs that some elements among Bahrain's Sunnis are seeking accommodation to focus on basic reforms aimed at helping all citizens, whatever their religious identity. These include a democratic form of governance, increased economic opportunity, and adequate housing for all. In addition, some figures have emerged outside the increasingly polarized extremes that make up the radical opposition and pro-government camps—those who claim loyalty but are also critical of all parties in the dispute.

One such figure is Abu Omar al Shafi'i, a prominent commentator on social media sites, including Twitter. The name al Shafi'i is a pseudonym, for the poster writes anonymously and only identifies himself as an "ordinary person and ordinary citizen" who "loves his nation of Bahrain." As a Sunni, he claims to have not been engaged politically until "the division was strong and extremism appeared clear to all," in the wake of events in February 2011.[44]

Al Shafi'i commented extensively on the crisis throughout 2012 by means of an active Twitter account, which he uses to engage in political dialogue, and through interviews and articles in the pro-government newspaper, *Al Watan*. He carved out an independent position critical at times of both pro- and antigovernment factions, and his commentaries highlighted a number of different phenomena and aspects of the conflict with a level of thoughtfulness and analytical clarity that sets him apart from partisans on either side. Through incisive political commentary that targets both the "extremist opposition parties" and the "militant loyalist parties,"[45] al Shafi'i has drawn an eager audience of more than 20,000 followers on Twitter, many of whom may welcome a political view outside the increasingly fragmented camps.

As much as the uprising in Bahrain was a response to the antiauthoritarian revolts in the Arab world, it was also driven by a history of religious discrimination and socioeconomic disparity between Shi'a and Sunni. In other words, the marginalization of the Shi'a in the public and economic spheres provoked political discontent at a time of great change in the Middle East.

For centuries, the Shi'a in Bahrain have fought for their rights and have, in general, been rebuffed by the ruling family, which has interpreted these demands by the majority sect in the country as a threat to the established order. To preserve the power of the minority Sunni population, the al Khalifa tribe has seen to it that the Shi'a are underrepresented in the most powerful positions in government ministries, and it has excluded the Shi'a, for the most part, from the security services, including the police. There is also well-documented discrimination in promotions in universities and in the medical profession, and in access to public housing.

The US State Department *July–December 2010 International Religious Freedom Report*, published in September 2011, stated:

> Although there were exceptions, the Sunni Muslim citizens often received preference for employment, particularly in sensitive government positions such as the security forces and the military. Only a few Shi'a citizens held significant posts in the defense and internal security arenas. . . . Although the police force reported it did not record or consider religious belief when hiring employees, Shi'a continued to assert they were unable to obtain government positions, especially in the security services, because of religious affiliation.[46]

The *2009 International Religious Freedom Report* noted:

> Shi'a were underrepresented in the Ministry of Education in both the leadership and in the ranks of head teachers who teach Islamic studies and supervise and mentor other teachers. At the secondary school level, out of more than a dozen Islamic studies head teachers, only two were Shi'a. Although there were many Islamic studies teachers who were Shi'a, school authorities discouraged them from introducing content about Shi'a traditions and practices and instructed them to follow the curriculum. . . .[47]

> Regional Sunni–Shi'a tensions had an impact on intra-Muslim relations. In general the Sunni Muslim minority enjoyed favored status. The private sector tended to hire Shi'a in lower paid, less skilled jobs. Educational, social, and municipal services in most Shi'a neighborhoods were inferior to those found in Sunni communities.[48]

The longstanding strategies among some within the Bahraini government to marginalize the Shi'a population were revealed in a startling document, which was leaked in 2006 and became known as the *Bandar Report*. According to this study, the objectives of these government figures included controlling the outcome of the second set of municipal and parliamentary elections in 2006, minimizing the influence of opposition forces by mobilizing the Sunni street against perceived Shi'a dominance, and manipulating the country's demographic balance.

The report was crafted by Salah al Bandar, a British–Sudanese citizen who was an adviser to the Ministry of Cabinet Affairs. Several government employees began to contact him in January 2006 about what they said was an organized campaign by elements within the state apparatus to raise sectarian tensions. Al Bandar spent most of 2006 investigating and acquiring financial documents that linked the various actors. In September 2006, he presented his report, which was published under the auspices of the Gulf Center for Democratic Development, to King Hamad, as well as to Western diplomats and the media. Al Bandar was promptly deported and threatened with criminal charges if he returned to Bahrain.[49]

The report alleges that this project was undertaken by a network led by Sheikh Ahmed bin Ateyalla al Khalifa, Minister of State for Cabinet Affairs, head of the Central Information Organization, and chairman of the executive committee overseeing the 2006 elections. The report claims Sheikh Ahmed's network had been active since October 2004, and in the 2 years between then and the report's release in summer 2006, the conspirators had undertaken a number of clandestine efforts, which cost an estimated $1.5 million.[50] Key elements of the alleged plot included the collection of intelligence on Shi'a opposition groups; coordinated efforts, through advertising and sermons in the mosques, to convert the Shi'a to Sunni Islam; the use of agent provocateurs to stir up sectarian tensions on social media; the creation of front groups, posing as nongovernmental organizations, to push the pro-Sunni line; and the preparation of propaganda materials to be published in the newspaper *Al Watan*, a pro-government publication. This latter tactic proved particularly effective, for the newspaper was whipping up Sunni public opinion against the Shi'a during the height of the uprising in 2011.

In interpreting the 216-page report, the Gulf Center for Democratic Development said the secret network was intended specifically to sabotage reform-minded figures within the government: "The attempt to control the composition of the political elite and dominate its direction and choices in accordance with a vision outside the framework of legal and constitutional legitimacy is considered a serious threat to the entire reform project of His Majesty the King and leads into a dark tunnel."[51]

This state-sponsored project of political, social, and economic marginalization of the Shi'a, which the Bandar Report revealed, has succeeded for the most part, for a long period of time. There are no official statistics available, but according to the Bahrain Center for Human Rights, an organization that is part of the opposition, 42.65% of the top positions in government are held by the royal family; 42.65% are held by other, nonroyal Sunnis; and only 14.7% are held by Shi'a. According to the same study, the Sunnis and the royal family make up 98% of the positions in the Bahraini security apparatus, and there are no Shi'a represented in the crown prince's office, the Supreme National Council of Defense, the National Guard, the Bahrain Defense Forces, or the Ministry of Interior.[52] A 2009 survey conducted by Justin Gengler found that 13% of Sunni households reported at least one member employed by the police or the military. No Shi'a male who offered occupational data said he was employed in the police or military.[53]

The nature of Bahrain's sectarianism poses serious obstacles to economic advancement on the part of the Shi'a population and subsequent development of a Shi'a middle class. Although there are no available government figures distinguishing the Sunni from the Shi'a, it is widely believed unemployment and underemployment are disproportionately higher among the Shi'a community compared with the national average.[54] In addition, a report issued in December 2012 by the US Department of Labor found evidence of improper restrictions on trade union freedoms, and political and sectarian-based discrimination against Shi'a workers.[55]

Two key figures within the Bahraini opposition movement—which is composed predominately of Twelver Shi'a—are the clerics Sheikh Isa Qassem and Sheikh Ali Salman, who was arrested in December 2014 and is serving a prison sentence. His sentencing was part of a government crackdown against al Wefaq leaders. Although Salman served a formal role as secretary-general of al Wefaq, Qassem's stature and connection to the movement derived from his status as the senior Shi'a figure in Bahrain.

Isa Qassem was born in the village of Diraz in 1940, the son of a fisherman. During the early 1960s, he went to the Iraqi shrine city of Najaf to further his religious studies, staying there for 4 years. He came back to Bahrain to teach for 2 years before returning to Najaf for additional study under Ayatollah Mohammed Baqer al Sadr.[56] After Bahrain's independence in 1971, Qassem was elected to the short-lived 1973 Parliament, and was considered one of the six members of the so-called religious bloc, which clashed regularly with the government over social measures.

During the early 1990s, he went to the Iranian city of Qom to pursue further studies in Islamic jurisprudence. Although affiliated more closely with Shi'a thought and figures in Iraq, Qassem's choice was dictated in part by geopolitical circumstances, given how Saddam Hussein's Baathist regime suppressed the Shi'a during the Iran–Iraq War and thereafter. Qassem returned in March 2001 after the beginning of King Hamad's announced reform project, announcing he would be stepping away from politics. In 2004, he founded the Ulama Council, which is broadly viewed as an extension of the Najaf clerical circles. Qassem has never held a formal position in al Wefaq; instead, he maintains informal influence through weekly sermons in the village of Diraz and in the activities of the Ulama Council.

Ali Salman, now serving a prison sentence and formerly the political head of al Wefaq, originally studied mathematics in Saudi Arabia before studying at a seminary in Qom from 1987 to 1992. When Qassem left Bahrain for Iran, he chose Salman to become the Friday prayer leader at his primary mosques. Salman became a national figure during the protests of the 1990s, and was jailed from December 1993 until January 1995. Thereafter, he moved to London, where he worked with the Bahrain Freedom Movement until being permitted to return to Bahrain after the start of the reform project.

One of the largest concerns among Western governments and analysts has been the possibility that the political end goal of al Wefaq and more radical Shi'a factions is to institute *velayat-e faqih*—a concern exacerbated by the fact that these two key figures in the opposition movement are clerics who spent substantial time in Iran. Despite this, there is little meaningful evidence to suggest this is the aim of the Bahraini opposition, although there may be outliers with more extreme ideologies. Nor does either Qassem or Salman appear to subscribe to the concept of direct clerical rule. This is a typical statement of Salman: "We have national demands that have nothing to do with Iran. We are proud of being a sensible, mature, and progressive political movement that doesn't need to take instructions from Iran or any other country."[57]

Yet, at times, Qassem has verged on expressing support for supreme clerical rule. In a sermon on June 8, 2007, Qassem, speaking about Ayatollah Khomeini and the Iranian Revolution, said: "If all Islamists, regardless of their sects, gathered around this man, this revolution, this state and the peoples of this nation followed them, Islam would have been on a fast track to total victory."[58]

A review of Qassem's sermons from 2010 to 2012 posted on al Wefaq's website, which is a selected collection of his public statements, indicates his discourse on the role of religion and the state has shifted slightly and become more liberal. For example, on October 15, 2010, Qassem stated directly that Islam should influence the political process: "Islam should influence politics and not politics influence Islam and whoever demonstrates a different interpretation to this truth is a liar."[59]

But after the Bahraini uprising began and Qassem used his pulpit in the mosque to inspire the Shi'a-dominated opposition, he became an avid supporter of democracy. On December 23, 2011, he said:

We have to insist on our religious and national unity and let our insistence aggravate whomever it aggravates. When our united people demand the democracy that allows it to change the constitution, its laws, government, and destiny, it is not demanding a Shiite or Sunni democracy. Democracy does not discriminate by sect and does not befriend a certain school of thought and reject another. Democracy, in a political sense, does not discuss sects and does not touch them. Democracy exists to bring fairness to the people and not to bring tyranny.[60]

If Qassem's sermons indicate his true beliefs, then he is clearly distancing himself from Iranian-style governance. The Islamic Republic has advanced clerical involvement in politics, which seemed to provide inspiration to the Arabs after the 1979 Revolution, but is now more of a liability, given Iran's track record 33 years later.

It is impossible to quantify the influence clerics in Iran or Iraq have on Bahrain's Shi'a. Nonetheless, some degree of clerical influence should be assumed. The Shi'a in Bahrain make regular trips to Qom, Najaf, and Karbala to visit the holy sites. The clerical networks in Iran influence the Shi'a in Bahrain and Iraq directly and indirectly. Since the Iranian Revolution in 1979, the Shi'a have staged street protests, many times inspired or instigated by clerics who were educated in Iran.

Thus, warnings by experts and US officials alike of greater Iranian involvement in the Bahraini opposition in the near future cannot be dismissed. The Iranians are in a position to fund the more radical youth who are in the opposition and who advocate regime change, which is in Iran's interest. Iran could provide the opposition with technical training and expertise in nearby Lebanon through Hezbollah. Some Bahraini opposition groups are now based in Beirut. Iran could also exploit the clerical networks that exist between the two countries. Such Iranian influence and intervention is likely if no serious steps toward reconciliation are taken. And it may not even have to be Iran that initiates the intervention. It is likely that when the Shi'a youth do not feel empowered to change the status quo peacefully, they will look for other means to do so.

CHAPTER SIX

SECTARIAN CONFLICT ON THE REGIONAL STAGE

When the Saudi government executed a Shi'a dissident cleric in late 2015, protests erupted across the Arab world, even in Lebanon, where he was virtually unknown. The particulars about Sheikh Nimr al Nimr—chiefly the fact that he fought for equal rights for Saudi Arabia's minority Shi'a population based primarily in the eastern province—were enough for Arab and Iranian Shi'a to take to the streets across the region in anger and frustration. Iranian protestors, almost certainly with some official sanction, ransacked the Saudi embassy in Tehran, and Saudi Arabia shortly thereafter cut off diplomatic ties with Iran. Although Sheikh Nimr identified much more with the Shi'a Arabs and the uprisings, the Saudi government portrayed him as an Iranian-backed terrorist. He had become a symbol for Shi'a across the Arab world as someone who fought for Shi'a rights, but among Iranians he represented the institutionalized repression that Sunni states commit against their Shi'a citizens.

The execution and its immediate aftermath both mirrored and intensified the grand contest between Iran and Saudi Arabia that has helped fuel sectarian sentiment in the Arab world for decades and reached greater heights after the Arab uprisings began. As the societal conflict unfolds, Iran and Saudi Arabia, and other states in the region, including Bahrain, Turkey, and the United Arab Emirates, encourage Shi'a–Sunni animosity to advance their own geopolitical aims, particularly with regard to the relationship with Iran.

For the Saudis, this focus on religious identity has proved particularly useful, for it has encouraged polarization and marginalization in the Kingdom to undermine the minority Shi'a population and stave off any mass uprising. Notably, the Saudi government moved overtly to exploit sectarian sentiment as a tool to ensure its stability as it watched the Arab uprisings topple some leaders in the region. About 10% to 15% of the Saudi population is Shi'a and, similar to Bahrain, it suffers from political and economic inequality with the majority Sunni population.

As with Saudi Arabia, the Islamic Republic of Iran, too, has found the upsurge in sectarian conflict and the renewed attention to personal religious identity an asset toward its strategic and geopolitical ends, although these forces have also compromised Iran's aging promise, dating back to the 1979 Revolution, to reinvigorate and lead a united Islamic world—Shi'a and Sunni together—against further Western encroachment.

Since the 2003 occupation of Iraq, as sectarian identity became a dominant feature of society—and then exploded across the region with the war that followed the revolution in Syria—the grassroots movements on the ground became the perfect fodder for some Sunni states to encourage religious differences for their own political ends. During the early years of the uprisings, even as the United States backed the Shi'a-led government in Iraq, Washington also gave support to attempts by Sunni Arab states to reverse Iran's gains as a result of Iran's intimate involvement in predominantly Shi'a Iraq.

But, as the uprisings continued, as the war in Syria tipped in Assad's favor, and as the Obama administration became determined to sign a nuclear deal with Iran, there was a perception among the Sunnis that the Shi'a were not only in ascendance but were effectively dominating four Arab capitals: Baghdad, Beirut, Damascus, and Sanaa. As part of this perception, some Sunnis held the United States responsible for what Jordan's King Abdullah famously coined as "the Shi'a Crescent" more than a decade ago. This notion gained new currency once the nuclear deal was concluded in 2015, which brought Iran back into the international community from its longstanding position as a pariah state vis-à-vis the West.

It was not uncommon, wherever I traveled in the Arab world throughout 2015, to hear Sunnis say the United States was an ally of Hezbollah, which Washington years ago declared a terrorist organization. Sunnis in northern Lebanon even commented they wanted to fight in Syria because the Shi'a and Iran were taking over the Arab world. Such sentiments were consistent with those of the Iraqi tribal leaders I met in Erbil, Iraq, who said they supported ISIS' takeover in parts of Iraq to reduce the power of the Shi'a-led government in Baghdad. And these same sentiments fill the Twitter-sphere, recasting today's rivalries in the imagery and rhetoric of historical sectarian grievance and helping to mobilize public opinion on all sides.

Time and time again, it was clear the geopolitics of the region and the grassroots struggle for religious identity were fueling one another. This, of course, complicates efforts to disentangle one from the other—to assess where social, economic, and political interests and pressures end, and sectarian and identity issues and sentiments begin. Yet, my travels and research have also convinced me, as illustrated in the preceding chapters, of the singular importance of these latter factors. Downplaying, dismissing, or ignoring outright the religious aspects of the conflicts and tensions seizing the region—as was largely the case with the Western media and political analyses of the so-called Arab Spring—threatens to thwart Western understanding and to complicate and even doom to failure any policy prescriptions that might flow from it. In the popular vernacular of American politics: sometimes, it really is *all about religion*.

Even traditional religious institutions, once content to remain largely outside the sectarian struggle, have joined the fray. Thus, the rising Salafists and other sheikhs at the venerable al Azhar Mosque and university in Cairo, historically a major center of mainstream Sunni thought and practice, have made known their animosity toward Iran and the Shi'a. During a trip former Iranian President Mahmoud Ahmadinejad made to Egypt in February 2013, a man hurled a shoe at him—a major insult among Muslims. The assailant was believed to be Syrian and angry over Iran's support for Assad. More significantly, Ahmadinejad was scolded when he visited al Azhar, Egypt's seat of Sunni scholarship. During the visit, Ahmadinejad was criticized publicly at a news conference by his hosts, who accused the Shi'a of interfering in Arab countries, including Egypt and Bahrain, and of discriminating against the minority Sunnis in Iran.

Sunni wariness toward Shi'a Iran has a long and varied history, and Sunni societies today recognize that Iranian backing for their sectarian brethren in the Arab world is hardly a development of the post-uprising era; it has been, in fact, part of the essence of the Islamic Republic since its founding. As a result, few ever credited Ayatollah Khomeini's declared vision of a pan-Islamic Middle East, with Iran at the fore, which would one day reconcile centuries of political and religious conflict among competing Muslim sects. Instead, both internally and externally, revolutionary Iran soon emerged as a powerful and influential source of pride and encouragement for the region's Shi'a populations, particularly in Lebanon and Bahrain.

With Khomeini's victories, first over the US-backed Shah and then over his secularist domestic rivals, Tehran created the first Shi'a state in the modern age, overcoming, as we have seen, the established traditions of quietism and noninvolvement in political affairs that long prevailed among Shi'a scholars and jurists. And since the formation of the Islamic Republic, Iran has historically exploited anti-Shi'a sentiment, portraying the Shi'a as victims, with Iran as their savior. The Iranians have pursued this rhetoric of suffering and martyrdom at the hands of the majority Sunni even as they placed boots on the ground in Syria to combat Sunni gains and efforts to topple their ally Assad.

Notwithstanding Iran's clear willingness to play the sectarian card, elite circles around Supreme Leader Khamenei apparently see in the Arab uprisings and their aftermath an opportunity to return to the revolutionary promise of a pan-Islamic awakening. "What has happened so far is significant," Khamenei said in a speech on January 30, 2012, to an audience at the Islamic Awakening and Youth Conference in Tehran, referring to the Arab uprisings.

For two hundred years, Westerners ruled the Islamic *ummah* by making use of their scientific advances. They occupied Islamic countries, some of them directly, some of them indirectly.... They humiliated the Islamic *ummah* as much as they could.... But the Islamic resolve of Muslim people and their presence wiped out all these impossible dreams and put an end to all these goals.[1]

The challenges inherent to such a broad vision—that is, the tensions between the traditional Shi'a quietist notions surrounding the Islamic *ummah* and the *Realpolitik* that may be required to realize it—are revealed on a regular basis by Iran's public alternation between declarations of peaceful intent and outright bellicosity. As much as Khamenei may stake his claim as leader of the Islamic world, Arab societies have their own demands and interests. Further complicating the prospects, of course, is the long and contradictory history between Shi'a Iran and the predominantly Sunni-ruled Arab states, a history grounded in mutual mistrust, rivalry, and recognition of the need to coexist. Numerous religious and political conflicts plague the perception of the Arab world toward Iran and vice versa.

Importantly, the Arab uprisings—regardless of their "failings" to give birth to Western-style liberal democracies—created new political and social space. Some brought to power longstanding Islamist political factions with their own histories, traditions, established infrastructure, and considered ideological views. Others simply raised the possibility of new forms of governance, outside the traditional choice of authoritarian dictatorship on the one hand and Iranian-style theocracy on the other.

Here, the case of Najaf, home to Iraq's Shi'a leadership and the source of much of its intellectual and theological influence, stands out. Freed from the repressive years under the secularist Baath Party, led for years by Saddam Hussein, Najaf has so far resisted successfully Iranian pressure to adopt its system of clerical rule. Instead, it has largely held on to its more traditional reading of Shi'a political thought and practice, albeit with some largely unsuccessful attempts—such as the *fatwa* creating the Shi'a militias—to play an overt role in Iraqi politics. The restoration of Najaf as a theological center, then, has effectively elevated it over the Iranian holy city of Qom in the eyes of the Arab

Shi'a. The Shi'a of Bahrain, for example, make frequent trips to visit the clerics in Najaf. This, in turn, has made it more difficult for Iran to advance its claim to be exclusive guardians of Shi'ism, and it demonstrates the degree to which the current confluence of blurred ideologies and combustible state rivalry fueling sectarian identities on the ground is remaking the Middle East today.

The stability and security of the modern Middle East, never to be taken for granted at the best of times, today face a profound challenge in the form of renewed sectarian hostility that can only compound the existing claims and counterclaims of regional states and societies. Contemporary geopolitical concerns, such as territorial demands, oil rights, and access to water, among others, are both fungible and time-bound. Today's crisis or *casus belli* can become tomorrow's basis for negotiation, settlement, or treaty. Likewise, today's ally can readily become tomorrow's enemy, and vice versa. Oil, still the lifeblood of industrialized and developing nations alike, will one day be largely supplanted or even replaced by newer, more efficient power technologies.

In contrast, religion and religious identity are, by their very nature, timeless—part and parcel in the eyes of believers of a universe that always was and always will be. Thus, sectarian conflict and outright violence are seemingly ever-present and prone to revival when conditions are ripe. They must, then, be managed, mitigated, or redirected whenever possible. This, however, poses a greater challenge in some religious traditions than in others.

In the case of Islam, central questions of authority and legitimacy remain largely unresolved. From its earliest days, the faith has struggled to define for the entirety of the *ummah* what it means to be a good Muslim, just as its history is dotted with figures claiming the absolute right to provide just such a definition to the exclusion of all others. This same quality is, paradoxically, also part of its strength, for it has allowed for considerable flexibility in interpretation, application, and ritual practice. Yet, it forces us to return to the question posed at the outset of this book: *Whose Islam is it?*

The answer, of course, remains a contested one, all the more so today in the wake of the Arab uprisings that have upended many of the social, political, and religious certainties that seemed to govern the Middle East at least since the final collapse of Western colonial rule. With many of the strictures on religious and political discourse essentially lifted, and with the acceleration of such discourse through social media such as Twitter, YouTube, and satellite television, it is hard to imagine anything in the foreseeable future but continued sectarian strife dominating the region, whether fueled by rival nations such as Sunni-led Saudi Arabia or Shi'a-ruled Iran, or by grassroots preachers and sheikhs such as those profiled earlier.

As I have argued here and elsewhere, the popular and widely accepted notion of an Arab Spring is dangerously misleading, with its unwarranted implication that the natural direction for popular uprisings against authoritarian rule is, and must be, something resembling Western democratic norms and ideals. Instead, the region's historical religious identity came to the fore, expressed either through the rise of Islamist political power or the emergence of the Salafists and other such ardently sectarian tendencies, or both.

One, albeit highly striking, marker of just how deep this realignment has been within Arab societies can be seen in the fact that the one-time rallying cry across the Muslim world—that of "resistance" to Israeli occupation of Palestine—has far less currency in Arab political life today than in the past. Instead, it is the sectarian fault line between the Sunni and Shi'a and the identity politics that grows out of that division that are now the key mobilizing forces.

SALAFIST TWEETS AND MAJOR EVENTS IN THE MIDDLE EAST

As part of this book, tweets of the scholars described in the preceding pages were also examined with an eye to their relationship to important events in 2013 that reflect the heightened Shi'a–Sunni conflict. The Twitter-sphere was particularly active during these events. Although it is difficult to form a direct causal relationship between the tweets and events on the ground, the tweets, as quoted here, show that events do escalate anti-Shi'a sentiments on Twitter.

APRIL 20, 2013: SYRIAN ARMY CAPTURES RADWANI-YAH, NEAR QUSAYR

"Reports from Syria said the four key villages of Qadesh, Mansouriyah, As'adiyah, and Radwani-yah—all lying around the town of Qusayr in Homs province on the border with Lebanon—were captured by government forces."[1]

ADNAN AL AROUR

- April 18, 2013 (263 retweets, 43 likes): Every sheikh who stood by the regime should be tried the way Bashar will be tried and every sheikh who took a neutral position shall be tried with cowardice. #Syria (https://twitter.com/AdnanAlarour/status/324969736339353600)
- April 21, 2013 (620 retweets, 70 likes): The international community wants to provide us with nonlethal weapons!! And they give

us communication tools to spy on us and pinpoint the locations of our fighters. #Syria (https://twitter.com/AdnanAlarour/status/326048671386984448)

MAY 19, 2013: HEZBOLLAH FIGHTERS IN SYRIA: THOUSANDS SENT TO ASSAD'S AID IN QUSAYR

"Syrian government forces backed by Lebanese fighters from the militant group Hezbollah pushed into parts of Qusayr, a strategic city long held by rebels, according to an antigovernment activist and pro-government news channels. Both sides called it one of the war's most intense ground battles. The fight inflamed regional tensions as Hezbollah plunged more deeply into the conflict in Syria."[2]

MOHAMAD AL AREFE

- May 20, 2013 (3,792 retweets, 309 likes): God grant victory to our people in #Qusayr, oh God help the fighters persevere and unite the hearts of the people of truth. (https://twitter.com/MohamadAlarefe/status/336256949010182144)
- May 20, 2013 (773 retweets, 130 likes): God forgive me and them, and give victory to our people in Syria and Qusayr, and everywhere. (https://twitter.com/MohamadAlarefe/status/336361635222532096)

SALEM AL RAFEI

- May 18, 2013 (3 retweets): The Shi'a of Qutayf in Saudi Arabia are participating in the killing of the Sunni people in Syria. (https://twitter.com/salemalrafei/status/335692986438529024)
- May 18, 2013 (2 retweets, 1 like): Oh God, be with our brothers in Qusayr and not against them. Grant them victory over the *kafirs*. (https://twitter.com/salemalrafei/status/335892216276979712)

- May 19, 2013 (5 retweets, 1 like): Don't be lazy or stingy in helping save your brothers in Qusayr. You hold the biggest weapon that anyone can have, that of prayer to God. (https://twitter.com/salemalrafei/status/336009343147327488)
- May 19, 2013 (3 retweets, 1 like): Breaking: Our heroes in Qusayr are dealing with the most gruesome of battles with the regime and Hezb al Lat. (https://twitter.com/salemalrafei/ status/336064514703388674)
- May 19, 2013 (4 retweets, 2 likes): I invite the Sunni people in all corners of the world to stand with their brothers in Qusayr. Pray for them and ask God to help them persevere. (https://twitter.com/salemalrafei/status/336080296413904897)
- May 19, 2013 (130 retweets, 7 likes): Our people in Qusayr are now fighting to rid tyranny and raise the word of God against those who worship the devil. (https://twitter.com/salemalrafei/status/336081390456168448)
- May 20, 2013: Qusayr will be your cemetery, Hezb al Shaytan. (https://twitter.com/salemalrafei/status/336534687461830660)

JUNE 5, 2013: QUSAYR CAPTURED BY SYRIAN GOVERNMENT AND HEZBOLLAH

"The Syrian army seized control of the strategic border town of Qusayr, in a major advance for Bashar al Assad's forces in the two-year civil war. Rebels said they had pulled out of Qusayr, which lies on a cross-border supply route with neighboring Lebanon and where they had fought fierce battles with government forces and Hezbollah guerrillas for more than two weeks. One Hezbollah fighter told Reuters that they took the town in a rapid overnight offensive, allowing some of the fighters to flee."[3]

"A car bombing in a part of Beirut dominated by the Shia group Hezbollah has led to at least 18 deaths and over 200 injured. The attack is seen as the latest echo of Syria's conflict in neighboring Lebanon."[4]

- June 4, 2013 (311 retweets, 33 likes): The Syrian people did not originally set out to kill the regime nor did deliberately set out on the sectarian path. They asked peacefully, but the regime forced the fighting against them and used sectarianism to kill them. (https://twitter.com/AdnanAlarour/status/341992558198652928)
- June 4, 2013 (985 retweets, 63 likes): If something happens in Syria and it falls in the hands of Iran, their coming goal is the Gulf and they have begun to implement this plan with Hezbollah's entrance into Syria. Iran has occupied Syria—a full occupation. (https://twitter.com/AdnanAlarour/status/342004054798499841)
- June 4, 2013 (1,549 retweets, 94 likes): If a chicken belonging to a Muslim crossed the Lebanese border they would have arrested it on charges of terrorism!! But the tanks and rockets of Hezb al Shaytan openly cross with an American order and an Iranian request and there is Arab silence!! (https://twitter.com/AdnanAlarour/status/342005432753201152)
- June 5, 2013 (706 retweets, 59 likes): The battle of #Qusayr will not change anything, it doesn't count for more than 1/400th of the territory of anger. If it fails, this will not affect our revolution, God willing. (https://twitter.com/AdnanAlarour/status/342223898600943617)
- June 5, 2013 (1,033 retweets, 78 likes): There was a withdrawal from Qusayr in the night, without losses worth mentioning and our fight is not in Qusayr nor for the land of Qusayr. Our battle is a battle of right and wrong and faith and *kufr*. (https://twitter.com/AdnanAlarour/status/342330856242835456)
- June 5, 2013 (921 retweets, 54 likes): Regardless of the withdrawal from Qusayr, we and God are the victors. We have gained more faith and more conviction in the truth of our doctrine. And we have unmasked the truth of the true enemies to the *ummah*. (https://twitter.com/AdnanAlarour/status/342340165357936641)

- June 6, 2013 (8,692 retweets, 1,478 likes): Whoever needs to support Qusayr or elsewhere with rice or sugar or other things, and your understanding is sufficient, reach us by phone at 00966598312678 for we have no one after God but you. (https://twitter.com/AdnanAlarour/status/342558612293570560)
- June 6, 2013 (1,075 retweets, 120 likes): I swear if we lose all of #Syria, and we die on the true doctrine, this is what God prefers and it is the ultimate victory. The victory after the victory of the true doctrine is the ultimate victory. (https://twitter.com/AdnanAlarour/status/342718037088157696)
- June 9, 2013 (1,180 retweets, 90 likes): "America has given Iraq to Iran on a plate of gold," according to Prince Saud Faysal. So who has now given Syria to Iran on a plate of blood? (https://twitter.com/AdnanAlarour/status/343753887334940673)
- June 9, 2013 (959 retweets, 73 likes): What is strange is that Arab and Islamic states hear Iranian agents and the *rawafid* saying "We will slay you and occupy Gulf states" and the Gulf states don't do anything about it!! (https://twitter.com/AdnanAlarour/status/343803883950325760)

MOHAMAD AL AREFE

- June 5, 2013 (789 retweets, 132 likes): Don't forget the jihadists of Syria in support and in prayer, from yesterday they have been bombarded with rockets by Iran and Hezb al Lat. (https://twitter.com/MohamadAlarefe/status/342186195566096384)
- June 5, 2013 (5,080 retweets, 442 likes): Oh Arab leaders, do you understand the danger of the situation in #Syria and #Qusayr? If you don't, this is a calamity! And if you do understand, the calamity is bigger! (https://twitter.com/MohamadAlarefe/status/342190666157285376)
- June 5, 2013 (1,748 retweets, 273 likes): After the victory of the Safavid order in Syria, God forbid, Iran will fight to occupy

the Gulf. They see us as *kafir* anyway!! (https://twitter.com/ MohamadAlarefe/status/342231738895966208)

- June 6, 2013 (611 retweets, 71 likes): #Hezbollah's doctrine and its supporters are *rawafid* Safavids, and their primary beliefs include: having many Imams, changing the words of the Koran, making the Imams Divine. (https://twitter.com/ MohamadAlarefe/status/342697284439527424)

- June 6, 2013 (611 retweets, 81 likes): And of #Hezbollah's doctrine: that the state is for the Imams only, excommunicating those who came before them, and cursing the caliphs Abu Bakr, Omar, and Othman. (https://twitter.com/MohamadAlarefe/status/342697738531643392)

- June 6, 2013 (591 retweets, 70 likes): #Hezbollah has expanded in Arab countries, there are branches in Bahrain and the Hijaz [Saudi Arabia] and Kuwait and Yemen and elsewhere that have yet to be discovered! (https://twitter.com/MohamadAlarefe/status/342699946878853120)

- June 6, 2013 (528 retweets, 61 likes): The relationship between #Hezbollah and Khomeini is one of a body to the soul, and the party has used it to spread Shi'ism in the Islamic world. (https://twitter.com/MohamadAlarefe/status/342700307639332864)

- June 6, 2013 (511 retweets, 69 likes): The *rawafid* Safavid #Hezbollah is taking over Sunni Mosques in Lebanon and changing their names. (https://twitter.com/MohamadAlarefe/status/342701436100042752)

- June 6, 2013 (1,080 retweets, 136 likes): A lot of people are fooled by #Hezbollah for three main reasons: ignorance of the Safavid *rawafid* doctrine, Hezbollah's concealment of their actions, and their astounding media. (https://twitter.com/MohamadAlarefe/status/342701909741801472)

- June 6, 2013 (380 retweets, 53 likes): The Assad regime has the ability to arm #Hezbollah politically in Lebanon, so this is why the Hezb stands by the regime today. (https://twitter.com/ MohamadAlarefe/status/342702445023096832)

- June 6, 2013 (653 retweets, 95 likes): This is #Hezbollah today fighting in Syria and Qusayr fighting with the *rawafid* Safavid Iranians and the Assad regime all together united in doctrine and hatred. http://arefe.ws/twitter/8b6d8a72.jpg: *Links to a photo of killed children.* (https://twitter.com/MohamadAlarefe/status/342703175557578752)

SALEM AL RAFEI

- June 3, 2013: Qusayr—the rebels are blocking attempts of a siege and have destroyed three tanks and killed nearly 35 members of Hezbollah. https://www.youtube.com/watch?v=VhzRDazzt8M (https://twitter.com/salemalrafei/status/341615417724391424)
- June 4, 2013: MTV: "Hezbollah" raises the amount for compensation … 50 thousand for each one killed. (https://twitter.com/salemalrafei/status/341807771857080320)
- June 4, 2013 (1 retweet): It really is revolution that has shown them in their true light, hypocrites who claim to belong to Islam when they kill Muslims. They claim to defend holy places and they bomb mosques. (https://twitter.com/salemalrafei/status/341959698918027267)
- June 5, 2013 (14 retweets, 2 likes): Qusayr has withstood more than 25 days against Russia and China and Iraq and Iran and Hezb al Shaytan and Bashar's gangs and Arabs letting them down. (https://twitter.com/salemalrafei/status/342302995993722880)
- June 5, 2013: A large and angry protest is taking place in Ain al Hilweh at this time to protest the Hezb al Shaytan's (Hezbollah) killing of our people in Syria. (https://twitter.com/salemalrafei/status/342345668494520320)
- June 5 2013 (6 retweets, 1 like): Of the positives of the battle of Qusayr: God has exposed Hezb al Shaytan more and more to people who used to believe them. The term Hezb al Shaytan is now replacing Hezbollah all over the world. (https://twitter.com/salemalrafei/status/342362404530819074)
- June 5, 2013 (2 retweets): They congratulate each other and fire shots into the air in jubilation and they don't know that the battle of Qusayr, for God, was not intended to make the regime fall. Its

point was to expose the fake resistance and remove God's name from their party and replace it with the devil. Before Qusayr it was called Hezbollah and before Qusayr it was called a resistance and after it, it has become a terrorist group. Before Qusayr, it defended people and the state, and after it, it became a killer. Its security zones will not remain safe after Qusayr. This small town in a short while has played its role and excelled. Don't be sad. (https://twitter.com/salemalrafei/status/342401723790422017)

NABIL AL AWADHY

- June 5, 2013 (1,293 retweets, 112 likes): The Muslim leaders have not realized the gravity of the situation. Qusayr is not just a city! This is the start of a dangerous war! Oh God, grant victory to your followers and let down all those who have let them down. (https://twitter.com/NabilAlawadhy/status/342187968859078656)
- June 5, 2013 (2,545 retweets, 157 likes): For your information, you who are the tails of Iran, the Free Syrian Army still controls more than 60% of Syrian land. And God willing, their victory is close. The tyrant will be defeated one day. (https://twitter.com/NabilAlawadhy/status/342201263489953792)
- June 5, 2013 (1,281 retweets, 91 likes): #Qusayr will remain a thorn in their beards. Their doctrinal war will burn them. (https://twitter.com/NabilAlawadhy/status/342203848817004544)
- June 5, 2013 (1,745 retweets, 100 likes): Oh God, we ask you to punish Iran and its followers. Iran stands behind every evil faced by the *ummah* today. Any regime that stands with them is of them! (https://twitter.com/NabilAlawadhy/status/342298517651456001)

JUNE 24, 2013: CLASHES BETWEEN THE LEBANESE ARMED FORCES AND AHMAD AL ASSIR

"At least 16 soldiers were killed and dozens wounded in Lebanon's southern city of Sidon over two days of intense fighting between the army and gunmen loyal to Salafist Sheikh Ahmad al Assir. Six soldiers were killed and 10 others injured in clashes that were sparked after supporters of the extremist cleric ambushed an army checkpoint. The number of casualties among Assir's gunmen is not yet known."[5]

SALEM AL RAFEI

- June 24, 2013 (6 retweets): Sheikh Salem al Rafei: We won't do anything to control the street. (https://twitter.com/salemalrafei/status/349112113035345921)
- June 24, 2013 (22 retweets): The Muslim Scholars Association invites all mosques in Lebanon to raise the calls in God's name in their minarets until the attack on Bilal bin Rabah Mosque ceases. (https://twitter.com/salemalrafei/status/349116837990109184)
- June 24, 2013 (10 retweets): Sheikh Salem al Rafei on the show *Ma Waraa al Khabar* on Al Jazeera Live: There is a plan to end Assir that came from Hezbollah and it is being implemented by the Army and members of the Hezb and Amal are participating in the bombing and attacking of the Bilal bin Rabah Mosque. (https://twitter.com/salemalrafei/status/349240297303195649)

NABIL AL AWADHY

- June 23, 2013 (2,013 retweets, 111 likes): This is what they have been planning.... After the millions that they have received from governments in the Gulf, the leaders of the Lebanese Army are conspiring with Hezb al Shaytan to kill the Sunni people, beginning with their sheikhs. (https://twitter.com/NabilAlawadhy/status/348810285341085697)
- June 23, 2013 (4,957 retweets, 292 likes): To the governments of the Gulf: where are the billions from your people that you have spent on Lebanon?!! Their weapons are being used against the Sunni people!! As usual, they are killing us with our money!! (https://twitter.com/NabilAlawadhy/status/348810824103624708)
- June 23, 2013 (1,657 retweets, 122 likes): Since the invasion of America of Iraq and it being given to the followers of Iran ... they have been killing Sunnis! And if Sunni people defend themselves,

they accuse them of sectarianism and terrorism!! (https://twitter.com/NabilAlawadhy/status/348813218325 6227840

- June 24, 2013 (962 retweets, 84 likes): What is strange is the silence of the Arab governments about what is happening in Lebanon!! Have they sold it like they sold Iraq and Syria?!!! (https://twitter.com/NabilAlawadhy/status/349086303670919168)

- June 24, 2013 (1,688 retweets, 152 likes): Iran wants to take attention away from Syria and shift it to Lebanon. The head of the snake does not know that Muslims will not give up on Iraq, or Syria, or Lebanon. And Iran will be returned to the Muslims!! (https://twitter.com/NabilAlawadhy/status/349090771653255169)

- June 24, 2013 (1,355 retweets, 85 likes): Do the Arab people know that Iranian Arabic-language satellite channels and Hezb al-Shaytan's channel are broadcast on Arab satellites!! They fight you with your money!! (https://twitter.com/NabilAlawadhy/status/349105826067275776)

AUGUST 21, 2013: GHOUTA CHEMICAL MASSACRE—AROUND 1,500 KILLED

"At least 1,300 people have been killed in a nerve gas attack on Syria's Ghouta region, leading opposition figure George Sabra said on Wednesday. In response, the opposition Syrian National Coalition called for an urgent U.N. Security Council meeting on the subject. 'I call on the Security Council to convene urgently,' National Coalition leader Ahmed al Jarba added to Al Arabiya news channel, condemning the Syrian army's bombardment of the Ghouta suburbs of Damascus as a 'massacre.'"[6]

ADNAN AL AROUR

- August 21, 2013 (1,422 retweets, 76 likes): What happened today with the use of chemical weapons is not a crime of the regime on its own but also the crime of the Security Council and the Arab League and everyone who does not support the Syrian people, both governments and people. (https://twitter.com/AdnanAlarour/status/370156688634302464)

- August 21, 2013 (671 retweets, 51 likes): If a thousand preachers in a thousand mosques have not been able to show the true colors of the world and the *rawafid* and the countries of human rights, the revolution has certainly exposed all of them in their true light. (https://twitter.com/AdnanAlarour/status/370156944612655104)

- August 21, 2013 (512 retweets, 37 likes): Where are those who personally bet against me that the regime wouldn't use chemical weapons?!!! (https://twitter.com/AdnanAlarour/status/370195676648714240)

- August 21, 2013 (2,711 retweets, 110 likes): The Salam Union under the oversight of Sheikh Adnan announces the launch of a campaign to buy face masks and protective medicine from poison gas, we look to God and then you for help in this campaign. (https://twitter.com/AdnanAlarour/status/370201194422996993)

- August 21, 2013 (2,595 retweets, 156 likes): The campaign will be called: Save a Muslim with a facemask, and our goal is to buy 100,000 masks, knowing that each one costs around 200 Saudi Riyals. (https://twitter.com/AdnanAlarour/status/370201342804914176)

- August 21, 2013 (3,753 retweets, 782 likes): You can support the campaign by donating money to the account at Rajhi Bank, IBAN: 261608010110546, SA0280000261608010110546. The account is in the name of Adnan Mohammad Mohammad Arour. (https://twitter.com/AdnanAlarour/status/370201698028908544)

- August 21, 2013 (752 retweets, 45 likes): What happened today in Ghouta is terrorism by the Assad gang, but it is with express international permission, and with permission from the Security Council. (https://twitter.com/AdnanAlarour/status/370287669688819713)

- August 21, 2013 (1,034 retweets, 89 likes): The Syrian people are our great loss, what is happening is divine wisdom, and it is written destiny, and God is testing us, and we must be patient and persevere. (https://twitter.com/AdnanAlarour/status/370289492403306496)

- August 22, 2013 (1,311 retweets, 80 likes): The #Save_a_Muslim_with_a_face_mask was launched yesterday and it aims to buy 100,000 face masks and preventative medicine from poisonous gases. (https://twitter.com/AdnanAlarour/status/370484239021510656)
- August 22, 2013 (3,441 retweets, 611 likes): You can support the #Save_a_Muslim_with_a_face_mask campaign by donating money to the account at Rajhi Bank, IBAN: 261608010110546, SA0280000261608010110546. The account is in the name of Adnan Mohammad Mohammad Arour. (https://twitter.com/AdnanAlarour/status/370484528671772672)
- August 22, 2013 (678 retweets, 72 likes): How can you blame the youth for falling into the trap of excommunicating other Muslims when they see these massacres! (https://twitter.com/AdnanAlarour/status/370635743661522944)
- August 22, 2013 (2,356 retweets, 164 likes): The US occupied Iraq because they thought it had chemical weapons, and today chemical weapons are openly being used in Syria and the US wants to first make sure that chemical weapons are being used. (https://twitter.com/AdnanAlarour/status/370649170354270208)

MOHAMAD AL AREFE

- August 21, 2013 (9,805 retweets, 521 likes): #Ghouta_is_being_exterminated_by_chemical_weapons God we look to you for strength, we ask you to punish the criminals and not show them your mercy. (https://twitter.com/MohamadAlarefe/status/370125947480977408)
- August 21, 2013 (5,330 retweets, 453 likes): It is not permissible for a Muslim to frighten another Muslim. Horrifying and scaring them is a great sin in itself, imagine how great a sin this bloodshed

and killing is. Woe to those who can grant these people victory and yet remained silent! pic.twitter/com/UBfvqvHw3Z: *Photo of people killed in the chemical attack.* (https://twitter.com/MohamadAlarefe/status/370148869344350208)

- August 21, 2013 (2,266 retweets, 131 likes): #Ghouta_is_being_exterminated_by_chemical_weapons. The world will keep watching our *ummah* being killed. Our people must bring victory to one another. (https://twitter.com/NabilAlawadhy/status/370037534601908225)
- August 21, 2013 (2,065 retweets, 117 likes): Where are the threats of the lying West if there was going to be a use of chemical weapons?!! Oh God, we all have no one but you. #Ghouta_chemical_massacre.#Ghouta_is_being_exterminated_by_chemical_weapons. (https://twitter.com/NabilAlawadhy/status/370039972641796096)
- August 21, 2013 (873 retweets, 48 likes): We have no one to rely on God, but you. #Ghouta_chemical_massacre #Eastern_Ghouta_massacre. (https://twitter.com/NabilAlawadhy/status/370043545240883200)
- August 21, 2013 (2,477 retweets, 197 likes): Enemies of the *ummah* let tyrants kill their people and burn the state, and they imprisoned a ruler [former Egyptian President Morsi] that the people had chosen. Oh God, our own people are our enemies. #Eastern_Ghouta_massacre. (https://twitter.com/NabilAlawadhy/status/370045166687502336)
- August 21, 2013 (5,933 retweets, 401 likes): If they paid one tenth of what they paid for the overthrow and killing of the people of #Egypt to jihadists in Syria, it would have been freed long ago! But it is the era of betrayal! #Ghouta_is_being_exterminated_by_chemical_weapons. (https://twitter.com/NabilAlawadhy/status/370047172172976128)
- August 21, 2013 (2,494 retweets, 202 likes): The video footage showing how children of Syria were killed by chemical weapons

should break all barriers of fear among our people. What is happening to them will happen to us one day if we remain silent!! (https://twitter.com/NabilAlawadhy/status/370047742753513472)

- August 21, 2013 (3,306 retweets, 166 likes): Oh God, to you we talk about our weakness, oh Merciful One, you are our source of power, and it is you we rely on. #Ghouta_is_being_exterminated_by_chemical_weapons. (https://twitter.com/NabilAlawadhy/status/370066688630218752)
- August 21, 2013 (2,733 retweets, 147 likes): Bashar did not commit his massacre today without a green light from tyrants like him and after safety from punishment by the international community. #Ghouta_is_being_exterminated_by_chemical_weapons. (https://twitter.com/NabilAlawadhy/status/370069869175128064)
- August 21, 2013 (1,897 retweets, 113 likes): And do not count God as ignorant to what the tyrants are doing. #Ghouta_is_being_exterminated_by_chemical_weapons. #Eastern_Ghouta_massacre. (https://twitter.com/NabilAlawadhy/status/370076888225443840)
- August 21, 2013 (2,246 retweets, 115 likes): Oh God, have mercy on their killed and accept them as martyrs and heal their wounds and give their families patience and perseverance oh Merciful One. #Ghouta_is_being_exterminated_by_chemical_weapons. #Eastern_Ghouta_massacre. (https://twitter.com/NabilAlawadhy/status/370077423607349248)
- August 21, 2013 (4,499 retweets, 202 likes): Oh God, misery is upon us and everything has become difficult and all the solutions are no longer working, we have no one but you God to help us. Oh God, save us all and save those in our *ummah* who are weak. #Ghouta_is_being_exterminated_by_chemical_weapons. (https://twitter.com/NabilAlawadhy/status/370079934900736000)

ADNAN AL AROUR

- December 5, 2013 (411 retweets, 48 likes): We are waiting for Hezbollah to take revenge for its commander in Israel, like they are taking revenge for Hussein in Syria against its women and children. Or are Muslim children considered to be more

criminal and *kafir* than Israelis, to Hezbollah? (https://twitter.com/
AdnanAlarour/status/408586204792492032)

2013 ESCALATION OF CRISIS IN IRAQ

During the months of 2013 leading to the escalation of the conflict in
Iraq in June 2014, which led to the radical group ISIS invading large
swathes of Iraq, al Arefe and al Arour were warning the Shi'a-led Maliki
government and calling for an end to the violence against the Sunnis.
Al Arour and al Arefe do not support extremist Sunni groups such as
ISIS; however, they are linked by their anti-Shi'a views. They have commented extensively on Twitter about the marginalization of the Sunnis
in Iraq, even as they call into question the religious legitimacy of ISIS,
which projects itself as a religious and political movement.

MOHAMAD AL AREFE

- October 5, 2013: Iraqis are our people and their blood runs
through our veins. Their history is of bravery, leadership, morals,
chivalry and generosity. #The_displacement_of_Sunni_people_in_
Iraq.*Link to a poster that says the cause is greater than a party or
an assembly or a sheikh or a thinker or a jihadist. It says that "our
cause" is the presence of Sunni people in Iraq.* (https://twitter.com/
MohamadAlarefe/status/386489045187981312/photo/1)

- June 2, 2013 (932 retweets, 118 likes): A statement from the
Iraqi jurisprudent assembly calling on the Islamic Cooperation
Association and Azhar in Egypt to defend the mosques of Sunni
people. *Link to a statement issued by the Fiqh Council of Senior
Scholars. The statement says that in light of the targeted killings
toward people praying in mixed areas in Baghdad, and attacks on
mosques and the government's inability to provide security for
these mosques, the Council calls upon the Islamic Cooperation
Association and Azhar to take a position on the massacres Iraqi
Sunnis are facing, whether in Baghdad or other Iraqi cities. The
Council calls on them to intervene and help protect the mosques*

and the people from sectarian militias who are tied to external powers. The Council also called on international human rights organizations to play their part in protecting Sunnis in Iraq against the extermination and genocide they faced and for which the government bears full responsibility. (https://twitter.com/MohamadAlarefe/status/341279251384897536/photo/1)

- April 26, 2013 (782 retweets, 142 likes): Yes to #justice_for_our_sons_in_Iraq. Everyone who can help them must exert their full energy in doing so. (https://twitter.com/MohamadAlarefe/status/327883460704342018)

THE SECTARIAN MESSAGING

The following selection of tweets from 2013 through 2015 for each cleric demonstrates that they fall under three categories: religious references, political references to events on the ground, and solicitations, either for fundraising purposes or political mobilization. As stated earlier, the religious references point to longstanding disputes between the Shi'a and Sunnis and are intended to portray the Shi'a as nonbelievers. In some cases, the tweets are fused with both political and religious commentaries. Data from Twitter were collected via www.twtrland. com. All figures are approximate.

RELIGIOUS REFERENCES

ADNAN AL AROUR

- October 14, 2015: retweeted @lord20077: @AdnanAlarour #Wisal @HazemAlarouur A Shi'i who was gifted [found the right path] at the hands of Shaykh Adnan al-Arour who has gifted many in Ahvaz. youtube.com/watch?v=o9_1KgCW_6s: *The video is about a supposed Shi'i caller phoning in from Ahvaz on the show* La'alhum Yahtdun *in which he talks about how and why he converted to Sunnism.* (https://twitter.com/lord20077/status/654397335762509824)
- December 15, 2013 (356 retweets, 49 likes): The Shi'a collect money publicly ... they kill publicly, their sectarianism reeks night and day, on the other hand the Sunnis...! (https://twitter.com/AdnanAlarour/status/412312003508584448)

- November 14, 2013 (607 retweets, 97 likes): The Shi'a say that Hussein (may God be pleased with him) knows the unknown, so we tell them if he knew the unknown why did he go to his fate?! So they remain silent with no answer. (https://twitter.com/AdnanAlarour/status/401055389430468608)
- November 14, 2013 (494 retweets, 63 likes): I think that the slapping for the Shi'a is a punishment from God to them with their hands because along with their forefathers they agreed to disappoint the biggest of martyrs (Hussein). (https://twitter.com/AdnanAlarour/status/401054613471633408)
- August 29, 2013 (642 retweets, 76 likes): I call on all Shi'a everywhere, make us understand, is killing children allowed? If you want to kill these children because they are the grandchildren of Mo'awiyya then I attest to God that you are *kafirs* and that you are the biggest *kafirs* God has ever created. (https://twitter.com/AdnanAlarour/status/373177538916274176)
- August 22, 2013 (622 retweets, 63 likes): How can you blame the youth for falling into the trap of excommunicating other Muslims when they see these massacres! If it wasn't for our firm rules, we would have excommunicated all the leaders one after the other. (https://twitter.com/AdnanAlarour/status/370635743661522944)
- June 9, 2013 (457 retweets, 34 likes): What is the relation of Hussein (may Allah be pleased with him) with the butchering of children in Qusayr? What is the relation of the killing of Hussein with the revolution in #Syria? (https://twitter.com/AdnanAlarour/status/343803025497923585)
- June 5, 2013 (963 retweets, 67 likes): There was a withdrawal from Qusayr in the night, without losses worth mentioning and our fight is not in Qusayr nor for the land of Qusayr. Our battle is a battle of right and wrong and faith and *kufr*. (https://twitter.com/AdnanAlarour/status/342330856242835456)
- May 26, 2013 (2,035 retweets, 54 likes): The Shi'a are the most *takfiri* of sects, for they cast out anyone who doesn't believe in their sect or doubts one of them or is allies with one

of their enemies. (https://twitter.com/AdnanAlarour/status/
338741253950808064)

- May 26, 2013 (586 retweets, 42 likes): The Mahdi according to the Shi'a doctrine is thirsty in the basement/hiding and is quenching his thirst with the blood of the Sunnis and they say in their books that there is nothing between the Mahdi and the Arabs except slaughter. (https://twitter.com/AdnanAlarour/status/338740597286375424)

- January 17, 2013 (837 retweets, 88 likes): We forbid the killing of a bird with no reason and we forbid the killing of ants and bees and they accuse us of sectarianism when they kill and butcher Muslims in the thousands and they're not sectarian!! #Syria (https://twitter.com/AdnanAlarour/status/291988415178756096)

MOHAMAD AL AREFE

- October 23, 2015 (1,856 retweets, 928 likes): Ali used to refuse betraying his in-law and the companions of the Prophet when Abu Bakr and Umar died. Ali ibn Abi Talib said, he who loves me should love them. (https://twitter.com/MohamadAlarefe/status/657602631951585281)

- October 21, 2015 (1,836 retweets, 1,025 likes): Ali named his son Umar, and his husband of his daughter Umar, and Hassan loved Umar and named on of his sons Umar and so did Hussein. (https://twitter.com/MohamadAlarefe/status/656882480549666821)

- October 29, 2015 (1,563 retweets, 652 likes): A message to the #Shi'is on the occasion of Ashura in four minutes: Dr. A'id al-Qarni, Dr. Sa'id al-Barik, and Dr. Mohamad al Arefe. https://www.youtube.com/watch?v=dD92scx2N24: *In the video addressed to Shi'is on the occasion of Ashura, al Arefe and other Saudi clerics talk about what the Quran does and doesn't say about Ashura.* (https://twitter.com/MohamadAlarefe/status/656488553078243328)

- October 20, 2015 (1,916 retweets, 942 likes): Oh #Shi'is. I swear to God that I pray for you and that I wish you well. Hitting and sadness on Ashura ... our masters from Ahl al-Bayt did not do this for the martyrdom of Ali nor Hussein. (https://twitter.com/MohamadAlarefe/status/656530741292048384)

- May 15, 2015 (4,240 retweets, 1,626 likes): Offense to our shaykh Ibn Baz, and lies about him at the Tehran international book fair. They say that he said: I am proud not to have seen the Prophet's grave for 40 years! (https://twitter.com/MohamadAlarefe/status/599286758388301824)

- September 20, 2014 (1,208 retweets, 486 likes): Strange! The explanation of [the beginning verses of surat Maryam in the Qu'ran]. If the #Prophet_of_God heard this, what would he say? Shi'i boys and girls, save yourselves. www.youtube.com/watch?v=01QhONdYOcc&sns=tw: *The video shows a Shi'i cleric explaining the meaning behind lone letters in the verses. He related the letters as symbolizing things relating to Karbala and Husayn.* (https://twitter.com/MohamadAlarefe/status/513436646692225025)

- September 20, 2014 (1,558 retweets, 475 likes): Shi'i boys and girls, you take your religion from this? I swear that I only want good for you. This is a Shi'i shaykh changing the verses of the Qu'ran. https://www.youtube.com/watch?v=moQxDjRdIq4&feature=youtu.be (https://twitter.com/MohamadAlarefe/status/513288526197043200)

- September 18, 2014 (2,114 retweets, 365 likes): I swear to God Ali would not accept this. Oh Shi'i youth, save yourselves. This one says: The Devil loves Ali ibn Abi Talib. youtube.com/watch?v=bGagI3WgBy4&sns=tw: *Audio of a Shi'i cleric saying that the devil likes the cousin and son-in-law of the Prophet.* (https://twitter.com/MohamadAlarefe/status/512559695869911040)

- September 2, 2014 (980 retweets, 316 likes): #Iran has called on them to believe that Ali is their God and that he will judge them on the Day of Judgment. Ali will not accept this. #Preventing_Converting_To_Shi'ism_In_Sudan. www.youtube.com/watch?v=w9NEeb-OWZo&feature=youtu.be: *A video of a Shi'i cleric saying that Ali ibn Abi Talib will "be our God on judgment day."* (https://twitter.com/MohamadAlarefe/status/506885562327105536)

- September 2, 2014 (752 retweets, 200 likes): #Iran has called on #Sudanese to excommunicate and curse the friends of the Prophet and those who love them, and accused the wives of the Prophet of obscenity. #Preventing_Converting_To_Shi'ism_In_Sudan. (https://twitter.com/MohamadAlarefe/status/506794104618242048)
- September 2, 2014 (1,595 retweets, 456 likes): I don't know a channel that has benefited Shi'is and informed them of the truth more than: #Wesal_TV, #Safa_TV, #Berhan_TV, #Ahwaz_TV. Congratulations to those who support them, may God bless them. (https://twitter.com/MohamadAlarefe/status/506766090299387904)
- September 2, 2014 (1,097 tweets, 290 likes): #Iran called on [the Sudanese] to kneel to others than God and praise humans as they praise God. #Preventing_Converting_To_Shi'ism_In_Sudan. (https://twitter.com/MohamadAlarefe/status/506882357627207681)
- September 2, 2014 (2,864 retweets, 525 likes): I swear to God that I wish goodness and truth for the #Shi'is. I know that a lot of them are unaware of the truth of the sect. God, gift us all with what pleases you. #Preventing_Converting_To_Shi'ism_In_Sudan. (https://twitter.com/MohamadAlarefe/status/506805201475366912)
- December 31, 2013 (tweeted by @KhalidALbakr, retweeted by @MohamadAlarefe): The #Shiite Council in #Najaf supports the military operation on the #Sunni people in #Anbar ... then they say: (we are not sectarian)...!! #Iraq. (https://twitter.com/KhalidALbakr/status/417958865318060032)
- December, 30, 2013 (tweeted by @YZaatreh, retweeted by @MohamadAlarefe): In Anbar, there is a battle to make the Sunni Arabs kneel, and after them all Iraqis. Maliki is practicing sectarian rallying to cover his failures on every front. He will never succeed. (https://twitter.com/YZaatreh/status/417728783068569601)
- October 2, 2013 (series of two tweets) (614 retweets, 98 likes): A report for the French newspaper *Le Monde*: (1) There is no such thing as temporary marriage for jihad. (2) This is an Iranian Syrian lie to distort the image of noble jihadists. (http://

new.elfagr.org/   Detail.aspx?nwsId=436044&secid=7&vid=2#).
Also (524 retweets, 66 likes): The Iranian and Syrian regimes
lied and created the #lie_of_temporary_marriage_for_jihad
and then slandered Muslim scholars by saying they had said it
was okay for a jihadist to marry his sister, mother or daughter
if the need arose. (https://twitter.com/MohamadAlarefe/status/
385456510077526016) (https://twitter.com/MohamadAlarefe/
status/385456897090150400)

- August 21, 2013 (4,972 retweets, 418 likes): It is not permissible
for a Muslim to frighten another Muslim. Horrifying and scaring
them is a great sin in itself, imagine how great a sin this bloodshed
and killing is. Woe to those who can grant these people victory
and yet remain silent! (https://twitter.com/ MohamadAlarefe/sta-
tus/370148869344350208)

- June 6, 2013 (496 retweets, 55 likes): The relationship between
#Hezbollah and Khomeini is one of a body to the soul, and the
party has used it to spread Shi'ism in the Islamic world. (https://
twitter.com/MohamadAlarefe/status/342700307639332864)

- June 6, 2013 (573 retweets, 69 likes): #Hezbollah's doctrine and
its supporters are *rawafid* Safavids, and their primary beliefs
include: having many Imams, changing the words of the Koran,
making the Imams Divine . . . to be continued. (https://twitter.com/
MohamadAlarefe/status/342697284439527424)

- June 6, 2013 (577 retweets, 79 likes): And of #Hezbollah's doctrine: that the state is for the Imams only, excommunicating
those who came before them, and cursing the caliphs Abu Bakr,
Omar and Othman. (https://twitter.com/MohamadAlarefe/status/
342697738531643392)

- June 6, 2013 (481 retweets, 66 likes): The *rawafid* Safavid
#Hezbollah are taking over Sunni Mosques in Lebanon and
changing their names. (https://twitter.com/MohamadAlarefe/sta-
tus/342701436100042752)

- June 2, 2013 (932 retweets, 118 likes): A statement from the Iraqi
jurisprudent assembly calling on the Islamic Cooperation Association

and Azhar to defend the mosques of Sunni people. (https://twitter.
com/MohamadAlarefe/status/341279251384897536/photo/1)

DAI AL ISLAM AL SHAHHAL

- December 2, 2013 (4 retweets): And we can't ignore any decision
  that targets the Sunni sect. (https://twitter.com/Daeislam/status/
  407638840678301697)
- September 28, 2013 (series of seven tweets): (1) The attack on
  our Sunni people and brothers in #Baalbek and their vulnerabil-
  ity at the hands of the organization called Hezbollah, a sectarian
  power whose purpose is to create war and sedition. (2) Sectarian
  sedition in #Lebanon is therefore normal to occur; the reactions
  are strong and uncontrollable toward the allies of this Hezb in
  different areas. (3) We hold Hezbollah and its allies accountable
  for the blood that's been spilled and the repercussions of this as
  well as the Lebanese state for its silence on the actions of the
  Hezb #Lebanon #Baalbek. (4) Like what is happening now in
  #Baalbek where sectarian claws do their deeds in Chiah and the
  Sunnis in Baalbek and the official security forces watch and do
  nothing #Lebanon. (5) Last night is so similar to May 7 and it
  appears that the state of Hezbollah asked the Lebanese state to
  come up with a security plan in Dahiye #Lebanon. (6) And under
  its rule so that it can have time to hit the opponents of the Syrian
  regime and Iranian project in Lebanon and ignite a Sunni–Shi'a
  sectarian war in the Arab and Islamic world #Lebanon. (7) So it
  is normal for Sunnis of the world not to be quiet on the Safavid
  project targeting the Sunni people in Syria and Lebanon and the
  area. The Information office of Sheikh #Shahhal. (https://twit-
  ter.com/Daeislam/status/384024148181540864) (https://twit-
  ter.com/Daeislam/status/384025933491236864) (https://twitter.
  com/Daeislam/status/384026557180035072) (https://twitter.
  com/Daeislam/status/384027274666053632) (https://twitter.
  com/Daeislam/status/384027997378207744) (https://twitter.
  com/Daeislam/status/384028662821310464) (https://twitter.com/
  Daeislam/status/384029411529728000)

- June 13, 2013 (7 retweets, 2 likes): Sheikh Dai al Islam #al-Shahhal: The Sunni people in #Lebanon are threatened, and we have warned of this, and we found no ears that listened. #The_stance_of_the_scholars_from_Syria. (https://twitter.com/Daeislam/status/345278963804946433)
- February 4, 2013 (6 retweets, 3 likes): From the statement of the Sheikh: the undermining of Sunni blood over and over on the hands of forces and officers of this organization compromises it … #Arsal #Lebanon. (https://twitter.com/Daeislam/status/298534426231570433)
- January 29, 2013 (4 retweets, 1 like): There is a lot of anger from the people of #Tripoli toward #Future movement because it gives priority to leaders and not to the interest of the Sunni sect. #TripoliLB. (https://twitter.com/Daeislam/status/296235023865094144)

SALEM AL RAFEI

- October 24, 2013 (26 retweets, 8 likes): God, I give you the city of knowledge of scholars Tripoli, God bring back its security and make its citizens safe, and take revenge upon those who seek to destroy it from the Ba'ath party criminals. (https://twitter.com/salemalrafei/status/393508244104433664)
- July 28, 2013 (1 like): Two and a half years it's been and we've been hearing and seeing photos of killing and torture and arrests of the Sunni people in Syria!!! On the hands of the criminal alliance … Today…. https://twitter.com/salemalrafei/status/350700428201168897)
- June 28, 2013 (7 retweets, 1 like): This is Sidon, the land of dignity, Sidon does not bow down to anyone but God … Sunnis do not bow down to anyone but God. God is Great. God is Great. fb.me/27i66h8vt (https://twitter.com/salemalrafei/status/350675338394734593)
- June 13, 2013 (3 retweets): al Qaradawi: Iran's rulers are helping Christians, and Christians are not Muslim, and the Shi'a are fighting us based on sect. They chant: "Oh Hussein," for they are polytheists. (https://twitter.com/salemalrafei/status/345148725582249985)

- June 4, 2013 (1 retweet): It really is the revolution that has shown their true light, hypocrites who claim to belong to Islam when they kill Muslims. They claim to defend holy places and they bomb mosques. (https://twitter.com/salemalrafei/status/341959698918027267)
- May 19, 2013 (124 retweets, 5 likes): Our people in Qusayr are now fighting battles between those whose allegiance is to God and who fight to remove tyranny and raise His name and those whose allegiance is to the Devil. (https://twitter.com/salemalrafei/status/336081390456168448)

BILAL BAROUDI

- December 28, 2013 (2 retweets, 2 likes): When will the Sunnis realize that they are targeted no matter how much they give up of their principles? Haven't we considered what happened to the Sunni people in Bosnia (and they didn't have any fundamentalist movement)? (https://twitter.com/AlsalamBilal/status/417021822899851264)

NABIL AL AWADHY

- July 6, 2013 (990 retweets, 130 likes): Wherever a Wahhabi is found, we must fight them to the death!! Watch how Iraqi Shiites are inciting to kill Muslims in Syria. (https://twitter.com/NabilAlawadhy/status/353463600259665921) A very dangerous video.
- June 22, 2013 (604 retweets, 42 likes): To the men of Iraq and its heroes: Maliki is still sending his Safavid soldiers to Syria to kill children and violate women and destroy the country!! (https://twitter.com/NabilAlawadhy/status/348559685491761152)
- April 23, 2013 (737 retweets, 64 likes): Why are monotheistic believers killed in Iraq?! On what guilt is their blood violated? And what religion is Maliki and his gangs using to do this? #The_Iraqi_Spring. #Hujaira_Massacre. (https://twitter.com/NabilAlawadhy/status/326614378478714880)
- April 4, 2013 (341 retweets, 31 likes): What I have seen in very painful footage far removed from humanity in #Iraq's prisons

and what Iraq has reached to today, is exactly what Americans wants in cooperating with the Safavids. (https://twitter.com/NabilAlawadhy/status/319811964111036416)

- April 4, 2013 (289 retweets, 28 likes): Iraq's prisons are filled with those oppressed and tortured and sectarianism controls the minds of those responsible for them. Videos of the torture are spreading without condemnation. The Safavids are following in the footsteps of the Americans! (https://twitter.com/NabilAlawadhy/status/319809729826275330)
- January 23, 2013 (186 retweets, 36 likes): @anti_kardashn: A report for BBC on the sectarian government in Iraq. http://www.bbc.com/arabic/multimedia/2013/01/130115_iraq_release_prisoners.shtml. #The_Iraqi_Spring. (https://twitter.com/NabilAlawadhy/status/294020039772880896)

POLITICAL REFERENCES

ADNAN AL AROUR

- September 27, 2015 (350 retweets, 185 likes): Is there a relation between the presence of a lot of Iranians in the #Mina_stampede and the maliciousness in their religion which calls to harm Muslims. https://www.youtube.com/watch?v=hNJCkvDiMec&feature=youtu.be: *It is audio of supposedly a Shi'i threatening that if a Shi'i were ever to be harmed, a bloodbath against pilgrims in the Hajj would ensue.* (https://twitter.com/AdnanAlarour/status/648161159388901376)
- September 15, 2015 (664 retweets, 261 likes): The Kingdom and Iran, between the cranes in the [Mecca] area, and the cranes of criminality, and between security officers coming to the aid of pilgrims and thugs going to kill them. youtube.com/watch?v=S2qh-Qo9Tk4&app=desktop: *An old documentry broadcast on Kuwaiti television about the 1987 Mecca incident.* (https://twitter.com/AdnanAlarour/status/643871452572332033)

- September 14, 2015 (440 retweets, 198 likes): Is Iran crying over the deaths in Mecca to keep people busy from its massacres in Iraq, Yemen, and Syria? Or is it to hide its *takfiri* bloody doctrine? Or is it just shameless? (https://twitter.com/AdnanAlarour/status/643518137665744897)

- August, 17, 2015 (915 retweets, 335 likes): This is the fruit of Nusayri-Safavid hatred, the Crusado-international scheme, and the Arab-Islamic disappointment. What are we waiting for? God, we have no one but you. #Duma_is_being_exterminated. (https://twitter.com/AdnanAlarour/status/633372905292873728)

- August 12, 2015 (360 retweets, 187 likes): A warning to our brothers in Aleppo: Lt. Suhayl Al-Hasan has fled from Sahl al-Ghab like a dog, heading toward Aleppo. A reward: One million liras for anyone who kills him . . . and five million to his battalion. (https://twitter.com/AdnanAlarour/status/631413003758477312)

- August 11, 2015 (260 retweets, 150 likes): We thank the people of Kafrayya for killing Hajj Abu Zaynab, a Hezbollah commander, when he and his soldiers wanted to commit rape. May God not please them in life nor in the afterlife. (https://twitter.com/AdnanAlarour/status/631171987243704321)

- August 11, 2015 (199 retweets, 146 likes): Did you ever wonder, oh wise one, why shots were fired on the people's protests and not on the Alawite protests? Isn't this sectarianism? Who is the sectarian one here? (https://twitter.com/AdnanAlarour/status/631174434120957952)

- August 11, 2015 (173 retweets, 128 likes): If the rumors the regime were spreading—that we want to kill any Alawite because he is Alawite—were true, we would have done so before the monster family raped the rule for we are far stronger and we are twenty times your number. (https://twitter.com/AdnanAlarour/status/631174940746715136)

- June 1, 2015 (429 retweets, 186 likes): We appreciate and thank the stances of the moderates of every sect, especially the Arab Shi'is who reject the exploitation by the Safavids who only seek sedition in the *ummah*. (https://twitter.com/AdnanAlarour/status/605436267858391040)

- May 24, 2015: retweeted @thtt2015: Arour is behind the incitement to kill Shi'is and this is the proof. Listen and watch: youtube/Do3DUvbWO7Y: *The video shows a speech by Sadrist leader Hazem al-A'raji. He can be heard calling on people to take up arms and fight every "filthy" Wahhabi.* (https://twitter.com/thtt2015/status/602590335341035520)

- April 30, 2015 (366 retweets, 246 likes): Jaysh al-Islam has frightened the regime. That's why enemies have tried to ruin its image. Its enemies are among the *rawafid*, spiteful Nusayris and those who are irreligious and hate Islam. (https://twitter.com/AdnanAlarour/status/593856891765166080)

- April 17, 2015 (1,331 retweets, 302 likes): We are very optimistic. Let everyone know that the number of those in the Saudi army is the same as that of all truthful Muslims in the world. #Operation_Decisive_Storm. (https://twitter.com/AdnanAlarour/status/589111010713186304)

- April 10, 2015 (525 retweets, 163 likes): The conspiracy in Iraq today is clear to everyone who sees. Bringing ISIS into Iraq as an excuse to form the Popular Mobilization [Forces] and deal a blow to the Sunni people and break the blockade on Iran and give it access to Iraq. (https://twitter.com/AdnanAlarour/status/586636995352399872)

- March 30, 2015 (689 retweets, 359 likes): A report for Shada channel exposing the speech of Hassan Nasrallah after #Operation_Decisive_Storm and his attack on Saudi Arabia, accusing it of supporting terror! https://www.youtube.com/watch?v=AZCU2ef5eRI&feature=youtu.be. *The video is a report by Shada channel in which they try to expose contradictions in a speech by Hezbollah about its ties to Iran and its role in Yemen.* (https://twitter.com/AdnanAlarour/status/582652605639172096)

- March 26, 2015 (839 retweets, 276 likes): The Kingdom's delayed intervention in Yemen was due to its wisdom and attempts at trying to reach a peaceful solution between the different sides. But the Houthis only wanted the murder, oppression and occupation of Yemen. (https://twitter.com/AdnanAlarour/status/581168710318211072)

- March 26, 2015 (1,378 retweets, 350 likes): Standing with the #Saudi army against sectarians, aggressors and violators of legitimacy is a religious duty. We suggest the formation of a badge of honor. #We_are_all_soldiers_of_the_two_sanctuaries. (https://twitter.com/AdnanAlarour/status/581078333351464961)

- March 26, 2015 (1,745 retweets, 455 likes): Oh God, bring victory to the soldiers of the Two Sanctuaries [Mecca and Medina] against the aggressor prostitutes, the enemies of Oneness and Sunnah and humanity. #Operation_Decisive_Storm. (https://twitter.com/AdnanAlarour/status/581021320005087233)

- March 18, 2015 (706 retweets, 186 likes): Despite our shortcomings and neglect of the causes of our Sunni brothers in #Occupied_Arab_Ahvaz, they insist to hold on to their religion and Arabism. #Ahvaz_rises_up. (https://twitter.com/AdnanAlarour/status/578233958405550081)

- February 19, 2015 (273 retweets, 146 likes): The fourth gift to the majoos and Al-Zamirah Hasan al-Shaytan [Hasan Nasrallah]. His prisoners curse him. youtube.com/watch?v=Bb5LkiY8Q2I (https://twitter.com/AdnanAlarour/status/568376534353846273)

- February 19, 2015 (252 retweets, 116 likes): Two presents for the majoos of Iran and their mercenaries. youtube.com/watch?v=abgpGxGoUFQ: *A video by Aleppo News showing the dead bodies of who it says are Syrian "government forces supported by Shi'i and Iranian militias."* (https://twitter.com/AdnanAlarour/status/568375580086784000)

- November 26, 2014 (371 retweets, 136 likes): To those who support or sympathize with Da'ish, you are *khawarij* like them. Stop giving your money to execute Muslims. (https://twitter.com/AdnanAlarour/status/537701375526711296)

- November 20, 2014 (257 retweets, 89 likes): The world was not only silent to the terrorism of the Shi'is and Nusayris, they supported them when they were sure that their swords were placed on

the necks of the Sunni people! (https://twitter.com/AdnanAlarour/
status/535536079789502464)

- November 20, 2014 (186 retweets, 69 likes): We must hasten to
search for a way out of the crisis in Yemen and work to bring back to
Yemen to the bosom of the Sunnis before we bite the fingers of regret.
(https://twitter.com/AdnanAlarour/status/535536247419047936)
- November 20, 2014 (207 retweets, 66 likes): The Shi'is have
plotted and promised and announced their plans! They carried
out a great deal of them and still some doubt their intention to
continue their plans. (https://twitter.com/AdnanAlarour/status/
535536604907982850)
- November 7, 2014 (232 retweets, 88 likes): Every Sunni that
attacks or curses or incites against is either ignorant, or is not
a Sunni and just wants to tarnish the Sunnis' image or he is a
malicious intruder who wants to create sedition between
Muslims and others. (https://twitter.com/AdnanAlarour/status/
530788180866265088)
- November 7, 2014 (243 retweets, 82 likes): If we look at the traps
set up for the Arabs after the Khomeini revolution, we see that they
are in the interest of expanding Iran. From the fall of Saddam, to
Da'ish, to the Houthis. (https://twitter.com/AdnanAlarour/status/
530766581131796480)
- November 7, 2014 (299 retweets, 92 likes): retweeted @
anwarmalek: Unfortunately, in the Arab world, there isn't a strategy and thinking center to combat the Safavid reach while we
find tens of them in #Iran and others specializing in exporting
the [Iranian] revolution. (https://twitter.com/anwarmalek/status/
530667889146466304)
- November 7, 2014 (179 retweets, 62 likes): Sectarian incitement
that incites sedition and attacks on another sect for its doctrine
is one thing, and is forbidden, and incitement that God has commanded against aggressor killers is another thing. (https://twitter.
com/AdnanAlarour/status/530770360325517312)
- November 5, 2014 (720 retweets, 118 likes): The Shi'is in
the Kingdom are blessed and not one of them is imprisoned

for his beliefs and not one of them was discriminated against in the workplace based on sect. Thank God for the Sunnis' blessing of justice. (https://twitter.com/AdnanAlarour/status/530068276907216897)

- November 5, 2014 (566 retweets, 111 likes): Compare between what the Kingdom offers to the people, especially in Syria in terms of services and aid, and what Iran provides of destruction and despair to know who works for goodness and who calls for peace. (https://twitter.com/AdnanAlarour/status/530063273261944832)
- November 5, 2014 (380 retweets, 106 likes): I challenge anyone to prove that Wesal [TV] and its likes have cursed any of the imams of the sects. It has opened the door of dialogue and understanding to all. (https://twitter.com/AdnanAlarour/status/530050024450060289)
- November 5, 2014 (1,273 retweets, 206 likes): Compare between the treatment of the Shi'is by the Kingdom, and the treatment of Sunnis by Iran to know who is sectarian. It's not allowed for one Sunni Mosque to be built in Tehran and hundreds of Sunnis are hanged. (https://twitter.com/AdnanAlarour/status/530065128150925312)
- October 23, 2014 (455 retweets, 152 likes): To everyone asking about the license of Al-Salam [organization] and Shada TV, we ask them, was Hezb al-Shaytan's [Hezbollah's] intervention in Syria licensed? Was the sectarian bombardment of children licensed? (https://twitter.com/AdnanAlarour/status/525376907068846080)
- October 15, 2014: retweeted @yahtadon: Watch tonight an important debate between Shaykh Farqad al-Kazyuni the agent of the Shi'is and Shaykh Adnan al Arour, the defender of the Sunni people on Wesal TV and Shada at 930 pm. (https://twitter.com/yahtadon/status/522439456133894144)
- October 3, 2014 (421 retweets, 94 likes): You can die of anger, you fools. The Saudis will continue to support Muslim causes, even if the Nusayris, *rawafid* and the irreligious hate it. (https://twitter.com/AdnanAlarour/status/518024754867888128)

- October 2, 2014 (146 retweets, 62 likes): Terrorists in the east are four: Zionists, Safavids, Nusayris, and Takfiris. (https://twitter.com/AdnanAlarour/status/517664286806532096)
- October 2, 2014: retweeted @yalshetewi: @awadalqarni On this day, on the Hijri year of 317, the *rawafid* stormed Mecca and killed more than 30,000 pilgrims at the Kaabah. (https://twitter.com/yalshetewi/status/517641941039579136)
- September 25, 2014: retweeted @tv_shada: Repeated violations committed by the Lebanese army and Hezbollah militias against Syrian refugees in Lebanon. (https://twitter.com/tv_shada/status/515201708071202817)
- September 24, 2014 (226 retweets, 82 likes): This is what the resistance front (Iran, Nusayris, Halish) have done, just as the Zionists did to the Palestinians except that the Zionists let them carry food. (https://twitter.com/AdnanAlarour/status/514775999653769216)
- September 19, 2014 (257 retweets, 67 likes): The terrorists of Halish [Hezbollah], Iraq and Iran have executed with their sectarian knives children and women and torn down holy places and done folds of what Da'ish has done. Oh God, stop their evil. (https://twitter.com/AdnanAlarour/status/512926640922308609)
- August 6, 2014 (587 retweets, 120 likes): In light of the clashes between civilians and the military, displaced Syrians have come under Lebanese army fire in coordination with Hezb alShaytan [Hezbollah], who burned their tents and killed their women and children. (https://twitter.com/AdnanAlarour/status/497134579933659136)
- December 29, 2013 (161 retweets, 36 likes): The most dangerous issue that ISIS is criticized about is that it refuses the rule of God. ISIS sees itself as a state and any jihadists other than them are seen to not be a part of that state. (https://twitter.com/AdnanAlarour/status/417379377769218049)
- December 15, 2013 (259 retweets, 38 likes): It is expected that they will accuse the jihadists of chemical weapons, Arour of terrorism, and that the *rawafid* and Hezb al Shaytan will be granted certificates of innocence by the Council of Betrayal and the

League of Disappointment. (https://twitter.com/AdnanAlarour/status/412313145651122176)

- December 5, 2013 (388 retweets, 42 likes): We are waiting for Hezbollah to take revenge for its commander in Israel, like they are taking revenge for Hussein in Syria against its women and children. Or are Muslim children considered to be more criminal and *kafir* than Israelis, to Hezbollah? (https://twitter.com/AdnanAlarour/status/408586204792492032)

- November 21, 2013 (100 retweets, 24 likes): We have demanded from ISIS for months to present the killers to legal courts and they have refused. Why are they not presenting these killers to the legal courts but are stalling instead? #Syria. (https://twitter.com/AdnanAlarour/status/403598894287695874)

- November 8, 2013 (360 retweets, 41 likes): The rebels aren't fighting the regime, the regime has fallen months ago, the rebels are fighting the Iranians and Hezb al Shaytan. (https://twitter. com/AdnanAlarour/status/398768286159998977)

- September 26, 2013 (298 retweets, 31 likes): At the time the Shi'a were covering Syria with crimes, the Saudis and the Qataris and the Kuwaitis and others were covering Syria with aid. (https://twitter.com/AdnanAlarour/status/383302136034902016)

- August 31, 2013: Oh honorable Shi'a, don't worry if Bashar and Hassan don't bomb, because Iran, whose leaders in their elections promised to throw Israel in the sea, will bomb, so leaders don't disappoint those who elected you. (https://twitter.com/AdnanAlarour/status/373590702753873920)

- August 31, 2013 (186 retweets, 20 likes): Oh honorable Shi'a and noble Christians, don't worry, for our leader Bashar and our Imam Hassan Khamenei will make us proud and bomb Tel Aviv before they bomb us. (https://twitter.com/AdnanAlarour/status/373588010132328448)

- August 21, 2013 (702 retweets, 42 likes): What happened today in Ghouta is terrorism by the Assad gang but it is with express international permission, and with permission from the Security Council. (https://twitter.com/AdnanAlarour/status/370287669688819713)

- August 21, 2013 (623 retweets, 44 likes): If a thousand preachers in a thousand mosques have not been able to show the true colors of the world and the *rawafid* and the countries of human rights, the revolution has certainly exposed all of them in their true light. (https://twitter.com/AdnanAlarour/status/370156944612655104)
- June 13, 2013 (600 retweets, 66 likes): The Arab League and most of its states are conspiring against the Syrian revolution, and if they had any honor they would have gone in and saved #Syria. (https://twitter.com/AdnanAlarour/status/345269227722264580)
- June 9, 2013 (907 retweets, 65 likes): What is strange is that Arab and Islamic states hear Iranian agents and the *rawafid* saying "we will slay you and occupy Gulf States" and the Gulf States don't do anything about it!! (https://twitter.com/AdnanAlarour/status/343803883950325760)
- June 9, 2013 (1,096 retweets, 82 likes): "America gave Iraq to Iran on a plate of gold," according to Prince Saud al Faisal. Who is now giving Syria to Iran on a plate of blood? (https://twitter.com/AdnanAlarour/status/343753887334940673)
- June 6, 2013 (*said by Arour, tweeted by 3ajel_ksa, retweeted by Arour*) #AlArour: The piling of Hezbollah and the regime on #Qusayr is because of their repeated defeats and failures. (https://twitter.com/3ajel_ksa/status/342729095924305920)
- June 5, 2013 (656 retweets, 54 likes): The battle of #Qusayr will not change anything, it doesn't count for more than 1/400th of the territory of anger. If it falls, this will not affect our revolution, God willing. (https://twitter.com/AdnanAlarour/status/342223898600943617)
- June 5, 2013 (859 retweets, 48 likes): Despite the withdrawal from Qusayr, we and God are the victors. We have gained more faith and more conviction in the truth of our doctrine. And we have unmasked the truth of the true enemies to the *ummah*. (https://twitter.com/ AdnanAlarour/status/342340165357936641)
- June 4, 2013 (922 retweets, 54 likes): If something happens in Syria and it falls in the hands of Iran, their coming goal is the Gulf and they have begun in implementing this plan with Hezbollah's

entrance into Syria. Iran has occupied Syria; a full occupation. (https://twitter.com/AdnanAlarour/status/342004054798499841)

- June 4, 2013 (293 retweets, 29 likes): The Syrian people did not originally go out to fight against the regime nor did they go out with sectarianism. They asked peacefully but the regime forced the fighting against them and used sectarianism to kill them. (https://twitter.com/AdnanAlarour/status/341992558198652928)

- June 4, 2013 (1,438 retweets, 84 likes): If a chicken belonging to a Muslim crossed the Lebanese border they would have arrested it on charges of terrorism!! But the tanks and rockets of Hezb al Shaytan openly cross with an American order and an Iranian request and Arab silence!! (https://twitter.com/AdnanAlarour/status/342005432753201152)

- May 30, 2013 (361 retweets, 36 likes): Do you want us to stay silent about Hezb al Shaytan's interference in #Syria so it will be ruled by the *rawafid* ... ?? (https://twitter.com/AdnanAlarour/status/340203331819544576)

- May 26, 2013 (506 retweets, 33 likes): We thank the noble Shi'a who stood by the Syrian revolution or who stood on the sidelines and did not join with Hezb al Shaytan to kill those who sheltered them and comforted them from Qusayr and elsewhere. (https://twitter.com/AdnanAlarour/status/338601076188135425)

- May 23, 2013 (544 retweets, 44 likes): Hezb al Shaytan penetrates borders and kills and slaughters and supports the falling army and the Safavids come from Isfahan through Iraq ... then you want us to stay silent?? (https://twitter.com/AdnanAlarour/status/337681942671683584)

- May 23, 2013 (633 retweets, 45 likes): Oh Arab rulers, why do you keep silent on the interference of Hezb al Shayan? (https://twitter.com/AdnanAlarour/status/337657134709870595)

- April 21, 2013 (575 retweets, 66 likes): The international community wants to provide us with nonlethal weapons!! And they give us communication tools to spy on us and pinpoint the locations of our fighters. #Syria. (https://twitter.com/AdnanAlarour/status/326048671386984448)

- April 18, 2013 (249 retweets, 36 likes): Every sheikh who stood by the regime will be tried alongside Bashar and every sheikh who took a neutral position shall be convicted of cowardice. #Syria. (https://twitter.com/AdnanAlarour/status/324969736339353600)
- April 11, 2013 (223 retweets, 37 likes): We ask all those who support ISIS, what is the ruling on those who don't pay homage to it and to those who are obedient to the unknown? The scholar issues fatwas based on knowledge and those who stray simply curse and accuse. (https://twitter.com/AdnanAlarour/status/322457044688977920)
- March 11, 2013 (698 retweets, 57 likes): God is Great, the small signs of the fall of the regime have shown, and the big signs are following, from them Hezb al Shaytan and Maliki's interference .... (https://twitter.com/AdnanAlarour/status/311228482657083392)
- March 7, 2013 (288 retweet, 30 likes): #America is the one who ignited sectarianism when it gave #Iraq to Iran and #Syria. (https://twitter.com/AdnanAlarour/status/309744878936530944)
- February 24, 2013 (366 retweets, 46 likes): If we only had what Hezb al Shaytan has from weapons and support, there would no longer be devils nor tyrants. #Syria. (https://twitter.com/AdnanAlarour/status/305751955236605952)

MOHAMAD AL AREFE

- October 27, 2015 (2,247 retweets, 950 likes): The Saudi Arab Kingdom will remain a compass for Muslims, its scholars and its people are all one. (https://twitter.com/MohamadAlarefe/status/658959783362482176)
- October 27, 2015 (1,365 retweets, 635 likes): If you want to find out the real criminal in any crime, look for who benefits. There is no one benefiting from the #Najran incident but Iran and its tails, and the Zionists and their supporters. (https://twitter.com/MohamadAlarefe/status/658959651921358848)
- September 2, 2015 (2,190 retweets, 920 likes): On YouTube, there are 645 clips openly inciting to kill Sunni people, based on texts and

books they refer to. And this was a quick tally we pulled up. This is besides the 121 channels in nine languages which fuel this. (https://twitter.com/MohamadAlarefe/status/639164199868862465)

- August 5, 2015 (1,315 retweets, 447 likes): Iranian channel IRINN, a government channel for Khamenei, has released a report about the influence of Persian Wesal Haq TV in the Iranian street. (https://twitter.com/MohamadAlarefe/status/628899302300090368)

- July 2, 2015 (1,074 retweets, 471 likes): A letter from the heart to those tricked by the Houthis. www.youtube.com/watch?v=RHCge ukHkss&feature=youtu.be: *The video is a public sermon given by al Arefe in which he addressed those supporting the Houthis and offering religious reasons as to why they should not support the Houthis. He adds that the "Persians are using you as mercenaries. They don't care if you live or die now or in the afterlife."* (https://twitter.com/MohamadAlarefe/status/616748990692921344)

- June 29, 2015 (1,857 retweets, 601 likes): #Iraq. Mos'ab Mosque-Salah al-Din 70; Sariya Mosque Dyali—50; Al-Juwayja market 40; the Sunni martyrs in the last 3 days. He says: Kill Sunnis and you will have heaven! www.youtube.com/watch?v=ziKUWNvQp-c: *It is a video of a Shi'i cleric, Hazem al-A'raji, saying that it is "your responsibility" to "arm Shi'is" and "kill filthy Wahhabis" and that if so "the doors of heaven will open for you."* (https://twitter.com/MohamadAlarefe/status/615464785937719297)

- June 28, 2015 (14,979 retweets, 3,514 likes): The first to have killed people in a mosque was Abu Lu'lu'a al-Majusi. He stabbed Umar and 13 of his companions, 7 of them died. And that's why #Iran made him a big deal and erected a shrine for him. (https://twitter.com/MohamadAlarefe/status/615245160436203520)

- June 22, 2015 (2,964 retweets, 1,169 likes): The targeting of the Sunni people and their brutal treatment in a lot of countries is becoming a daily occurrence! Action by Ulama and Islamic associations is a duty. May God release them. #Roumieh_prison. (https://twitter.com/MohamadAlarefe/status/612990072057655296)

- June 17, 2015 (3,618 retweets, 1,110 likes): Arbitrary sectarian arrest! Then false confessions taken by hateful Safavid sectarians. #Execution_of_7,000_Iraqi_Sunnis. (https://twitter.com/MohamadAlarefe/status/611301011282599936)

- May 30, 2015 (9,917 retweets, 3,479 likes): #Burning_of_a_Sunni_man. What our people in Iraq have faced, at the hands of sectarian militias, of burning, homelessness, violation, imprisonment and humiliation ... an issue that needs to be resolved immediately. (https://twitter.com/MohamadAlarefe/status/604785619324293121)

- May 24, 2015 (3,754 retweets, 1,990 likes): Thousands of enemy intelligence accounts use Sunni and Shi'i and IS names to spread falsehoods and incite sedition and curse and excommunicate. Don't engage with them. (https://twitter.com/MohamadAlarefe/status/602584484672737280)

- May 9, 2015 (2,339 retweets, 1,391 likes): They have 120 Safavid channels, and with that, they try to tarnish the image of Wesal al-Haq. The warn about it, imprison those who follow it, and hang up in their face! (https://twitter.com/MohamadAlarefe/status/597020365978607617)

- May 9, 2015 (16,622 retweets, 4,427 likes): Tehran is the only capital in the world with no Sunni Mosque. The Iranian parliament has nine Jews and four Zoroastrians and not one Sunni. Even though there are 22 million Sunnis in Iran! (https://twitter.com/MohamadAlarefe/status/597102368778358785)

- April 25, 2015 (2,480 retweets, 831 likes): Arab Persian channels have huge reach and are influential on most Persians. They have helped thousands of them find the right path. Follow them, enter their sites and message them to support them. (https://twitter.com/MohamadAlarefe/status/591876220926627841)

- April 19, 2015 (3,379 retweets, 1,134): Our people in Ahvaz have been patient and struggled fighting for their beliefs and land for 90 years, and the Persian Safavids tortured them. (https://twitter.com/MohamadAlarefe/status/589801599406514178)

- April 19, 2015 (1,084 retweets, 582 likes): Yesterday's meeting: They [the Houthis] spoke to us about pictures spread which claimed to be of people killed in #Operation_Decisive_Storm. They said: We know our country and what it looks like and our citizens and these are the crimes of Bashar [al-Asad] and the Safavids. (https://twitter.com/MohamadAlarefe/status/589803671099080704)

- April 12, 2015 (2,373 retweets, 1,652 likes): Reports have been distributed that centers, mosques and schools built by Gulf states in Africa and elsewhere have been taken over by Safavids years ago. They should be won back. (https://twitter.com/MohamadAlarefe/status/587333153473171456)

- April 10, 2015 (3,419 retweets, 1,347 likes): 41 Safavid Persian channels are helping stray Persian speakers and inject them [with hatred] against us. Let's support the 4 Sunni Persian channels: Nour, Kalima, Tawhid, Wesal. (https://twitter.com/MohamadAlarefe/status/586467558741520385)

- March 27, 2015 (3,989 retweets, 1,829 likes): #Wesal_TV. Its efforts are distinguished in resisting the Safavid reach. A nonprofit channel. Blessed are those who support it. (https://twitter.com/MohamadAlarefe/status/581534380746653696)

- March 26, 2015 (9,366 retweets, 3,394 likes): The Houthis have killed people, destroyed mosques, brought destruction to the role of the Qur'an, insulted the Qur'an, stole, looted. There had to be an #Operation_Decisive_Storm. (https://twitter.com/MohamadAlarefe/status/581153870597873664)

- March 25, 2015 (15,715 retweets, 4,732 likes): #Operation_Decisive_Storm, a wise decision from a wise man. May God bring victory to our soldiers over this transgressor and support them and keep them. (https://twitter.com/MohamadAlarefe/status/580984848203972608)

- March 17, 2015 (16,484 retweets, 2,085 likes): God, protect our brothers in Ahvaz. Bless them and protect them. How nice they are when they feel with their Muslim brothers and welcome Hilal club. (https://twitter.com/MohamadAlarefe/status/577886045003350016)

- September 26, 2014 (3,048 retweets, 535 likes): Why aren't there Shi'is in Guantanamo? Why aren't Shi'i charity groups closed down? (https://twitter.com/MohamadAlarefe/status/515471701195235329)

- September 23, 2014 (2,515 retweets, 396 likes): #Save_Yemen. (https://twitter.com/MohamadAlarefe/status/514354750255423488)
- September 2, 2014 (931 retweets, 272 likes): The secret of Muslims today. The cultural attaché for #Iran in #Sudan has been closed for leaving its cultural work and inviting people to Shi'ism. #Preventing_Converting_To_Shi'ism_In_Sudan. (https://twitter.com/MohamadAlarefe/status/506792993508978688)
- September 2, 2014 (994 retweets, 284 likes): #Iran has called on them to spread sin in the name of enjoying women! God forbid that Sudan's chaste women see this. #Preventing_Converting_To_Shi'ism_In_Sudan. (https://twitter.com/MohamadAlarefe/status/506882522140385280)
- September 2, 2014 (1,171 retweets, 253 likes): #Iran has called on them to excommunicate Muslims and said that there aren't 1.5 billion Muslims but that instead there aren't more than 53 million Muslims (who are Shi'is). #Preventing_Converting_To_Shi'ism_In_Sudan. (https://twitter.com/MohamadAlarefe/status/506881229330067456)
- August 23, 2014: #Syria: The jihadis thwarted an advance made by the regime's Nusayri army at the #Central_Aleppo_prison. They destroyed a tank and killed 14 Nusayri soldiers and from Hezb al-Lat [Hezbollah], among them a high-ranking officer. (https://twitter.com/MohamadAlarefe/status/503433240749678592)
- October 31, 2013 (tweeted by @YZaatreh, retweeted by @MohamadAlarefe): Iranian tyranny; from Damascus' countryside to other areas in Syria, and even Iraq and Yemen. This won't stop without a Saudi-Turkish understanding, but ... !!! (https://twitter.com/YZaatreh/status/396004385534115840)
- June 6, 2013 (728 retweets, 99 likes): #Hezbollah, the Safavid party, was founded in Lebanon in 1982 and branched out from the Shi'ite movement Amal that killed Muslims in Sabra and Chatila. (https://twitter.com/MohamadAlarefe/status/342696782930780160)
- June 6, 2013 (362 retweets, 47 likes): Hassan Nasr al Lat of #Hezbollah said that the religious source for them was Iran and that gave them a religious and legal cover to fight with

weapons. (https://twitter.com/MohamadAlarefe/status/342698
811757563904)

- June 6, 2013 (455 retweets, 51 likes): Ibrahim al Amine, a leader in
  #Hezbollah, said that they don't consider themselves a part of Iran,
  that instead Iran was Lebanon and Lebanon was Iran. (https://twit-
  ter.com/MohamadAlarefe/status/342699468187107328)

- June 6, 2013 (559 retweets, 65 likes): #Hezbollah has expanded in
  Arab countries, there are branches in Bahrain and Hijaz and Kuwait
  and Yemen and elsewhere that have yet to be discovered! (https://
  twitter.com/MohamadAlarefe/status/342699946878853120)

- June 6, 2013 (382 retweets, 52 likes): Khomeini gave Iranian officials the task of keeping him up to date on the movements of the
  rawafid Safavid work in Lebanon and #Hezbollah leaders are only
  appointed by Iran. (https://twitter.com/MohamadAlarefe/status/
  342700906195865602)

- June 6, 2013 (554 retweets, 76 likes): The previous secretary
  general of #Hezbollah Subhi al Tufaili: Hezbollah is the one
  who guarded the borders of Israel. https://www.youtube.com/
  watch?v=l8emZ60VmEY: *A video of former secretary-general
  of Hezbollah Subhi al-Tufayli in which he says that Hezbollah's
  weapons serve to protect Israel on the border.* (https://twitter.
  com/MohamadAlarefe/status/342701111876145152)

- June 6, 2013 (1,009 retweets, 122 likes): A lot of people are fooled
  by #Hezbollah for three main reasons: ignorance of the Safavid
  rawafid doctrine, Hezbollah's concealment of their actions, and
  their astounding media. (https://twitter.com/MohamadAlarefe/
  status/342701909741801472)

- June 6, 2013 (364 retweets, 49 likes): The Assad regime has
  the ability to arm #Hezbollah politically in Lebanon, so this is
  why the Hezb stands by the regime to day. (https://twitter.com/
  MohamadAlarefe/status/342702445023096832)

- June 6, 2013 (618 retweets, 93 likes): This is #Hezbollah today fighting
  in Syria and Qusayr fighting with the *rawafid* Safavid Iranians and the
  Assad regime all together united in doctrine and hatred. http://arefe.ws/
  twitter/8b6d8a72.jpg: *It links to an image of children's corpses strewn*

across the ground. Their faces are blurred out. (https://twitter.com/
MohamadAlarefe/status/342703175557578752)

- June 5, 2013: After the victory of the Safavid order in Syria,
God forbid, Iran will fight to occupy the Gulf. They see us
as *kafirs* anyway!! (https://twitter.com/MohamadAlarefe/sta-
tus/342231738895966208)

- June 5, 2013: Oh Arab leaders, do you understand the danger of
the situation in #Syria and #Qusayr? If you don't, this is a calamity! And if you do understand, the calamity is bigger! (https://
twitter.com/MohamadAlarefe/status/342190666157285376)

NABIL AL AWADHY

- July 13, 2015 (676 retweets, 293 likes): In only three hours, your
donations have covered 37% of the project #Sponsoring_of_Syrian_
orphans to sponsor 100 orphans. Help us now https://www.alnajat.
org.kw/m/Projects/show/1915 (https://twitter.com/NabilAlawadhy/
status/620725544359866368)

- June 26, 2015 (3,376 retweets, 835 likes): #Bombing_of_AlSadek_
Mosque. A criminal sinful act, whoever did it!! Oh God, punish those
who want what is bad for us, and preserve our security and bring us all
together. Condolences to the families of the victims and the wounded.
(https://twitter.com/NabilAlawadhy/status/614381439669252096)

- August 20, 2013 (5,553 retweets, 373 likes): If they had paid one
tenth of what they have paid to overthrow and kill the people of
#Egypt to the jihadists in Syria, it would have been freed long ago!
But this is the era of betrayal. #Ghouta_is_being_exterminated_
by_chemical_weapons. (https://twitter.com/NabilAlawadhy/sta-
tus/370047172172976128)

- June 24, 2013 (1,277 retwets, 75 likes): Do the Arab people know about the Iranian satellite channels broadcasting
in the Arabic language and Hezb al Shaytan's channels who
are broadcasting via Arabic satellites!! They are fighting you
with your money! (https://twitter.com/NabilAlawadhy/status/
349105826067275776)

- June 24, 2013: Sanioura: "the Army must remove all militants from #Sidon." And what about the areas of Hezb al Shaytan?!! Will you demonstrate your manhood in them too?! (https://twitter.com/NabilAlawadhy/status/3490868442a20215296)
- June 24, 2013 (1,577 retweets, 130 likes): Iran wants to take attention away from Syria and shift it to Lebanon. The head of the snake does not know that Muslims will not give up on Iraq, or Syria, or Lebanon. And Iran will be returned to the Muslims!! (https://twitter.com/NabilAlawadhy/status/349090771653255169)
- June 24, 2013 (678 retweets, 44 likes): The Lebanese Army does not want a truce! And they don't care about the wounded even if they were children or women!! They only answer to and submit to Hezb al Shaytan!! (https://twitter.com/NabilAlawadhy/status/349082008456138752)
- June 24, 2013 (886 retweets, 73 likes): What is strange is the silence of the Arab governments about what is happening in Lebanon!! Have they sold it like they sold Iraq and Syria?!!! (https://twitter.com/NabilAlawadhy/status/349086303670919168)
- June 23, 2013: Since the American invasion of Iraq and it being given to the followers of Iran ... they have been killing Sunnis! And if Sunni people defend themselves, they accuse them of sectarianism and terrorism!! (https://twitter.com/NabilAlawadhy/status/348813218325 6227840)
- June 23, 2013 (1,859 retweets, 96 likes): This is what they have been planning ... after the millions that they have received from governments in the Gulf, the leaders of the Lebanese Army are conspiring with Hezb al Shaytan to kill the Sunni people, beginning with their sheikhs. (https://twitter.com/NabilAlawadhy/status/348810285341085697)
- June 23, 2013 (4,617 retweets, 272 likes): To the governments of the Gulf, where are the billions from your people that you have spent on Lebanon?!! Their weapons are being used against the Sunni people!! As usual, they are killing us with our money!! (https://twitter.com/NabilAlawadhy/status/348810824103624708)

- June 5, 2013 (1,226 retweets, 101 likes): The Muslim leaders have not realized the gravity of the situation. Qusayr is not just a city! This is the start of a dangerous war! Oh God, grant victory to your followers and let down all those who have let them down. (https://twitter.com/NabilAlawadhy/status/342187968859078656)
- June 5, 2013 (2,368 retweets, 136 likes): For your information, you who are the tails of Iran, the Free Syrian Army still controls more than 60% of Syrian land. And God willing, their victory is close. The tyrant will be defeated one day. (https://twitter.com/NabilAlawadhy/status/342201263489953792)
- June 5, 2013 (1,196 retweets, 81 likes): #Qusayr will remain a thorn in their beards. Their doctrinal war will burn them. (https://twitter.com/NabilAlawadhy/status/342203848817004544)
- June 5, 2013: Oh God, we ask you to punish Iran and its followers. Iran stands behind every evil faced by the *ummah* today. Any regime that stands with them is of them! (https://twitter.com/NabilAlawadhy/status/342298517651456001)

DAI AL ISLAM AL SHAHHAL

- December 5, 2013 (1 retweet): We ask not to grant the opportunity to those who want the army to clash with the Sunni people. #Tripoli. (https://twitter.com/Daeislam/status/408721194792521728)
- December 2, 2013 (5 retweets): Mikati sells Tripoli and we can't read this decision as anything but targeting the Sunni sect and especially its stronghold Tripoli and we will work to abort this plan and smash it politically. (https://twitter.com/Daeislam/status/407562390730203136)
- June 23, 2013 (23 retweets, 1 like): #Lebanon falls hour after hour completely in the grip of #Hezb_elLat, and what is dangerous is they are fighting the Sunni people with the hands of the Army, as it appears to us clearly. #Sidon #Tripoli. (https://twitter.com/Daeislam/status/348904537442119680)
- May 17, 2013 (tweeted by @muhanna93, retweeted by Shahhal): The *rawafid* of Qutayf are fighting with Iran and Hezb al Shaytan and Bashar in Syria. And this is the evidence:

https://twitter.com/FSAUnited/status/335473556945244162/ photo/1: *Links to leaflet posted by an FSA Twitter account, which is a death notice for Shi'i fighter who died "defending" the Sayyida Zaynab shrine.* (https://twitter.com/muhanna93/status/335485884344442880)

- January 29, 2013 (39 retweets, 5 likes): The Sunni sect is in need of overcoming personal interest, given that it is targeted politically and security wise from Iranian armed militias in #Lebanon. (https://twitter.com/Daeislam/status/296236047485001729)

- January 29, 2013 (27 retweets, 4 likes): The operation to make #Tripoli arms free will not apply to Jabal Mohsen considering it is a follower of Hezbollah. This operation therefore, will not be successful unless Hezbollah is stripped of its weapons. #Lebanon. (https://twitter.com/Daeislam/status/296239882681073664)

SALEM AL RAFEI

- June 29, 2013 (49 retweets, 2 likes): Haaretz: Iran and Israel are an eternal alliance—Haaretz paper states that Israel needs Iran. . . . http://www.aljazeera.net/news/presstour/2012/8/26/آترس-ناريإ-وإارسيئاي-لحف-يدبأ (https://twitter.com/salemalrafei/status/350876398879117312)

- June 29. 2013 (6 retweets, 1 like): "Hezbollah" removes Syrians from Abra—More than ten Syrians have been stopped by "Hezbollah" during the clashes. . . . fb.me/2FDCbsUOO (https://twitter.com/salemalrafei/status/350880817767120896)

- June 29, 2013 (9 retweets, 1 like): The Muslim Scholars Association from Abra: If those in positions of power do not respond to our demands, we will consider them against the Sunni people in Lebanon and we will declare civil disobedience in all Sunni areas. (https://twitter.com/salemalrafei/status/350945195837239296)

- June 25, 2013 (18 retweets, 2 likes): Dr. Faisal al Kassem: I didn't know Lebanon had an Army until Nahr al Bared Camp was destroyed and when Bilal bin Rabah Mosque was captured in Sidon. (https://twitter.com/salemalrafei/status/349491063855128576)

- June 24, 2013 (3 retweets): Sheikh Salem al Rafei on Al Jazeera in the show *Ma Wara' Al Khabar* live: The state is weak in front of Hezbollah and it only becomes strong when it comes to us. (https://twitter.com/salemalrafei/status/349236879620710401)

- June 24, 2013 (10 retweets): Sheikh Salem al Rafei on the show *Ma Waraa Al Khabar* on Al Jazeera Live: There is a plan to end Assir that came from Hezbollah and it is being implemented by the Army and members of the Hezb and Amal are participating in the bombing and attacking of the Bilal bin Rabah Mosque. (https://twitter.com/salemalrafei/status/349240297303195649)

- June 24, 2013 (5 retweets): *Al Mustaqbal*: The spread of agents for Hezb al Lat at the American Roundabout near Ain al Hilweh Camp. (https://twitter.com/salemalrafei/status/348942171753312256)

- June 24, 2013 (7 retweets, 1 like): *Al Mustaqbal*: 4 dead and 15 injured for Hezb al Lat in clashes in Sidon were moved to the Raii' Hospital and the Hezb is hiding information from security forces. (https://twitter.com/salemalrafei/status/348939920305442816)

- June 18, 2013 (1 retweet): *Al Mustaqbal* Newspaper: 5,000 Shi'a Iraqis fight with the Assad forces—Syrian sources revealed the participation of about.... http://www.almustaqbal.com/v4/Article.aspx?Type=np&Articleid=575630(https://twitter.com/salemalrafei/status/346879891616174080)

- June 5, 2013: Of the positives of the battle of Qusayr: God has exposed Hezb al Shaytan more and more to people who used to believe them. The term Hezb al Shaytan is now replacing Hezbollah all over the world. (https://twitter.com/salemalrafei/status/342362404530819074)

- June 5, 2013 (12 retweets, 2 likes): Qusayr has withstood more than 25 days against Russia, China, Iraq, Iran and Hezb al Shaytan and Bashar's militias and the disappointment of the Arabs!! Of what downfall do they speak!!! (https://twitter.com/salemalrafei/status/342302995993722880)

- June 5, 2013 (1 retweet): They congratulate each other and fire shots into the air in jubilation and they don't know that the battle of Qusayr, for God, was not intended to make the regime fall. Its point was to expose the fake resistance and remove God's name from their party and replace it with the devil. Before Qusayr it was called Hezbollah and before Qusayr it was called a resistance and after it, it has become a terrorist group. Before Qusayr, it defended people and the state, and after it, it became a killer. Its security zones will not remain safe after Qusayr. (https://twitter.com/salemalrafei/status/342401723790422017)

- May 20, 2013 (2 retweets): Qusayr will be your cemetery, Hezb alShaytan.(https://twitter.com/salemalrafei/status/336534687461830660)
- May 19, 2013 (4 retweets): Information about civil disobedience and anger between the people in Dahiye after information about Hezb fighters being wounded in Syria last night. (https://twitter.com/salemalrafei/status/336229704086478848)

BILAL BAROUDI

- November 13, 2013 (4 retweets, 1 like): When will our people in the Gulf realize that the American Iranian bonding happened at the same time Nasrallah threatened the Gulf? They have to change their plans in facing them before they are raided by the plots. (https://twitter.com/AlsalamBilal/status/400717990708396033)
- April 19, 2013 (1 retweet, 1 like): US support for the Syrian opposition includes nonlethal military weapons. Isn't this conditional nonlethal aid strange? Why does the West want to prolong death in Syria? (https://twitter.com/AlsalamBilal/status/325334526840684545)

UTILITARIAN REFERENCES

ADNAN AL AROUR

- January 24, 2015 (639 retweets, 171 likes): Those of you who do well, your money won't go to waste. The heroes of Daraa and Al-Qunaytirah have cut off the biggest road on the occupier. Congratulations to the Syrians and those with them. The victory is big. (https://twitter.com/AdnanAlarour/status/559058262335582208)
- December 29, 2013 (214 retweets, 48 likes): More than 30 journalists have been arrested in Aleppo by ISIS and some of them are journalists for Liwaa al Tawhid while others are journalists for

the Shada channel. I challenge ISIS to prove just one allegation against these people. (https://twitter.com/AdnanAlarour/status/417382117635407873)

- June 6, 2013 (8,158 retweets, 1,267 likes): Whoever wants to support Qusayr and the others with aid and rice and sugar and other things ... and your understanding is sufficient. You can connect with us by phone on 00966598312678/ for after God, we only have you. (https://twitter.com/AdnanAlarour/status/342558612293570560)

- April 12, 2013 (245 retweets, 128 likes): Sheikh Adnan #AlArour talks about the ISIS issue, 2013-4-11: https://www.youtube.com/watch?feature=player_embedded&v=w3Inu8GzccE, #Jabhat_al_Nusra. #Syria. (https://twitter.com/AdnanAlarour/status/322643391689142273)

- April 12, 2013 (130 retweets, 25 likes): Will ISIS unite or create divisions? Should we advise those who wish to divide to be with the ones who want to unite? (https://twitter.com/AdnanAlarour/status/322674518147620864)

- April 11, 2013 (168 retweets, 32 likes): All those who support ISIS and their methods should leave the lands of tyrants and live under them and this is according to their origins. (https://twitter.com/AdnanAlarour/status/322460047995195392)

MOHAMAD AL AREFE

- March 23, 2015 (4,479 retweets, 1,661 likes): Excommunicating believers and finding ways to shed their blood and take their money is a huge crime, so be wary. (https://twitter.com/MohamadAlarefe/status/580046077639835648)

- December 30, 2013 (968 retweets, 159 likes): Our people in #Iraq are in a difficult time, saving them is a duty, they are being killed and are homeless and hungry. (https://twitter.com/MohamadAlarefe/status/417862138750046208/photo/1)

- November 1, 2013 (tweeted by @OmawiLive, retweeted by @MohamadAlarefe): The rawafid assemble Shi'a women whose aim is to provide temporary marriage for Shi'a fighters. #enter-tainment_jihad.pic.twitter.com/h5sHsZ8hNx. It is important to share this picture. (https://twitter.com/OmawiLive/status/396126578578849792)

- October 22, 2013: #Our_prisoners_in_Iraq, a case that needs justice immediately, I thank brother Tamer al Balheed @thamr33 head of the committee for the prisoners for his efforts. (https://twitter.com/MohamadAlarefe/status/392730339635777536)

- October 5, 2013 (862 retweets, 122 likes): Iraqis are our people and their blood runs through our veins. Their history is of bravery, leadership, morals, chivalry and generosity. #The_displacement_of_Sunni_people_in_Iraq. (https://twitter.com/MohamadAlarefe/status/386489045187981312/photo/1)

- October 3, 2013 (tweeted by @alajmi_saad, retweeted by @MohamadAlarefe): A statement from Sheikh Abdallah al Sa'ad about the #forced_displacement_of_the_Sunni_people_in_Iraq. An invitation to unite. http://twitmail.com/email/781004497/16/ (https://twitter.com/alajmi_saad/status/385982103844028416)

- October 1, 2013 (tweeted by @Muslim_LTI, retweeted by @MohamadAlarefe): Statistics: Ethnic cleansing of the Sunni "Arabs" in #Iraq.... Share the tweet as much as you can.... #retweet #share #tweetinaphoto. https://twitter.com/Muslim_LTI/status/385140700263624704/ photo/1 (https://twitter.com/Muslim_LTI/status/385140700263624704)

- June 5, 2013: I will give a sermon this Friday about Syria and the crimes of Hezb al Lat in the past and now, and the crimes of the Safavid *rawafid* in history, and the importance of jihad. (https://twitter.com/MohamadAlarefe/status/342228620254785536)

- June 5, 2013: Don't forget the jihadists of Syria in support and in prayer, from yesterday they have been bombarded with rockets by Iran and Hezb al Lat. (https://twitter.com/MohamadAlarefe/status/342186195566096384)

- May 20, 2013 (3,575 retweets, 277 likes): God grant victory to our people in #Qusayr, Oh God help the fighters persevere and unite the hearts of the people of truth. (https://twitter.com/ MohamadAlarefe/status/336256949010182144)

- May 20, 2013 (743 retweets, 123 likes): God forgive me and them, and give victory to our people in Syria and Qusayr, and everywhere. (https://twitter.com/MohamadAlarefe/status/ 336361635222532096)
- April 26, 2013 (782 retweets, 142 likes): Yes to #justice_for_our_ sons_in_Iraq. Everyone who can help them must exert their full energy in doing so. (https://twitter.com/MohamadAlarefe/status/ 327883460704342018)

NABIL AL AWADHY

- July 13, 2015 (676 retweets, 293 likes): In only three hours, your donations have covered 37% of the project #Sponsoring_of_ Syrian_orphans to sponsor 100 orphans. Help us now. https:// www.alnajat.org.kw/m/Projects/show/1915 (https://twitter.com/ NabilAlawadhy/status/620725544359866368)
- July 13, 2015 (380 retweets, 155 likes): #Al_Najat_Group have a project to sponsor 100 Syrian orphans at the cost of 18,000 dinars. Donations are taken electronically and open to all. https://www.alna-jat.org.kw/m/Projects/show/1915. #Sponsoring_of_Syrian_orphans. (https://twitter.com/NabilAlawadhy/status/620665832385871872)
- July 12, 2015 (370 retweets, 279 likes): Ghars Voluntary Group announces in coordination with Al-Rahma al-Alamiyya (Global Mercy) a project called Bread for Hope to support and give work to refugees. @Ghars_Q8. (https://twitter.com/NabilAlawadhy/sta-tus/620329029451669504)
- April 25, 2015 (1,268 retweets, 423 likes): Yemen is calling for help. Blessed are those who help in feeding the widows and the poor. http://www.khaironline.net/sorry.aspx. #Help_Yemen. (https:// twitter.com/NabilAlawadhy/status/592016493098835968)
- January 7, 2015 (4,820 retweets, 618 likes): #The_cold_in_ Damascus_is_painful. And the refugee children are freezing from the cold. The campaign of Global Mercy, the cost of heating is 30 Kuwaiti dinars. The website is http://www.khaironline.net/

SharedProjects/DonateForSharedProject.aspx. (https://twitter.com/
NabilAlawadhy/status/552914541688786944)

- August 21, 2013 (2,117 retweets, 115 likes): #Ghouta_is_
being_exterminated_by_chemical_weapons The world will keep
watching our *ummah* being killed. Our people must bring victory to one another. (https://twitter.com/NabilAlawadhy/status/
370037534601908225)

- August 21, 2013 (1,925 retweets, 98 likes): Where are the threats of
the lying West if there was going to be a use of chemical weapons?!!
Oh God, we all have no one but You. #Ghouta_chemical_massacre.
#Ghouta_is_being_exterminated_by_chemical_weapons.   (https://
twitter.com/NabilAlawadhy/status/370039972641796096)

- August 21, 2013 (815 retweets, 42 likes): We have no one to rely on God,
but you. #Ghouta_chemical_massacre. #Eastern_Ghouta_massacre.
(https://twitter.com/NabilAlawadhy/status/370043545240883200)

- August 21, 2013 (2,321 retweets, 174 likes): Enemies of the *ummah*
left tyrants to kill their people and burn the state, and they imprisoned a ruler that the people had chosen. Oh God, our own people
are our enemies. #Eastern_Ghouta_massacre. (https://twitter.com/
NabilAlawadhy/status/370045166687502336)

- June 4, 2013: An invitation to attend a symposium tomorrow . . . .
"Hezb al Lat . . . and sectarian terrorism." pic.twitter.com/
I4vIBsCsh5: *Leaflet advertising a discussion by Kuwaiti clerics
on "Hezb al Lat and its sectarian terror."* (https://twitter.com/
NabilAlawadhy/status/341996059859496960)

- March 2, 2013 (357 retweets, 30 likes): Dangerous words from
Sobhi al Tufaili! For your information, he is the founder of what is
called Hezbollah. #Syria. youtu.be/CUETtP-wegM (https://twitter.
com/NabilAlawadhy/status/307943595812462593)

DAI AL ISLAM AL SHAHHAL

- June 28, 2013 (25 retweets, 1 like): Sheikh Shahhal to Annahar: The
anger of the street will continue until we receive the bodies and
the prisoners are released. #Sidon. #Tripoli. #Lebanon. (https://
twitter.com/Daeislam/status/350602478720516096)

- June 24, 2013 (5 retweets, 1 like): I say it honestly they want to humiliate them.... I invite the men of the Sunni sect to unite.... #Tripoli. #Sidon. (https://twitter.com/Daeislam/status/349253957014659073)
- June 24, 2013 (4 retweets, 1 like): I will never forget May 7. I cannot forget my sect. #alShahhal. (https://twitter.com/Daeislam/status/349254343096143873)
- June 24, 2013 (8 retweets, 1 like): #al-Shahhal: Why have four Sheikhs been attacked in Beirut in one day; who is pushing things to escalate?!!! (https://twitter.com/Daeislam/status/349263588101324800)
- June 13, 2013 (2 retweets, 2 likes): A word for the Sheikh Dai al Islam #al-Shahhal in the festival of victory for #Syria in which he speaks about the duty to rescue the Sunni people in Syria. #Cairo. http://t.co/dFH96kFk5x: *A screenshot of a TV from Al Jazeera TV showing a conference for Ulama who want to "bring victory to the Syrian people."* (https://twitter.com/Daeislam/status/345263770165194752)
- June 6, 2013 (series of nine tweets): (1) The developments in #Tripoli are forcing those in positions of responsibility to move fast before the situation deteriorates quickly after which it will be hard to realize #AlShahhal. (2) What is undoubted is that there are sound people in the Army who don't like evil and don't wish it, so it is asked of those not to provide opportunities to the Syrian regime and its allies #AlShahhal. (3) We invite them to hamper the opportunities of the allies of the Syrian regime in Dahiye and in Rabieh and those who try to belittle the organization of the army and its legitimacy #AlShahhal. (4) The allies of the Syrian regime are trying to use the Lebanese Army as much as possible to kill the Sunni people much like the Syria regime is doing to the Syrian people. #Syria #AlShahhal. (5) From here, we ask everyone in the Army and outside it to look at the public interest and to exercise caution.... #Lebanon #Syria #AlShahhal. (6) We don't have much time and may they know that undermining people's dignity and blood in a provocative way is absolutely unacceptable

#AlShahhal. (7) Is the objective to incriminate the Sunnis???!!! And we advise the youth of #Tripoli and elsewhere not to waste their energy. #Lebanon #Syria #AlShahhal. (8) Let's all work to unite our class which our enemies are trying so hard to penetrate and divide, and let all the Sunni people and the youth of Islam cooperate to unite the word. (9) And to bring victory to the vulnerable of our Sunni sect in all #Lebanon and in all organizations and bodies. #Tripoli. (https://twitter.com/Daeislam/status/342690418309349377) (https:// twitter.com/Daeislam/status/342736952530989057 (https://twitter .com/Daeislam/status/342738928710864896) (https://twitter .com/Daeislam/status/342740700833652737) (https://twitter. com/Daeislam/status/342741261951852544) (https://twitter. com/Daeislam/status/342742310519443458 (https://twitter.com/ Daeislam/status/342743352682352640) (https://twitter.com/ Daeislam/status/342744315774263296) (https://twitter.com/ Daeislam/status/342745277008060604160)

- May 23, 2013 (50 retweets, 4 likes): There are strong clashes between the Sunni people in #Tripoli #Lebanon and al Nasiriyyeen (Alawites of Syria). This clash will play a role in determining the balance of power in the region. Your prayers and support. (https:// twitter.com/Daeislam/status/337695454483578880)
- May 22, 2013 (81 retweets, 10 likes): I sent my son to #Qusayr for victory or martyrdom. But what is being rumored about his martyrdom isn't true, for he is in good health fighting the enemy as best he can. #AlShahhal. (https://twitter.com/Daeislam/status/ 337234617063063553)
- February 3, 2013 (tweeted by @dr-aboubakr, retweeted by Shahhal): Save #Arsal from the conspiracy of Hezbollah and the regime in #Syria. Save the #Sunni people in #Lebanon @sonnaleb3. (https://twitter.com/dr_aboubakr/status/298132288389124096)

SALEM AL RAFEI

- July 2, 2013 (19 retweets, 3 likes): Sheikh Salem al Rafei: the Army is colluding with "Hezbollah" to kill the Sunni people, and does the Army allow itself to call on a militia against the Sunnis? Does this Army respect itself? (https://twitter.com/salemalrafei/status/352021692182310913)

- July 2, 2013 (15 retweets, 3 likes): A new scandal: New evidence and testimony of Abra residents confirms Hezb Iran bombs Bilal bin Rabah and its surrounding area. https://www.youtube.com/watch?v=HS5enoXN1Jw: *A TV report from LBC on the Abra clashes interviewing a resident who said that Hezbollah militants came to his house during the Abra clashes and told him they were from Hezbollah.* (https://twitter.com/salemalrafei/status/352161897958748160)

- June 29, 2013 (53 retweets, 4 likes): The Association of Muslim Scholars: We say to each Muslim not to turn themselves in to the security forces should they request, so you don't die under torture in their prisons. (https://twitter.com/salemalrafei/status/350976308567752707)

- June 29, 2013 (81 retweets, 11 likes): Association of Muslim Scholars: After the facts, photos and live testimonies were taken from the people in Saidon, members of Hezb Iran were implicated fb.me/3029f1Sru (https://twitter.com/salemalrafei/status/350979233264316416)

- June 28, 2013 (10 retweets, 3 likes): Sheikh Salem al Rafei, may God preserve him, speaks today: the second message to "Hezbollah:" We say to Hezb al Shaytan: your leader.... fb.me/6nJVxH65S (https://twitter.com/salemalrafei/status/350639700601602049)

- June 28, 2013 (5 retweets, 1 like): Sheikh Salem al Rafei, may God preserve him, directs a message to the youth: when defending the honor of the Sunnis, we will be in the front lines and you will not accept any less from us. (https://twitter.com/salemalrafei/status/350580654020370433)

- June 28, 2013 (8 retweets, 2 likes): A message to the Lebanese Army: We say to the Lebanese Army that "Hezbollah" has publically [sic] declared war on Sunnis in Syria and it appears that fb.me/HPUB4TGG (https://twitter.com/salemalrafei/status/350628731733286913)

- June 9, 2013: A message to those not going to jihad after the massacres of the regime in Qusayr and Banyas and after the raising of Shiite flags in Qusayr.... fb.me/M7tSZITk (https://twitter.com/salemalrafei/status/343652414496329729)
- June 5, 2013: A large and angry protest is taking place in Ain al Hilweh at this time to protest the Hezb al Shaytan's killing of our people in Syria. (https://twitter.com/salemalrafei/status/342345668494520320)
- June 4, 2013: MTV: "Hezbollah" raises the amount of compensation ... 50 thousand for each one killed. (https://twitter.com/salemalrafei/status/341807771857080320)
- May 19, 2013: Information says: Tens of wounded for the Iranian Hezb al Shaytan in hospitals in Beqaa and Beirut and their Facebook pages are asking for blood types of all kinds. And it is said that the biggest leaders of the Hezb have gone to the Lebanese Syrian borders to raise the morale of the killers. (https://www.facebook.com/sheikhsalemrafei/posts/658554070825608)
- May 19, 2013 (3 retweets, 1 like): Breaking news: Our heroes in Qusayr are dealing with the most gruesome of battles with the regime and Hezb al Lat. (https://twitter.com/salemalrafei/status/336064514703388674)

BILAL BAROUDI

- December 28, 2013 (2 retweets, 1 like): Our battle is a battle of existence and presence and identity, our existence is in our principles, our presence is in our stances, and our identity is in our pride of belonging. He who loses his identity has no existence or presence. (https://twitter.com/AlsalamBilal/status/417022607549300736)
- June 28, 2013 (37 retweets, 6 likes): He who thinks that the campaign in Sidon is to clamp down on the phenomenon on Ahmad al Assir is blind. It is a campaign that began in the streets of Baghdad and its last stop is Mecca. Wake up!! (https://twitter.com/AlsalamBilal/status/350587981431701505)

- June 8, 2013 (1 retweet): http://www.masjedalsalam.com/node/194: Friday's sermon from Salam Mosque entitled: Who fell in Qusayr?? For Sheikh Bilal Baroudi. (https://twitter.com/AlsalamBilal/status/343558482521382912)

- March 1, 2013: @lordonasis http://www.masjed- alsalam.com/node/183: This week's Friday sermon entitled: Who is seeking sedition? For Sheikh Bilal Baroudi from Salam Mosque. (https://twitter.com/AlsalamBilal/status/307461793658322944)

- February 9, 2013 (tweeted by @YZaatreh, retweeted by Bilal Baroudi): Nouri al Maliki: "The Alawites in Syria are fighting with their women and men in order to stay." An open incitement for them to keep on killing. This is rudeness and hostility towards the Syrian people. (https://twitter.com/YZaatreh/status/300195999530491904)

- January 12, 2013: http://www.masjedalsalam.com/ node/177: Friday's sermon for Sheikh Bilal Baroudi from Salam Mosque entitled: This Is Hezbollah. (https://twitter.com/AlsalamBilal/status/290173205023432706)

NOTES

INTRODUCTION

1. It should be noted here that the Shi'a, who only emerged in any meaningful sense well after the death of their own champion Ali ibn Abi Talib, the last of the four *Rashidun*, reject any notion of a Rightly Guided Caliphate.

2. Naser Ghobadzdeh and Shahram Akbarzadeh. "Sectarianism and the Prevalence of 'Othering' in Islamic Thought," *Third World Quarterly* 36 (2016): 700.

3. Max Weiss, *In the Shadow of Sectarianism: Law, Shi'ism and the Making of Modern Lebanon* (Cambridge: Harvard University Press, 2010), 12.

4. Graham Fuller and Rend Rahim Francke, *The Arab Shi'a: The Forgotten Muslims* (New York: St. Martin's Press, 1999), 55.

5. Weiss, *In the Shadow of Sectarianism*, 187.

6. Pew Forum on Religion and Public Life. "The World's Muslims: Unity and Diversity," PewForum.org (August 9, 2012), http://www.pewforum.org/Muslim/the-worlds-muslims-unity-and-diversity-executive-summary.aspx. In this context, it is worth noting that the rhetoric of militant Sunni movements, such as al Qaeda, reserve at least as much venom for the Shi'a as they do for America and its allies.

7. Ibid.

8. Erling Ladewig Petersen, *Ali and Muawiya in Early Arab Tradition: Studies on the Genesis and Growth of Islamic Historical Writing Until the End of the Ninth Century* (Copenhagen: Munksgaard, 1964), 177–179.

9. Yitzhak Nakash, *Reaching for Power: The Shi'a in the Modern Arab World* (Princeton: Princeton University Press, 2006), 18–19.

10. Wael B. Hallaq, *The Impossible State: Islam, Politics, and Modernity's Moral Predicament* (New York: Columbia University Press, 2013), 51.

11. Ibid., 50–52.

12. Pew Research Center, "The Future of the Global Muslim Population: Projections for 2010-2030," http://www.pewforum.org/files/2011/01/FutureGlobalMuslimPopulation-WebPDF-Feb10.pdf.

13. Fuller and Rahim Francke, *The Arab Shi'a*, 10.

14. Petersen, *Ali and Muawiya in Early Arab Tradition*, 13.

CHAPTER I

1. M. Litvak, "Madrasa and Learning in 19th-Century Najaf and Karbala," in *The Twelver Shi'a in Modern Times, Religious, Cultural and Political History*, ed. Rainer Brunner and Werner Ende (Leiden: Brill, 2001), 58–59, 70.

2. Ibid.

3. For a discussion of Iranian clerical opposition to Khomeini's notion of *velayat-e faqih*, see Geneive Abdo and Jonathan Lyons, *Answering Only to God: Faith and Freedom in 21st-Century Iran* (New York: Henry Holt, 2003), 19–55.

4. Video of al Karbalai reading the fatwa, https://www.youtube.com/watch?=m6dsSEDSjQ.

5. The complete text of the statement, http://www.sistani.org/Arabic/archive/24915/.

6. http://www.iraqinews.com/features/0-000-volunteers-respond-to-sistani-s-fatwa/.

7. http://www.bbc.com/arabic/multimedia/2014/06/140619_iraq_Shi'a_volunteers.

8. Interviews with author in 2014 and 2015.

9. Ibid.

10. Fanar Haddad, *Shi'a-Centric State Building and Sunni Rejection in Post-2003 Iraq* (Washington, DC: Carnegie Endowment for International Peace, 2015), 1.

11. Ibid., 6.

12. Fanar Haddad, *The Hashd: Redrawing the Military and Political Map of Iraq* (Washington: Middle East Institute, April 9, 2015),

http://musingsoniraq.blogspot.com/2015/05/will-hashd-al-shaabi-change-face-of.html.

13. Interview with author, Najaf, November 2015.

14. http://alhayat.com/Articles/8395991/-تجاوز-عراقي-باسيج--في-العراق--الشعبي-الحشد .فتوى--الجهاد-الكفائي-.

15. http://www.aljazeera.net/encyclopedia/movementsandparties/2015/3/9/الحشد-الشعبي.

16. http://a lhayat.com/Articles/8395991/-تجاوز-عراقي-باسيج--في-العراق--الشعبي-الحشد .فتوى--الجهاد-الكفائي-.

17. Adnan Abu Zeed, "Controversy Surrounds Alleged Violations of Shiite Forces in Tikrit," *Al Monitor*, April 23, 2015, http://www.al-monitor.com/pulse/originals/2015/04/iraq-tikrit-liberation-popular-mobilization-violations.html.

18. Interview with author, April 2015.

19. Amnesty International, *Absolute Impunity: Militia Rule in Iraq* (London, 2014), 4.

20. Ibid., 6.

21. http://www.al-monitor.com/pulse/originals/2015/03/iraq-sistani-righteous-jihad-fatwa-popular-mobilization.html.

22. http://a lhayat.com/Articles/8395991/-تجاوز-عراقي-باسيج--في-العراق--الشعبي-الحشد .فتوى--الجهاد-الكفائي-.

23. http://www.al-monitor.com/pulse/originals/2015/03/iraq-sistani-righteous-jihad-fatwa-popular-mobilization.html.

24. http://a lhayat.com/Articles/8395991/-تجاوز-عراقي-باسيج--في-العراق--الشعبي-الحشد .فتوى--الجهاد-الكفائي-.

25. Dexter Filkins, "The Shadow Commander," *The New Yorker*, September 30, 2013.

26. http://a lhayat.com/Articles/8395991/-تجاوز-عراقي-باسيج--في-العراق--الشعبي-الحشد .فتوى--الجهاد-الكفائي-.

27. http://www.aljazeera.com/news/middleeast/2014/06/mapping-out-iraq-fighting-groups-201462494731548175.html.

28. Official statement, http://www.newsalgalibon.net/index.php/2013-02-26-22-41-36/2013-02-26-22-42-13/3148-2014-06-24-06-51-55.html.

29. http://raseef22.com/politics/2015/02/25/iraqi-militias-identity-and-affiliation/.

30. Faleh A. Jabar, *The Shi'ite Movement in Iraq* (London: Saqi Books, 2003), 15.

31. Benedict Anderson, *Imagined Communities* (London: Verso, 2006), 11.

32. Cited in Mahmoud Ayoub, *Redemptive Suffering in Islam: A Study of the Devotional Aspects of Ashura in Twelver Shi'ism* (The Hague: Mouton, 1978), 118–119.

33. Heinz Halm, *Shi'ism*, 2nd ed., trans. Janet Watson and Marian Hall (Edinburgh: Edinburgh University Press, 2004), 6.

34. Ibid., 16.

35. Quoted in Ayoub, *Redemptive Suffering in Islam*, 58.

36. Islam reveres Jesus, along with the other Biblical prophets, but rejects his deification, as well as the Christian concept of the Trinity, which in Muslim eyes smacks of the sin of polytheism.

37. Graham E. Fuller and Rend Rahim Francke, *The Arab Shi'a: The Forgotten Muslims* (New York: St. Martin's Press, 1999), 18.

38. Andrew Newman, *The Formative Period of Twelver Shi'ism: Hadith Discourse between Qum and Baghdad* (Richmond, UK: Curzon Press, 2000), 1.

39. John Obert Voll, *Islam: Continuity and Change in the Modern World* (Syracuse: Syracuse University Press, 1994), 19.

40. Abdo and Lyons, *Answering Only to God*, 27–29.

41. Interview with author, Najaf, November 2015.

CHAPTER 2

1. Interview with author, Cairo, November 2012.

2. Quintan Wiktorowicz, "Anatomy of the Salafi Movement," *Studies in Conflict and Terrorism* 29 (2006): 207, note 1.

3. Ahmad Moussalli, "Wahhabism, Salfism, and Islamism: Who Is the Enemy?" *Conflicts Forum*, January (2009).

4. For example, Wiktorowicz ("Anatomy of the Salafi Movement") divides global Salafists into "purists, politicos, and jihadis" (209–239). See also Christopher M. Blanchard, "The Islamic Tradition of Wahhabism and Salafiyya," Congressional Research Service, RS21695 (Routledge: Taylor and Francis Group, January 25, 2006).

5. Wiktorowicz, "Wahhabism, Salfism, and Islamism," 208.

6. Cited in Bernard Haykel, "On the Nature of Salafi Thought and Action," in *Global Salafism: Islam's New Religious Movement*, ed. Roel Meijer (New York: Columbia University Press, 2009), 34.

7. Wiktorowicz, "Wahhabism, Salfism, and Islamism: Who is the Enemy?," 219.

8. Roel Meijer, "Introduction," in *Global Salafism: Islam's New Religious Movement*, ed. Roel Meijer (New York: Columbia University Press, 2009), 4.

9. Ibid., 42.

10. Haykel, "On the Nature of Salafi Thought and Action," 36.

11. Mohammad 'Ibn Abd al Wahhab, al Radd 'alaal'rafida, quoted in Guido Steinberg, "Jihadi-Salafism and the Shi'is," in *Global Salafism: Islam's New Religious Movement*, ed. Roel Meijer (New York: Columbia University Press, 2009), 113.

12. Guido Steinberg, "Jihadi-Salafism and the Shi'is," 113.

13. Ali Abdallah, "Salafiyyaa Sooryawal Thawra [Syria's Salafists and the Revolution]," *Al Jumhuriya*, last modified December 12, 2013, http://therepublicgs.net/2013/12/12/.

14. Laurence Louer, *Transnational Shi'a Politics: Religious and Political Networks in the Gulf* (New York: Columbia University Press, 2008), 196–197.

15. Ibid.

16. Ali Abdel-Aal, "Salafiyyat Lubnan … Al Nasha'awal Tatawor [Lebanese Salafism … Foundation and Development]," March 2010, http://lojainiat.com/main/Content.

17. Ibid.

18. Ibid.

19. Ibid.

20. Ibid.

21. Mohammad M. Alloush, "Waqe' al Salafiyya fi Lubnan [The Salafist Reality in Lebanon]," *Al Jumhuriya*, September 8, 2012, http://therepublicgs.net/2013/12/12/.

22. Yehya al Kobeissi, "Al Salafiyya fil Iraq: Takalobat al Dakhelwa Tajathobat al Kharej [Salafism in Iraq: Internal Vicissitudes and External Enticements]," (Doha: Al Jazeera Center for Studies, May 6, 2013), 5, http://studies.aljazeera.net/ResourceGallery/media/Documents/2013/5/6/201356103854252734Salafism%20in%20Iraq.pdf.

23. Ibid., 9, 11.

24. Ibid., 8.

25. Ibid.
26. Interview with author, Amman, Jordan, 2014.
27. Sabbah Yassin, interview with the author, Amman, Jordan, October 2014.
28. http://studies.aljazeera.net/en/events/2014/01/201412194433987696.htm.

CHAPTER 3

1. "Hiwar Shabakat Alloukehmaa' Fadilat al Shaykh Dai al Islam al Shahhal [Alloukeh Network's Conversation with Sheikh Dai al Islam al Shahhal]," *Alukah*, February 10, 2011, http://www.alukah.net/world_muslims/0/29541/.
2. Omayma Abdel-Latif, "Lebanon's Sunni Islamists: A Growing Force," no. 6 (Washington, DC: Carnegie Endowment for International Peace, 2008).
3. Nour Samaha, "Lebanon's Sunnis Search for a Savior," Al Jazeera, June 15, 2013, http://www.aljazeera.com/indepth/features/2013/06/201361511501527272727.html.
4. Marc Lynch, Deen Freelon, and Sean Aday, "Syria's Socially Mediated Civil War," *Peaceworks* 91 (2014), 27.
5. Oliver Roy, *Globalized Islam: The Search for a New Ummah* (New York: Columbia University Press, 2006), 113.
6. It is worth noting here that the Shi'a, too, feel historical grievances, as well as the effects of being a perennial minority, albeit a considerable one, within the larger *ummah*. It is not for nothing that the ruling Iranian clerics remind their fellow believers regularly that this struggle is as real today as it was centuries ago, when proto-Sunni forces slaughtered Imam Hussein, the younger son of Ali and champion of what would become the Shi'a, as summed up in the common slogan, "Every day is Karbala."
7. Adnan al Arour, Twitter Post, November 14, 2013, https://twitter.com/AdnanAlarour/status/401055389430468608. Here, al Arour is mocking the Third Imam of the Shi'a, Hussein, whose martyrdom at Karbala in 680 helped transform proto-Shi'a dissenters into a distinct Muslim sect. According to the Shi'a, Hussein knowingly went to his death at the

hands of the overwhelming forces of the Sunni Caliph. The motif of the unwinnable, but noble, struggle is integral to the Shi'a worldview.

8. Ibn Marjana is another name for Ubaydullah bin Ziyad, who helped prepare the Sunni army to fight Hussein at Karbala.

9. Abdul Rahman Dimashqiah, Twitter Post, August 17, 2013, https://twitter.com/DrDimashqiah/status/368508952629104640.

10. Salem al Rafei, Twitter Post, June 4, 2013, https://twitter.com/salem-alrafei/status/341959698918027267.

11. Mohammad al Arefe, Twitter Post, June 6, 2013, https://twitter.com/MohamadAlarefe/status/342700307639332864.

12. Mohammad al Arefe, Twitter Post, June 5, 2013, https://twitter.com/MohamadAlarefe/status/342231738895966208.

13. http://www.arabnews.com/node/402266.

14. Official website of Sheikh Mohammad A. Al-Areefi, last modified 2013, http://arefe.ws/ar/index.php?com=content&id=1.

15. Excerpt from a Friday sermon by Mohammad al Arefe: "Saudi Cleric Muhammad Al-Arifi Vilifies Shiites, Calling Iraqi Ayatollah Sistani 'an Infidel,' " MEMRI, December 11, 2009, http://www.memritv.org/clip_transcript/en/2336.htm.

16. "Sheikh Mohammad al Arefe: The Problem of the Shiites and Sunnis," YouTube, May 15, 2011, https://www.youtube.com/watch?v=bavl3Y_LS78.

17. Mohammad al Arefe, Twitter Post, December 31, 2013, https://twitter.com/KhalidALbakr/status/417958865318060032.

18. Official website of Sheikh Mohammad A. Al-Areefi.

19. "Fight or Flight? Saudi Cleric Heads to London After Call for Jihad in Syria," *Al Arabiya*, June 22, 2013, http://english.alarabiya.net/en/News/middle-east/2013/06/22/Fight-or-flight-Saudi-cleric-heads-to-London-after-calling-for-Jihad-in-Syria.html.

20. Cahal Milmo, "Sunni vs. Shi'a ... in Gerrard's Cross: New Mosque Highlights Growing Tensions Among British Muslims," *The Independent*, June 24, 2013, lhttp://www.independent.co.uk/news/uk/home-news/sunni-vs-Shi'a-in-gerrards-cross-new-mosque-highlights-growing- tensions-among-british-muslims-8671969.htm.

21. Jessica Elgot, "Controversial Saudi Preacher Mohammad Al-Arefe Denies Anti-Shi'a Stance and Defends UK Visit," *Huffington Post*

UK, June 28, 2013, http://www.huffingtonpost.co.uk/2013/06/28/mohammad-al-arefe_n_3517727.html.

22. "Does Islam Allow Men to Beat Their Wives, Explained by Mohammad al Arifi," YouTube, May 14, 2009, http://www.youtube.com/watch?v=klSeoGY4jqE.

23. "Sheikh Mohammad al-Arefe: Why Did Aisha Get Married So Young?" YouTube, March 7, 2013, http://www.youtube.com/watch?v=-jDHnRRDE.

24. "Al Arefe Prohibits Girls from Sitting Alone with their Fathers," YouTube, April 19, 2011, http://www.youtube.com/watch?v=HUdLtIJ4YnA.

25. "Top Saudi Cleric Says Twitter Is for Clowns," Al Jazeera, March 24, 2013, http://www.aljazeera.com/news/middlee-ast/2013/03/20133246150585567.html.

26. Adnan al Arour, Twitter Post, June 6, 2013, https://twitter.com/AdnanAlarour/status/342558612293570560.

27. Ibid.

28. "Sheikh al Arour Challenges the Shi'a with Three Questions," YouTube, March 9, 2013, https://www.youtube.com/watch?v=OGKoO2dTcBw.

29. Adnan al Arour, Twitter Post, August 31, 2013, https://twitter.com/AdnanAlarour/status/373588010132328448.

30. Adnan al Arour, Twitter Post, May 23, 2013, https://twitter.com/AdnanAlarour/status/337681942671683584.

31. Adnan al Arour, Twitter Post, May 26, 2013, https://twitter.com/AdnanAlarour/status/338741253950808064.

32. Adnan al Arour, Twitter Post, May 26, 2013, https://twitter.com/AdnanAlarour/status/338740597286375424.

33. Adnan al Arour, Twitter Post, January 1, 2014, https://twitter.com/AdnanAlarour/status/418457033759653888.

34. Salman al Odah, Twitter Post, February 26, 2015, https://twitter.com/salman_alodah/status/571025969927958528.

35. http://www.nytimes.com/2014/04/05/world/middleeast/conservative-saudi-cleric-salman-al-awda.html?_r=0.

36. Forum post about Nabil al Awadhy on Badiouh.com, http://www.badiouh.com/vb/showthread.php?t=9471.

37. Elizabeth Dickinson, "Shaping the Syrian Conflict from Kuwait," *Foreign Policy*, December 4, 2013.

38. Nabil al Awadhy, Twitter Post, June 22, 2013, https://twitter.com/NabilAlawadhy/status/348559685491761152.

39. "Sheikh Nabil al Awadi Accounts the Rulers of the Muslims for Their Betrayal against Syrians," YouTube, August 30, 2012, https://www.youtube.com/watch?v=JccjmC1tmrU#t=70.

40. "World Famous Sheikh Nabeel al Awadi: Syria Is a Sign of a Coming Great Change," Nahda Productions, March 14, 2012, http://nahdaproductions.org/islamic-revival/arab-world/item/573-world-famous-sh-nabeel-alawadi-syria-is-a-sign-of-a-coming-great-change-beautiful-words.

41. "Man Howwa Al Shaykh Nabil al Awadhy [Who Is Sheikh Nabil Al Awadhy?]," Google Answers (Arabic), August 19, 2011, http://ejabat.google.com/ejabat/thread?tid=49b46c7004a0db06.

42. "Sirat Al Shaykh Nabil al Awadhy [Sheikh Nabil Awadhy's Biography]," Mohazarat.net, http://www.mohazarat.net.qa/in- dex21.htm.

43. See, for example, Sami Alrabaa, "Radical Muslim Chaplains Root Cause of Islamic Fanaticism and Terror," Islam-Watch.org, February 14, 2009, http://www.islam-watch.org/Sami/Radical-Muslim-Chaplains-Islamic-Fanaticism-and-Terror.htm.

44. Nabil al Awadhy, Twitter Post, June 5, 2013, https://twitter.com/NabilAlawadhy/status/342203848817004544.

45. Nabil al Awadhy, Twitter Post, June 23, 2013, https://twitter.com/NabilAlawadhy/status/348813218325622784O.

46. Nabil al Awadhy, Twitter Post, June 24, 2013, https://twitter.com/NabilAlawadhy/status/349090771653255169.

47. Abdel-Latif, "Lebanon's Sunni Islamists," 13.

48. "Scores Dead in North Lebanon Twin Blasts," Al Jazeera, last modified August 24, 2013, http://www.aljazeera.com/news/middleeast/2013/08/201382311249855388.html.

49. Antoine Amrieh and Mohammed Zaataril, "Soldiers Killed in Akkar After Tripoli Protests," *The Daily Star*, April 9, 2014, http://www.dailystar.com.lb/News/Lebanon-News/2014/Apr-09/252760-soldiers-killed-in-akkar-after-tripoli-protests. ashx#axzz3HTJnuejM.

50. Ibid.

51. "Lebanon's Armed Forces Under Fire," *The Economist*, April 15, 2014, http://www.economist.com/blogs/pomegranate/2014/04/lebanons-armed-forces.

52. "Machnouk, Salafist Sheikh Discuss Tripoli Security," *The Daily Star*, April 4, 2014, http://www.dailystar.com.lb/News/Lebanon-News/2014/Apr-04/252284-army-makes-more-arrests-in-tripoli.ashx.

53. "Salafist Leader Says Won't Abandon Syrian Rebels," *The Daily Star*, April 6, 2012, https://www.google.com/?gws_rd=ssl#q=%E2%80%9CSalafist+Leader+Says+Won%E2%80%99t+Abandon+Syrian+Rebels%2C%E2%80%9D+.

54. Tim Whewell, "Lebanese Families Drawn into Syrian Conflict," BBC, June 18, 2013. http://www.bbc.com/news/world-middle-east-22938132.

55. "Al Shahhal Denies Call for Jihad, Says Salafists Pose No Threat," Naharnet, March 8, 2013, http://m.naharnet.com/stories/en/74768-al-shahhal-denies-calls-for-jihad-says-salafists-pose-no-threat.

56. Radwan Mortada, "Lebanon: Rival Salafist Sheikhs Seek Unity," *Al Akhbar*, April 1, 2013, http://english.al-akhbar.com/node/15405.

57. Abdel-Latif, "Lebanon's Sunni Islamists," 17.

58. Lucy Fielder, "Tripoli Rumbles On," *Al Ahram*, August 2008, http://weekly.ahram.org.eg/2008/911/re4.htm.

59. Ahmad Moussalli, "Wahhabism, Salfism, and Islamism: Who Is the Enemy?" *Conflicts Forum*, January (2009).

60. "Speech of Sheikh Salem al Rafei at the Iraqi Spring Festival," YouTube, April 5, 2013, https://www.youtube.com/watch?v=tY9Hrhwqfog.

61. "Salem al Rafei for Annahar: Phenomenon of the Captive Sheikh and the Elimination of Presence in Tripoli," Annahar, June 25, 2013, http://www.annahar.com/article/44388.

62. "Death Toll Rises to 42 in Tripoli, Lebanon Explosions," *Ya Libnan*, August 23, 2013.

63. Mariam Kharouny and Alasdair MacDonald, "Sermons on Syria Fan Mideast Sectarian Flames," Reuters, June 7, 2013, http://www.reuters.com/article/2013/06/07/us-syria-crisis-muslims-idUSBRE95613320130607.

64. "At a Tripoli Blast Site, Residents Shoulder State's Burden," *Syria Deeply*, August 26, 2013, http://beta.syriadeeply.org/2013/08/tripoli-blast-site-residents-shoulder-states-burden-2/.

CHAPTER 4

1. Interviews with author 2014 and 2015, Tripoli and Beirut.

2. Interview with author, Beirut, February 2015.

3. Bassel F. Salloukh, Rabie Barakat, Jinan S. al Habbal, Lara W. Khattab, and Shoghig Mikaelian, *The Politics of Sectarianism in Postwar Lebanon* (London: Pluto Press, 2015), 156.

4. Interview with author, Beirut, February 2016.

5. Ben Hubbard, "Saudis Cut Off Funding for Military Aid to Lebanon," *New York Times*, February 19, 2016, http://www.nytimes.com/2016/02/20/world/middleeast/saudis-cut-off-funding-for-military-aid-to-lebanon.html.

6. "Sixteenth Annual Report of the Secretary-General to the Security Council on the Implementation of Security Council Resolution 1559," October 17, 2012, http://www.un.org/ga/search/view_doc.asp?symbol=S/2012/773.

7. *Al Akbar*, May 21, 2012.

8. Interview with the author, Beirut, June 2012.

9. Interview with the author, Jabal Mohsen, June 2012.

10. Ibid.

11. Samia Nakhoul, "Analysis: Killing of Security Chief Raises Fears for Lebanon," Reuters, October 21, 2012, http://www.reuters.com/article/2012/10/21/us-lebanon-explosion-turmoil-idUSBre89K0DV20121021.

12. Nadine Elahi, "Nothing Will Be the Same," *Now Lebanon*, October 25, 2012, https://now.mmedia.me/lb/en/reportsfeatures/nothing_will_be_the_same.

13. "Hezbollah Denies Responsibility for Killing Hassan," *Ya Liban*, October 20, 2012, http://www.yalibnan.com/2012/10/20/hizbollah-denies-responsibility-for-killing-hassan/.

14. "Tripoli Death Toll Rises to 12," *Al Akbar*, August 21, 2012.

15. Imad Salamey, "The Double Movement & Post-Arab Spring Consociationalism," *Muslim World* 106(1) (2016): 187–204.

16. Hassan Nasrallah, quoted by BBC World News, July 3, 2011.

17. Hilal Khashan, "Hezbollah's Plans for Lebanon," *The Middle East Quarterly* Spring (2013): 81–86.

18. Quoted in Hilal Kashan, "Will Syria's Strife Rip Lebanon Apart?" *The Middle East Quarterly* 20 (2013): 79.

19. Interview with the author, Beirut, June 27, 2012.

20. Kamal S. Salibi famously applied this Biblical reference, taken from John 14:2, to Lebanon's patchwork of religious and ethnic groups. See his *A House of Many Mansions: The History of Lebanon Reconsidered* (Berkeley: University of California Press, 1990).

21. The Jafari School of Law is followed by most Shi'a. It takes its name from Jafar al Sadeq, the Sixth Imam of the Twelver Shi'a.

22. Max Weiss, *In the Shadow of Sectarianism: Law, Shi'ism, and the Making of Modern Lebanon* (Cambridge: Harvard University Press, 2010), 187.

23. Given the sensitivities in Lebanon to identity politics, it is little wonder that no official census that would define citizens by religion or sect has been carried out since the 1932 survey.

24. Yitzak Nakash, *Reaching for Power: The Shi'a in the Modern Arab World* (Princeton: Princeton University Press, 2006), 105.

25. Ibid., 114.

26. Graham E. Fuller and Rend Rahim Francke, *The Arab Shi'a: The Forgotten Muslims* (New York: Palgrave, 2001), 204.

27. Ibid., 209.

28. Hezbollah officials declined to be interviewed for this project. E-mail message, Beirut, June 2012.

29. Afif Diab, "Bekaa Salafi Leader: Wishing to Build Bridges," *Al Akhbar*, October 12, 2012.

30. Anonymous, interview with the author, Beirut, June 2012.

31. Interview with the author, Beirut, June 25, 2012.

32. Interview with author, Tripoli, June 2015.

33. International Crisis Group, "Tentative Jihad: Syria's Fundamentalist Opposition," CrisisGroup.org, October 12, 2012, http://www.crisis-group.org/en/regions/middle-east-north-africa/egypt-syria-lebanon/syria/131-tentative-jihad-syrias-fundamentalist-opposition.aspx.

34. The irony of this strategy is that the Salafists generally do not recognize the Alawites as Muslims, yet they use Alawite behavior in Syria to generalize about the latent intentions of all Shi'a Muslims. Of course, the more radical among them do not accept the Shi'a either.

35. Interview with the author, Tripoli, June 2012.

36. Interview with the author, Tripoli, September 27, 2012.

37. "Islamic Thoughts," May 30, 2011, http://www.youtube.com/watch ?v=DPeArLcjrv8&feature=related.

38. "ShamNews24," May 13, 2012, http://www.youtube.com/ watch?v=2GIe29pKA_8&feature=related.

39. Interview with the author, Sidon, June 2012.

40. Interview with the author, Beirut, June 2012.

41. Mohammad Zaatari, "Search Warrants Issued against Assir Supporters," *The Daily Star,* November 20, 2012, http://www.dai-lystar.com.lb/News/Politics/2012/Nov-20/195600-search-warrants-issued-against-assir-supporters.ashx#axzz2CfzqIhx.

42. Bernard Rougier, *Everyday Jihad: The Rise of Militant Islam Among Palestinians in Lebanon* (Cambridge: Harvard University Press, 2007), 31–32.

43. Interview with the author, Sidon, September 29, 2012.

44. Interview with the author, Beirut, September 2012.

CHAPTER 5

1. http://www.state.gov/documents/organization/236806.pdf.

2. Graham E. Fuller and Rend Rahim Francke, *The Arab Shi'a: The Forgotten Muslims* (New York: St. Martin's Press, 1999), 121.

3. Ibid.

4. Ibid.

5. "Report of the Bahrain Independent Commission of Inquiry," 26.

6. Fuller and Francke, *The Arab Shi'a*, 126–27.

7. International Crisis Group, "Bahrain's Sectarian Challenge," Crisisgroup. org, May 6, 2005, http://www.crisisgroup.org/en/publication-type/media-releases/2005/mena/bahrains-sectarian-challenge.aspx.

8. Luay Bahry, "The Socioeconomic Foundations of the Shiite Opposition in Bahrain," *Mediterranean Quarterly* 11 (2000): 131.

9. International Crisis Group, "Popular Protests in North Africa and the Middle East (III): The Bahrain Revolt," *Middle East/North Africa Report* 105 (2011): 2.

10. Ibid.

11. Bahry, "The Socioeconomic Foundations of the Shiite Opposition in Bahrain," 131.

12. Human Rights Watch, "Routine Abuse, Routine Denial: Civil Rights and the Political Crisis in Bahrain," hrW.org, 1997, http://www.hrw.org/reports/1997/07/01/routine-abuse-routine-denial.

13. Fuller and Francke, *The Arab Shi'a*, 135.

14. King Hamad bin Isa al Khalifa, "Stability Is a Prerequisite for Progress," *Washington Times*, February 8, 2011, http://www.washingtontimes.com/news/2011/apr/19/stability-is-prerequisite-for-progress/.

15. The Center for the Preserving and Publishing the Works of Grand Ayatollah Sayyid Ali Khameni, "Supreme Leader's Speech to Participants of 'Islamic Awakening and Youth Conference,'" January 30, 2012, http://english.khamenei.ir/index.php?option=com_content&task=view&id=1580&Itemid=16.

16. Ayatollah Saafi Gulpaygani, "A Warning Letter from Ayatollah Gulpaygani to King Abdullah," *Shi'a Post*, March 30, 2012, http://en.Shi'apost.com/2012/03/30/a-warning-letter-from-ayatollah-gulpaygani-to-king-abdullah/.

17. Anonymous sources interviewed by author, Kuwait, December 2012.

18. "Kuwait Naval Units Join Bahraini Mission: 'Plot Foiled,'" *Arab Times*, March 21, 2011, http://www.arabtimesonline.com/NewsDetails/tabid/96/smid/414/ArticleID/167009/reftab/36/Default.aspx.

19. Anonymous leader interviewed by author's researcher, Manama, February 2013.

20. Saqer al Khalifa interviewed by author, Manama, December 15, 2012.

21. Ali Fakhro interviewed by author, Manama, March 2012.

22. Anonymous. Interviewed by author, Manama, April 2012.

23. Ali al Khalifa interviewed by author, Manama, April 2012.

24. "Saudi Women Rally in Support of Bahrain Revolution Leaders," *Pakistan Today*, September 9, 2012, http://www.pakistantoday.com.pk/2012/09/09/news/foreign/saudi-women-rally-in-support-of-bahrain-revolution-leaders/.

25. Un Galani, "Saudis Wouldn't Gain Much from a Union with Bahrain," Reuters, May 2, 2012, blogs.reuters.com/breakingviews/2012/05/02/.

26. Laurence Louer, *Transnational Shia Politics: Religious and Political Networks in the Gulf* (Columbia University Press, 2008), 206.

27. Dubai al Arabiya, "Gates Accuses Iran of Complicating Things in Bahrain," *Al Arabiya English*, March 24, 2011, http://english.alarabiya.net/articles/2011/03/24/142891.html.

28. Closed meeting at the US State Department attended by author, March 2011.

29. Anonymous US official interviewed by author, Washington, DC, January 3, 2013.

30. International Crisis Group, "Popular Protest in North Africa and the Middle East: Bahrain's Rocky Road to Reform," Middle East/North report no. 111–28, (2011), 3.

31. Mahmoud Cherif Bassiouni, Nigel Rodley, Badria al Awadhi, Philippe Kirsch, and Mahnoush H. Arsanjani, "Report of the Bahrain Independent Commission of Inquiry," Manama, November 23, 2011, http://www.bici.org.bh/BICIreporteN.pdf.

32. Cherif Bassiouni interviewed by author via e-mail, January 8, 2013.

33. Anonymous. Interviewed by author, Manama, April 2012.

34. "Report of the Bahrain Independent Commission of Inquiry," 365.

35. Anonymous. Interviewed by author, Manama, April 2012.

36. Barack Obama, "Remarks by President Obama in Address to the United Nations General Assembly," Address, United Nations, New York, NY, September 21, 2011.

37. Anonymous. Interviewed by author, Manama, April 2012.

38. Anonymous. Interviewed by author, Beirut, September 2012.

39. Anonymous. Interviewed via Skype, December 2012.

40. Abdul Hakim al Subhi interviewed by author's researcher, Manama, December 2012.

41. "Report of the Bahrain Independent Commission of Inquiry," 400–401.

42. Khalil Marzooq interviewed by author, Manama, April 2012.

43. Justin Gengler, "How Radical Are Bahrain's Shi'a?" *Foreign Affairs*, May 15, 2011, http://www.foreignaffairs.com/articles/67855/justin-gengler/how-radical-are-bahrains-Shi'a.

44. "Abu Omar al Shafi'i: My Views Represent Me Alone . . . the Sunni Street Is 'Lost' and 'Opposition' Needs 'Courage.' " *Al Watan*, December 18, 2012, http://www.alwasatnews.com/3755/news/read/723919/1.html.

45. Abu Omar al Shafi'i, "Readings in the Political Landscape, Exploring Scenarios to Solve the Bahraini Crisis, Part Two," *ALSHAF3EE* December 13, 2012, http://www.alshaf3ee.blogspot.com/2012/12/blog-post_13.html.

46. US Department of State, "International Religious Freedom Report," September 13, 2011, http://www.state.gov/j/drl/rls/irf/2010_5/168261.htm.

47. US Department of State, "International Religious Freedom Report," October 26, 2009, http://www.state.gov/j/drl/rls/irf/2009/127345.htm.

48. Ibid.

49. Hassan M. Fattah, "Report Cites Bid by Sunnis in Bahrain to Rig Elections," *New York Times*, October 2, 2006, http://www.nytimes.com/2006/10/02/world/africa/02iht-web.1002bahrain.2997505.html?pagewanted=all&_r=0.

50. Salah al Bandar, "Bahrain: The Democratic Option & Exclusion Mechanisms," *Gulf Center for Democratic Development*, September (2006): 31, https://docs.google.com/file/d/18MyshDhDSioxI4bcJySrW-WfxavOScMbPlYa2wPwBc1XYFLPswooh_Kh_u_dX/edit?hl=en_US.

51. Ibid., 7.

52. Bahrain Center for Human Rights, "Discrimination in Bahrain: The Unwritten Law," September 2003, http://www.bahrainrights.org/files/BChrreportonDiscrimination.pdf.

53. Justin Gengler, "Bahrain's Sunni Awakening," *Middle East Research and Information Project*, January 17, 2012, http://www.merip.org/mero/mero011712.

54. Steven Wright, "Fixing the Kingdom: Political Evolution and Socioeconomic Challenges in Bahrain," *Center for International and Regional Studies*, Georgetown University, Occasional Paper no. 3 (2008): 10.

55. "Public Report of Review of US Submission 2011-01 (Bahrain)," December 20, 2012, http://www.dol.gov/ilab/programs/otla/20121220Bahrain.pdf.

56. Wasam al Saba'a, "Displaced People from the Countryside: 'The Religious Bloc' in the Parliament of 1973," *Al Wasat*, October 22, 2010, http://www.alwasatnews.com/2968/news/read/493809/1.html.

57. Andrew Hammond, "Interview: Bahrain Shi'ite Leader Says Backs Royal Family," Reuters, May 29, 2011, http://www.reuters.com/article/2011/05/29/bahrain-shiite-idAFLDe74SoC720110529?sp=true.

58. Ed Husain, ed. "Iran's Man in Bahrain," Council on Foreign Relations, April 27, 2012, http://blogs.cfr.org/husain/2012/04/27/irans-man-in-bahrain/.

59. "Israel Is Mocking the Arab Regimes," http://alwefaq.net/index.php?show=news&action=article&id=4109.

60. Al Waefaq, "What Freedom Is Left for the People?" http://alwefaq.net/cms/?p=6085.

CHAPTER 6

1. Mwali Alkhamenei, "Speech of Imam Khamenei," YouTube video, February 1, 2012, http://www.youtube.com/watch?v=hCzkQVllBeY.

APPENDIX A

1. "Syrian Army Captures Strategic Villages Near Lebanon Border," *Press TV*, April 20, 2013, http://www.presstv.com/detail/2013/04/20/299361/syrian-army-captures-key-villages/.

2. Anne Bernard and Hwaida Saad, "Hezbollah Aids Syrian Military in Key Battle," *New York Times*, May 13, 2013, http://www.nytimes.com/2013/05/20/world/middleeast/syrian-army-moves-to-rebel-held-qusayr.html?pagewanted=all&_r=0.

3. Erika Soloman, "Syrian Army Captures Strategic Border Town of Qusair," Reuters, June 5, 2013, http://www.reuters.com/article/2013/06/05/us-syria-crisis-town-idUSBRE95406220130605.

4. "Car Bomb Blast in Beirut Kills at Least 20, Injures Dozens," *Time*, August 15, 2013, http://world.time.com/2013/08/15/car-bomb-blast-in-beirut-kills-at-least-20-injures-dozens/.

5. "Sidon Clashes Kill 16 Soldiers as Assir Remains at Large," *Al Akhbar*, June 24, 2013, http://english.al-akhbar.com/node/16219.

6. "Syrian Opposition: 1,300 Killed in Chemical Attack on Ghouta Region," *Al Arabiya*, August 21, 2013, http://english.alarabiya.net/en/News/middle-east/2013/08/21/Syrian-activists-at-least-500-killed-in-chemical-attack-on-Eastern-Ghouta.html.

SELECTED BIBLIOGRAPHY

As you will recognize readily, much of the research for this book was carried out through interviews with local religious figures and other non-state actors, as well as through analysis of social media, such as Twitter, YouTube, and popular blogs, all of which are playing an ever-increasing role in the public life of the Muslim Middle East. Details of these sources can be found in the chapter notes. In addition, the following works proved useful in the preparation of this work.

Abdallah, Ali. "Salafiyyoo Sooryawal Thawra [Syria's Salafists and the Revolution]." *Al-Jumhuriya*, December 12, 2013. http://aljumhuriya. net/22395.

Abdel-Aal, Ali. "Salafiyyat Lubnan: Al Nasha'awal Tatawor [Lebanese Salafism: Foundation and Development]." *Al Fajr News*, March 7, 2010. http://www.turess.com/alfajrnews/28767.

Abdo, Geneive. *No God But God: Egypt and the Triumph of Islam.* New York: Oxford University Press, 2000.

Abdo, Geneive, and Jonathan Lyons. *Answering Only to God: Faith and Freedom in Twenty-First-Century Iran.* New York: Henry, 2003.

Abdo, Geneive, and Reza H. Akbari. "Morsi Is Just Not That into Iran." *Foreign Policy*, August 30, 2012. http://mid-east.foreignpolicy.com/ posts/2012/08/30/morsis_just_ not_that_into_iran_0.

Abouzeid, Rania. "A Spasm of Violence: How Lebanon Is Threatened by Syria's rebellion." *Time,* May 21, 2012. http://www.time.com/time/ world/article/0,8599,2115386,00.

Abu Zeed, Adnan. "Controversy Surrounds Alleged Violations of Shiite Forces in Tikrit." *Al Monitor*, April 23, 2015. http://www.al-monitor.com/pulse/originals/2015/04/iraq-tikrit-liberation-popular-mobilization-violations.html.

Ajami, Fouad. "Lebanon: The Prospects: Lebanon and Its Inheritors." *Foreign Affairs* 63 (1984): 778–799.

Akbari, Reza H., and Jason Stern. "The Triangle of Conflict: How Bahrain's Internal Divisions Inhibit Reconciliation." Washington, DC: The Institute for Middle East Studies, Elliot School of International Affairs, 2012. http://www.gwu.edu/~imes/assets/docs/Capstone%20Papers%20-%202012/Akbari,%20Stern.pdf (accessed January 9, 2013).

Akhavi, Khody. "Lebanon: Violence in Beirut Polarizes Sunni and Shi'a Groups." *Interpress Service*, May 15, 2008. https://www.highbeam.com/doc/1G1-179045672.html.

Al Arabiya, "Fight or Flight? Saudi Cleric Heads to London after Call for Jihad in Syria." June 22, 2013. http://english.alarabiya.net/en/News/middle-east/2013/06/22/Fight-or-flight-Saudi-cleric-heads-to-London-after-calling-for-Jihad-in-Syria.html.

Al Bandar, Salah. "Bahrain: The Democratic Option & Exclusion Mechanisms." Manama, Bahrain: Gulf Center for Democratic Development, n.d.

Al Jazeera. "Top Saudi Cleric Says Twitter Is for Clowns." March 24, 2013. http://www.aljazeera.com/news/middleeast/2013/03/201332461505585567.html.

Al Khalifa, Hamad bin Isa bin Salman. "Stability Is Prerequisite for Progress." *Washington Times*, April 19, 2011. http://www.washingtontimes.com/news/2011/apr/19/stability-is-prerequisite-for-progress/.

Al Kobeissi, Yehya. "Al Salafiyya fil Iraq: Takalobat al Dakhelwa Tajathobat al Kharej [Salafism in Iraq: Internal Vicissitudes and External Enticements]." Doha: Al Jazeera Center for Studies, 2013.

Al Najjar, Ghanim. "Struggle over Parliament in Kuwait." Carnegie Endowment for International Peace, 2006. http://carnegieendowment.org/2008/08/18/struggle-over-parliament-in-kuwait/6bgo.

Al Rashed, Abdul Rahman. "Kuwait: Who Is the Authority?" *Al Arabiya*, November 16, 2012. http://english.alarabiya.net/views/2012/11/16/249876.html (accessed December 11, 2012).

Alnahas, Ibrahim Mahmoud Yaseen, "Continuity and Change in the Revolutionary Iran Foreign Policy: The Role of International and Domestic Political Factors in Shaping the Iranian Foreign Policy, 1979–2006." PhD diss., University of West Virginia, 2007.

Alpeyrie, Jonathan. "Syria's War Spills over into Lebanon." *The Middle East* 430 (2012). http://www.thefreelibrary.com/Syria%27s+war+spills+over+into+Lebanon.-a0286114529 (accessed December 4, 2012).

Amnesty International. "Absolute Impunity: Militia Rule in Iraq." London: Amnesty International, 2014. https://www.amnesty.org.uk/sites/default/files/absolute_impunity_iraq_report.pdf.

Amrieh, Antoine, and Mohammed Zaataril. "Soldiers Killed in Akkar after Tripoli Protests." *The Daily Star*, April 9, 2014. http://www.dailystar.com.lb/News/Lebanon-News/2014/Apr-09/252760-soldiers-killed-in-akkar-after-tripoli-protests.ashx.

Anderson, Benedict. *Imagined Communities*. London: Verso, 2006.

Asmar, Christine, Maroun Kisirwani, and Robert Springborg. "Clash of Politics or Civilizations? Sectarianism among Youth in Lebanon." *Arab Studies Quarterly* 21 (1999): 35–64.

Ayoub, Mamoud. *Redemptive Suffering in Islam: A Study of the Devotional Aspects of Ashura in Twelver Shi'ism*. The Hague: Mouton, 1978.

Bahgat, Gawdat. "Peace in the Persian Gulf: The Shi'is Dimension." *Peace and Change* 24 (2002): 76–90.

Bahri, Luayy. "The Socioeconomic Foundations of the Shiite Opposition in Bahrain." *Mediterranean Quarterly* 11 (2000): 129–143.

Barnard, Anne. "Loyalty to Syria Chief Could Isolate Hezbollah." *New York Times*, April 5, 2012.

Barzegar, Kayhan. "Iran and the Shiite Crescent: Myths and Realities." *Brown Journal of World Affairs* 15 (2008): 87–99.

_____. "Regionalism in Iran's Foreign Policy." *Journal of Central Eurasian Studies* 2 (2010): 23–40.

_____. "The Shi'a Factor in Iran's Foreign Policy." Tehran: Center for Strategic Research, 2008. http://www.csr.ir/departments.aspx?lng=en&abtid=07&&depid=74&semid=1421 (accessed October 17, 2012).

Blanchard, Christopher M. "The Islamic Tradition of Wahhabism and Salafiyya." Washington, DC: Congressional Research Service, January 25, 2006.

Blanford, Nicholas. "In Lebanon, a Worrying Sectarian Spillover from Syria." *The Christian Science Monitor*, June 3, 2012. http://www.csmonitor.com/World/Middle-East/2012/0603/In-Lebanon-a-worrying-sectarian-spillover-from-Syria.

_____. "Lebanese Join the Free Syrian Army's Struggle." *The Daily Star*, May 30, 2012. http://www.dailystar.com.lb/News/Politics/2012/May-30/175072-lebanese-join-the-free-syrian-armys-struggle.ashx.

_____. "Lebanon: The Shiite Dimension." In *The Islamists Are Coming: Who They Really Are*, edited by Robin Wright, 109–118. Washington, DC: United States Institute of Peace, 2012.

Bronner, Ethan, and Michael Slackman. "Saudi Troops Enter Bahrain to Help Put Down Unrest." *New York Times*, March 14, 2011. http://www.nytimes.com/2011/03/15/world/middleeast/15bahrain. html.

Brookings Institution. "From Tribunal to Turbulence: Lebanon and the Middle East's Multiple Challenges." Doha: The Brookings Doha Center, October 20, 2010. http://www.brookings.edu/~/media/events/2010/10/20-lebanon/1020_lebanon_transcript.pdf (accessed December 4, 2012).

Brown, Nathan. "The Beginning of Real Politics in Kuwait?" Washington, DC: Carnegie Endowment for International Peace, December 13, 2006. http://www.carnegieendowment.org/2008/08/13/beginning-of-real-politics-in-kuwait/6bfz (accessed December 11, 2012).

_____. "Democracy Works—Only Very Slowly." *New York Times*, July 4, 2007. http://www.nytimes.com/2007/07/04/opinion/04iht-edbrown.1.6485071. html.

_____. "Kuwait's 2008 Parliamentary Elections: A Setback for Democratic Islamism?" Washington, DC: Carnegie Endowment for International Peace, 2008. http://www.carnegieendowment.org/files/brown_kuwait2. pdf (accessed December 11, 2012).

_____. "Kuwaiti Democracy in Crisis." Washington, DC: Carnegie Endowment for International Peace, May 18, 2009. http://carnegieendowment.org/2009/05/18/kuwaiti-democracy-in-crisis/97k (accessed December 11, 2012).

_____. "Moving out of Kuwait's Political Impasse." Washington, DC: Carnegie Endowment for International Peace, 2009. http://carnegieendowment.org/2007/06/25/moving-out-of-kuwait-s-political-impasse/1nlp (accessed December 11, 2012).

_____. "Post-revolutionary Al-Azhar." Washington, DC: Carnegie Endowment for International Peace, 2011. http://carnegieendowment. org/files/al_azhar.pdf (accessed January 14, 2012).

_____. "Kuwait's Short 19th Century." *Foreign Policy* (2012). http://mideast.foreignpolicy.com/posts/2011/12/15/kuwaits_short_19th_century (accessed December 15, 2012).

Chatah, Mohamad, and Marwan Muasher. "Lebanon on the Margins of the Arab Spring." Paper presented at the Carnegie Endowment for International Peace, Washington, DC, February 3, 2012. http://carnegieendowment.org/2012/02/03/lebanon-on-margins-of-arab-spring (accessed December 4, 2012).

Chelkowski, Peter, and Hamid Dabashi. *Staging a Revolution: The Art of Persuasion in the Islamic Republic.* New York: New York University Press, 2000.

Daou, Rita. "Lebanon's Maronite Christian Head Sparks Syria Debate." *Your Middle East,* September 13, 2011, sec X. http://www.yourmiddleeast.com/news/lebanons-maronite-christian-head-sparks-syria-debate_1538.

Dickinson, Elizabeth. "Shaping the Syrian Conflict from Kuwait." *Foreign Policy* (2013). http://foreignpolicy.com/2013/12/04/shaping-the-syrian-conflict-from-kuwait/ (accessed December 12, 2013).

Diwan, Kristin Smith. "Kuwait: Too Much Politics, or Not Enough?" *Foreign Policy* (2011). http://foreignpolicy.com/2011/01/10/kuwait-too-much-politics-or-not-enough/.

_____. "Kuwait's Constitutional Showdown." *Foreign Policy* (2011). http://mideast.foreignpolicy.com/posts/2011/11/17/kuwaits_constitutional_showdown (accessed December 11, 2012).

_____. "Kuwait's Balancing Act." *Foreign Policy* (2012). http://foreignpolicy.com/2012/10/23/kuwaits-balancing-act/ (accessed December 11, 2012).

Elgot, Jennifer. "Controversial Saudi Preacher Mohammad Al-Arefe Denies Anti-Shia Stance and Defends UK Visit." *Huffington Post UK,* June 28, 2013. http://www.huffingtonpost.co.uk/2013/06/28/mohammad-al-arefe_n_3517727.html.

Fattah, Hassan M. "Report Cites Bid by Sunnis in Bahrain to Rig Elections." *New York Times,* October 2, 2006. http://www.nytimes.com/2006/10/02/world/middleeast/02bahrain.html?pagewanted=print.

Fordham, Alice. "Syria's Sectarian Splits Creep into Lebanon." *Washington Post,* May 15, 2012. https://www.washingtonpost.com/world/middle_east/syrias-sectarian-splits-creep-into-lebanon/2012/05/15/gIQAlpGQSU_story.html.

Fuller, Graham E., and Rend Rahim Francke. *The Arab Shi'a: The Forgotten Muslims.* New York: St. Martin's Press, 1999.

Galani, Una. "Saudis Wouldn't Gain Much from a Union with Bahrain." Reuters. May 2, 2012. http://blogs.reuters.com/breakingviews/2012/05/02/saudis-wouldnt-gain-much-from-a-union-with-bahrain/.

Gause, F. Gregory III. "Kuwait's Elections Don't Solve Its Political Crisis." *Foreign Policy* (2009). http://foreignpolicy.com/2009/05/17/kuwaits-elections-dont-solve-its-political-crisis/.

_____. "The Year the Arab Spring Went Bad." *Foreign Policy* (2012). http://foreignpolicy.com/2012/12/31/the-year-the-arab-spring-went-bad/.

Gengler, Justin. "How Radical Are Bahrain's Shi'a?" *Foreign Affairs* (2011). https://www.foreignaffairs.com/articles/bahrain/2011-05-15/how-radical-are-bahrains-shia.

_____. "Bahrain's Sunni Awakening." Washington, DC: Middle East Research and Information Project, January 17, 2012. http:// www.merip.org/mero/mero011712.

George, Marcus. "Iran's Revolutionary Guards Commander Says Its Troops in Syria." Reuters, March 16, 2012. http://www.reuters.com/article/us-iran-syria-presence-idUSBRE88F04C20120916

Ghabra, Shafeeq. "Balancing State and Society: The Islamic Movement in Kuwait." *Middle East Policy* 5 (1997): 58–72.

_____. "Kuwait and the Dynamics of Socio-economic Change." *The Middle East Journal* 51 (1997): 358–372.

Ghobadzdeh, Naser, and Shahram Akbarzadeh. "Sectarianism and the Prevalence of 'Othering' in Islamic Thought." *Third World Quarterly* 36 (2015): 691–704.

Gulpaygani, Ayatollah Saafi. "A Warning Letter from Ayatollah Gulpaygani to King Abdullah." *The Shi'a Post,* March 30, 2012.

Haddad, Fanar. "The Hashd: Redrawing the Military and Political Map of Iraq." Washington, DC: The Middle East Institute, April 9, 2015. http://www.mei.edu/content/article/hashd-redrawing-military-and-political-map-iraq.

_____. "Shi'a Centric State Building and Sunni Rejection in Post-2003 Iraq." Washington, DC: Carnegie Endowment for International Peace, January 7, 2016. http://carnegieendowment.org/2016/01/07/shia-centric-state-building-and-sunni-rejection-in-post-2003-iraq/is5w.

Halm, Heinz. *Shi'ism.* 2nd ed., translated by Janet Watson and Marian Hall. Edinburgh: Edinburgh University Press, 2004.

Haykel, Bernard. "On the Nature of Salafi Thought and Action." In *Global Salafism: Islam's New Religious Movement*, edited by Roel Meijer, 33–57. New York: Columbia University Press, 2009.

Hazran, Yusri. "The Shiite Community in Lebanon: From Marginalization to Ascendancy." Waltham: Crown Center for Middle East Studies, Brandeis University, Issue Brief no. 37, June 2009. http://www.brandeis.edu/crown/publications/meb/MeB37.pdf.

Hearst, David. "Kuwait's Protests Remind Us of the Arab Spring's True Spirit." *The Guardian*, November 2, 2012. http://www.theguardian.com/commentisfree/2012/nov/02/kuwait-protests-arab-spring.

Hiltermann, Joost. "A New Sectarian Threat in the Middle East?" *International Review of the Red Cross* 868 (2007): 795–808.

Hokayem, Emile. "Lebanon's Little Syria." *Foreign Policy* (2012). http://foreignpolicy.com/2012/05/15/lebanons-little-syria/ (accessed December 4, 2012).

Hubbard, Ben, and Elizabeth A. Kennedy. "Violence in Syria Spills over into Lebanon." Associated Press, May 21, 2012.

Hudson, Michael. *The Precarious Republic: Political Modernization in Lebanon*. New York: Random House, 1968.

Human Rights Watch. "Routine Abuse, Routine Denial: Civil Rights and the Political Crisis in Bahrain." New York: Human Rights Watch, 1997. http://pantheon.hrw.org/legacy/reports/1997/bahrain/.

———. "Bahrain: Court Upholds Convictions of Medics." New York: Human Rights Watch, 2012.

Hunter, Shireen. *Iran and the World: Continuity in a Revolutionary Decade*. Bloomington: Indiana University Press, 1990.

Husain, Ed. "Iran's Man in Bahrain." New York: Council on Foreign Relations, April 27, 2012. http://blogs.cfr.org/husain/2012/04/27/irans-man-in-bahrain/.

Hutchins, David. "Analysis: Why Arab Springs Falter—Bahrain." Voice of America, May 16, 2012. http://www.voanews.com/content/is_arab_spring_over_in_bah-rain/666797.html.

International Crisis Group. "Bahrain's Sectarian Challenge." May 6, 2005. http://www.crisisgroup.org/en/regions/middle-east-north-africa/iraq-iran-gulf/bahrain/040-bahrains-sectarian-challenge.aspx (accessed January 14, 2013).

_____. "Tentative Jihad: Syria's Fundamentalist Opposition." October 12, 2012. http://www.crisisgroup.org/~/media/Files/Middle%20east%20 North%20Africa/Iraq%20Syria%20Lebanon/Syria/131-tentative-jihad-syrias-fundamentalist-opposition (accessed December 5, 2012).

Ismail, Raihan. "Lebanon at a Tripwire." Beirut/Brussels: Crisis Group, December 21, 2006. http://www.crisisgroup.org/en/regions/middle-east-north-africa/syria-lebanon/lebanon/b020-lebanon-at-a-tripwire. aspx (accessed December 4, 2012).

_____. "Nurturing Instability: Lebanon's Palestinian Refugee Camps." Beirut/ Brussels: Crisis Group, February 19, 2009. http://www.crisisgroup.org/en/ regions/middle-east-north-africa/israel-palestine/084-nurturing-instability-lebanons-palestinian-refugee-camps.aspx (accessed December 4, 2012).

_____. "Lebanon's Politics: The Sunni Community and Hariri's Future Current." Beirut/Brussels: Crisis Group, May 26, 2010. http://www.crisisgroup.org/en/publication-type/media-releases/2010/mena/lebanon-s-politics-the-sunni-community-and-hariri-s-future-current.aspx (accessed December 4, 2012).

_____. "New Crisis, Old Demons in Lebanon: The Forgotten Lessons of Bab-Tebbaneh/Jabal Mohsen." Beirut/Brussels: Crisis Group, October 14, 2010. http://www.crisisgroup.org/en/regions/middle-east-north-africa/ egypt-syria-lebanon/lebanon/B29-new-crisis-old-demons-in-lebanon-the-forgotten-lessons-of-bab-tebbaneh-jabal-mohsen.aspx (accessed December 4, 2012).

_____. "Popular Protests in North Africa and the Middle East (III): The Bahrain Revolt." Brussels: Crisis Group, April 6, 2011. http://www. crisisgroup.org/en/regions/middle-east-north-africa/iraq-iran-gulf/bahrain/105-popular-protests-in-north-africa-and-the-middle-east-iii-the-bahrain-revolt.aspx (accessed January 14, 2013).

_____. "Popular Protest in North Africa and the Middle East (VIII): Bahrain's Rocky Road to Reform." Brussels: Crisis Group, July 28, 2011. http:// www.crisisgroup.org/en/regions/middle-east-north-africa/iraq-iran-gulf/ bahrain/111-popular-protest-in-north-africa-and-the-middle-east-viii-bahrains-rocky-road-to-reform.aspx (accessed January 14, 2013).

_____. *Saudi Clerics and Shi'a Islam*. New York: Oxford University Press, 2016.

Jabar, Faleh A. *The Shiite Movement in Iraq*. London: Saqi Books, 2003.

Jadaliyya Reports. "Bahraini 'Coalition for a Republic' Issues First Statement." Jadaliyya, March 9, 2011. http://www.jadaliyya.com/pages/index/839/bahraini.

Karouny, Mariam. "Syria Rebels Kidnap 13 Lebanese Shi'ites." Reuters, May 22, 2012. www.reuters.com/article/us-syria-lebanon-idUSBRE84L11520120522.

Katzman, Kenneth. "Bahrain: Reform, Security, and U.S. Policy." Washington, DC: Congressional Research Service, March 21, 2011. http://fpc.state.gov/documents/organization/159344.pdf (accessed January 9, 2013).

Kechichian, Joseph A. "Lebanon Premier Appeals for Calm as Cleric Shot Dead." Gulf News, May 21, 2012. http://gulfnews.com/news/mena/lebanon/lebanon-premier-appeals-for-calm-as-cleric-shot-dead-1.1025522.

Keddie, Nikki R. Scholars, Saint, and Sufis. Berkeley: University of California Press, 1972.

Kennedy, Elizabeth A. "Violence in Syria Spills over into Lebanon." The Guardian. May 21, 2012.

Kharouny, Mariam, and Alasdair MacDonald. "Sermons on Syria Fan Mideast Sectarian Flames." Reuters, June 7, 2013. http://www.reuters.com/article/us-syria-crisis-muslims-idUSBRE95613320130607.

Khashan, Hilal. "The Religious and Political Impact of Sayyid M. H. Fadlallah on Arab Shi'ism." The Journal of Shi'a Islamic Studies 3 (2010): 427–441.

———. "The View from Syria and Lebanon: Middle Eastern Upheavals." Middle East Quarterly 18 (2011): 25–35.

Limba, Mansoor. "Theoretical Viewpoints of Imam Khomeini in the Realm of Foreign Policy (Part I)." Islamic Thought Foundation. http://imam-khomeini.com/web1/english/showitem.aspx?cid=2491&pid=2843 (accessed December 10, 2012).

Litvak, Meyer. "Madrasa and Learning in 19th-Century Najaf and Karbala." In The Twelver Shia in Modern Times: Religious, Cultural and Political History, edited by Rainer Brunner and Werner Ende, 58–78. Leiden: Brill, 2001.

Lorenz, Andrea W. "Kuwait Begins Its Return to Democracy." The Washington Report on Middle East Affairs (October 1992).

Louër, Laurence. Transnational Shi'a Politics: Religious and Political Networks in the Gulf. New York: Columbia University Press, 2008.

_____. "Houses Divided: The Splintering of Bahrain's Political Camps." Washington, DC: Carnegie Endowment for International Peace, April 4, 2012. http://carnegieendowment.org/sada/2012/04/04/houses-divided-splintering-of-bahrain-s-political-camps/a6ej (accessed December 05, 2012).

Lynch, Marc. "Kuwait's Moment of Truth." *Foreign Policy* (2012). http://foreignpolicy.com/2012/11/01/kuwaits-moment-of-truth/ (accessed December 11, 2012).

Lynch, Marc, Deen Freelon, and Sean Aday, "Syria's Socially Mediated Civil War." Washington, DC: United States Institute of Peace, 2014. http://www.usip.org/publications/syria-s-socially-mediated-civil-war.

Mackey, Sandra. *The Iranians: Persia, Islam and the Soul of a Nation.* New York: Dutton, 1996.

McDowall, Angus. "Bahrain Crown Prince Calls for Talks with Opposition." Reuters, December 8, 2012. www.reuters.com/article/us-bahrain-politics-idUSBRE8B704H20121208.

Meijer, Roel. "Introduction." In *Global Salafism: Islam's New Religious Movement*, edited by Roel Meijer, 1–32. New York: Columbia University Press, 2009.

Milmo, Cahil. "Sunni vs. Shi'a ... in Gerrard's Cross: New Mosque Highlights Growing Tensions among British Muslims." *The Independent*, June 24, 2013.

Mir-Khalili, Seyed Javad. "Imam Khomeini's Viewpoints on Iranian Foreign Policy." *Iran Review* (2008). http://www.iranreview.org/content/Documents/Imam_ Khomeini%e2%80%99s_Viewpoints_on_Iranian_Foreign_Policy.htm (accessed December 10, 2012).

Mohazarat.net. "Sirat Al Shaykh Nabil Al Awadhy [Sheikh Nabil Awadhy's Biography]." http://www.mohazarat.net.qa/index21.htm.

Monroe, Steve L. "Salafis in Parliament: Democratic Attitudes and Party Politics in the Gulf." *The Middle East Journal* 66 (2012): 409–424.

Moshaver, Ziba. "Revolution, Theocratic Leadership and Iran's Foreign Policy: Implications for Iran–EU relations." *International Review of International Affairs* 3 (2003): 283–305.

Motaparthy, Priyanka. "Jailed for Tweeting in Kuwait." *Foreign Policy* (2012). http://mideast.foreignpolicy.com/posts/2011/08/24/in_kuwait_jailed_for_tweeting (accessed December 11, 2012).

Moubayed, Sami. "A Turning Point in Lebanon." *Huffington Post*, August 8, 2012. http://www.huffingtonpost.com/sami-moubayed/a-turning-point-in-lebano_b_1578715.html.

_____. "Lebanon's New Wild Card: Shaker Al-Barjawi?" *Huffington Post*, May 24, 2012. http:// www.huffingtonpost.com/sami-moubayed/hizballahs-new-proxy-shak_b_1541589.html (accessed December 4, 2012).

Moussalli, Ahmad. "Wahhabism, Salafism, and Islamism: Who Is the Enemy?" Washington, DC: Conflicts Forum, January 2009.

Naharnet Newsdesk. "Al Shahhal Denies Call for Jihad, Says Salafists Pose No Threat." March 8, 2013. http://m.naharnet.com/stories/en/74768-al-shahhal-denies-calls-for-jihad-says-salafists-pose-no-threat.

Nakash, Yitzhak. *Reaching for Power: The Shi'a in the Modern Arab World*. Princeton: Princeton University Press, 2006.

Newman, Andrew. *The Formative Period of Twelver Shi'ism: Hadith Discourse between Qum and Baghdad*. Richmond, UK: Curzon Press, 2000.

Norell, Magnus. "A Boatload of Trouble." *Foreign Policy* (2009). http://foreign-policy.com/2009/11/09/a-boatload-of-trouble/ (accessed December 4, 2012).

_____. "Realities of the UN in Lebanon." Washington, DC: Washington Institute for Near East Policy. January 27, 2009. http://www.washingtoninstitute.org/policy-analysis/view/realities-of-the-un-in-lebanon (accessed December 4, 2012).

Norton, Augustus Richard. "Hizballah: From Radicalism to Pragmatism?" *Middle East Policy Council* 5 (1998): 147–158. http://almashriq.hiof.no/lebanon/300/320/324/324.2/hizballah/norton.html (accessed December 4, 2012).

Okruhlik, Gwenn. "The Identity Politics of Kuwait's Election." *Foreign Policy* (2012). http://foreignpolicy.com/2012/02/08/the-identity-politics-of-kuwaits-election/ (accessed December 11, 2012).

Omayma, Abdel-Latif. "Lebanon's Sunni Islamists: A Growing Force." Washington, DC: Carnegie Endowment for International Peace, February 4, 2008. http://carnegie-mec.org/2008/02/04/lebanon-s-sunni-islamists-growing-force.

Pew Forum on Religion & Public Life. "The World's Muslims: Unity and Diversity." Washington, DC: PEW Research Center, August 9, 2012. http://www.pewforum.org/files/2012/08/the-worlds-muslims-full-report.pdf.

Porter, Gareth. "Iran's Regional Power Goal Is Rooted in Shi'a Ties." *Interpress Service*, December 16, 2008. https://www.highbeam.com/doc/1G1-190746813.html (accessed December 4, 2012).

Posner, Michael H. "Implementation of the Bahrain Independent Commission of Inquiry Report." Washington, DC: Bureau of Democracy, Human Rights, and Labor.

Testimony before the Tom Lanthos Human Rights Commission Hearing. August 1, 2012. http://www.state.gov/j/drl/rls/rm/2012/195516.htm.

Project on Middle East Democracy (POMED). "One Year Later: Assessing Bahrain's Implementation of the BICI Report." Washington, DC: POMED, November 2012. http://pomed.org/wordpress/wp-content/uploads/2012/11/POMED_BahrainReport_web-FINAL.pdf.

Project on Middle East Political Science (POMEPS). "Arab Uprisings: The New Salafi Politics." October 16, 2012. Washington, DC: POMEPS. http://pomeps.org/wp-content/uploads/2012/10/POMEPS_BriefBooklet14_Salafi_web.pdf (accessed December 5, 2012).

Radwan, Mortada. "Lebanon: Rival Salafist Sheikhs Seek Unity." *Al Akhbar*, April 1, 2013. english.al-akhbar.com/node/15405.

Rizzo, Helen, Katherine Meyer, and Ali Yousef. "Extending Political Rights in the Middle East: The Case of Kuwait." *Journal of Political and Military Sociology* 35 (2007): 177–197.

Roberts, David. "Kuwait's War of Words with Iraq." *Foreign Policy* (2011). http://foreignpolicy.com/2011/07/20/kuwaits-war-of-words-with-iraq/.

Rougier, Bernard. *Everyday Jihad: The Rise of Militant Islam among Palestinians in Lebanon*. Cambridge: Harvard University Press, 2007.

Roy, Oliver. *Globalized Islam: The Search for a New Ummah*. New York: Columbia University Press, 2006.

Salem, Paul. "Kuwait: Politics in a Participatory Emirate." *Carnegie Papers* 3 (2007): 1–19. http://www.carnegieendow-ment.org/files/cmec3_salem_kuwait_final1.pdf.

Salibi, Kamal S. *A House of Many Mansions: The History of Lebanon Reconsidered*. Berkeley: University of California Press, 1988.

Samii, Abbas William. "Shiites in Lebanon: The Key to Democracy." *Middle East Policy* 13 (2006): 30–37.

Schenker, David. "To Retaliate or Not: Hizballah's Calculus Following a Strike on Iran." Washington, DC: The Washington Institute for Near

East Policy, March 14, 2012. http://www.washingtoninstitute.org/policy-analysis/view/to-retaliate-or-not-hizballahs-calculus-following-a-strike-on-iran (accessed December 04, 2012).

Shahine, Alaa. "Lebanon Clashes Reach Beirut after Anti-Syrian Cleric Death." *Bloomberg*, May 12, 2012. http://www.bloomberg.com/news/articles/2012-05-21/lebanon-clashes-reach-beirut-after-anti-syrian-cleric-s-killing.

Shayji, Abdullah. "Kuwait: A Democratic Model in Trouble." Washington, DC: Carnegie Endowment for International Peace, February 3, 2009. http://carnegieendowment.org/sada/2009/02/03/kuwait-democratic-model-in-trouble/8xiq (accessed December 11, 2012).

Smith, Lee. "A Talk with Samir Geagea, Head of the Lebanese Forces." *The Weekly Standard*, May 10, 2012. http://www.weeklystandard.com/a-talk-with-samir-geagea-head-of-the-lebanese-forces/article/644312.

Tabler, Andrew. "The Washington–Beirut–Damascus Triangle (Part II)." Washington, DC: The Washington Institute for Near East Policy. March 17, 2009. http://www.washingtoninstitute.org/policy-analysis/view/the-washington-beirut-damascus-triangle-part-ii (accessed December 04, 2012).

Telhami, Shibley. "Hezbollah's Power Play." *The National Interest*, January 13, 2011. http://nationalinterest.org/commentary/hezbollahs-power-play-4721 (accessed December 04, 2012).

Ulrichsen, Kristian Coates. "Kuwait's Uncertain Path." *Foreign Policy* (2012). http://mideast.foreignpolicy. com/posts/2012/09/26/kuwait_s_uncertain_path (accessed December 11, 2012).

_____. "Political Showdown in Kuwait." *Foreign Policy* (2012). http://mideast.foreignpolicy.com/posts/2012/06/20/political_showdown_in_kuwait (accessed December 11, 2012).

US State Department. "International Religious Freedom Report 2009: Bahrain." October 26, 2009. http://www. state.gov/j/drl/rls/irf/2009/127345.htm.

Van Pelt, Mary Cubberly. "The Sheikhdom of Kuwait." *The Middle East Journal* 4 (1950): 12–26.

Voll, John O. *Islam: Continuity and Change in the Modern World*. Syracuse: Syracuse University Press, 1994.

Wehrey, Frederic. "The March of Bahrain's Hardliners." Washington, DC: Carnegie Endowment for International Peace. May 31, 2012. http://carnegieendowment.org/2012/05/31/march-of- bahrain-s-hardliners/bozr.

Weiss, Max. *In the Shadow of Sectarianism: Law, Shi'ism, and the Making of Modern Lebanon.* Cambridge: Harvard University Press, 2010.

_____. "Practicing Sectarianism in Mandate Lebanon: Shi'a Cemeteries, Religious Patrimony, and the Everyday Politics of Difference." *Journal of Social History* 43 (2010): 703–733.

Wheeler, Deborah L., and Lauren Mintz. "The Internet and Political Change in Kuwait." *Foreign Policy* (2010). http://foreignpolicy.com/2010/04/15/the-internet-and-political-change-in-kuwait/ (accessed December 11, 2012).

Whewell, Tim. "Lebanese Families Drawn into Syrian Conflict." BBC, June 18, 2013. http://www.bbc.com/news/world-middle-east-22938132.

Wiktorowicz, Quintan. "Anatomy of the Salafi Movement." *Studies in Conflict and Terrorism* 29 (2006): 207–239.

Wright, Robin, and Peter Baker. "Iraq, Jordan See Threat to Election from Iran." *The Washington Post*, December 8, 2004.

Wright, Steven. "Fixing the Kingdom: Political Evolution and Socio-economic Challenges in Bahrain." Occasional paper no. 3. Center for International and Regional Studies, Georgetown University, 2008. https://repository.library.georgetown.edu/handle/10822/558295.

INDEX

Page numbers followed by t indicate a reference to a tweet